Emily Rice grew up in the same village as the first witch to be executed in England, Agnes Waterhouse. After researching the local witch, Emily became fascinated in history, and her history teachers encouraged an interest in female historical figures. So, with the help of her research and analytical skills gained from her studying at the University of York, Emily spent the 2020 Lockdown writing her first book, *Women Forgotten in History*. This was to shed some light on the fascinating lives of lesser-known women in history.

For all the Forgotten Women.

Emily Rice

WOMEN FORGOTTEN IN HISTORY

AUSTIN MACAULEY PUBLISHERS™

LONDON * CAMBRIDGE * NEW YORK * SHARJAH

Copyright © Emily Rice 2023

The right of Emily Rice to be identified as author of this work has been asserted by the author in accordance with sections 77 and 78 of the Copyright, Designs and Patents Act 1988.

All rights reserved. No part of this publication may be reproduced, stored in a retrieval system, or transmitted in any form or by any means, electronic, mechanical, photocopying, recording, or otherwise, without the prior permission of the publishers.

Any person who commits any unauthorised act in relation to this publication may be liable to criminal prosecution and civil claims for damages.

A CIP catalogue record for this title is available from the British Library.

ISBN 9781398462922 (Paperback)
ISBN 9781398462939 (ePub e-book)

www.austinmacauley.com

First Published 2023
Austin Macauley Publishers Ltd®
1 Canada Square
Canary Wharf
London
E14 5AA

Thank you to all my family and friends for the support you have given me, and to my history teachers, who inspired my passion for history. I would like to thank those who made the publication of this book possible; those who suggested titles and historical women to include in this book; and everyone who has shown enthusiasm and supported me throughout this process. I am extremely grateful to you all.

Table of Contents

Introduction	13
Pharaoh Hatshepsut (1507–1458 BCE)	14
Sappho (630–570 BCE)	18
Empress Lü Zhi (241–180 BCE)	22
Trưng Trắc and Trưng Nhị (12–43 CE)	28
Empress Jingū (169–269 CE)	32
St Agnes of Rome (291–304 CE)	36
Hypatia of Alexandria (370–415 CE)	39
Liu Chuyu (446–465 CE)	44
Queen Seondeok of Silla (606–647 CE)	47
Empress Wu Zetian (624–705 CE)	53
Pope Joan (818–857 CE)	63
Murasaki Shikibu (978–1014 CE)	66
Empress Matilda (1102–1167 CE)	70
Hōjō Masako (1156–1225 CE)	76
Queen Tamar the Great (1166–1213 CE)	82
Queen Isabella (1295–1358 CE)	89
Christine de Pizan (1364–1430 CE)	98
Agnes Waterhouse (1503–1566 CE)	105
Gráinne O'Malley (1530–1603 CE)	110

Lady Katherine Grey (1540–1568 CE)	117
Countess Elizabeth Báthory (1560–1614 CE)	122
Mary Frith (1584–1659 CE)	127
Artemisia Gentileschi (1593–1653 CE)	132
Queen Anne (1665–1714 CE)	137
Nanny of the Maroons (1686–1755 CE)	144
Empress Elizaveta Petrovna (1709–1762 CE)	149
Elizabeth Sugrue (1740–1807 CE)	156
Sybil Ludington (1761–1839 CE)	159
Wang Zhenyi (1768–1797 CE)	163
Ching Shih (1775–1844 CE)	167
Mary Baker (1792–1864 CE)	171
Policarpa Salavarrieta (1795–1817 CE)	175
Sojourner Truth (1797–1883 CE)	179
Mary Anning (1799–1847 CE)	184
Pine Leaf (1806–1854 CE)	191
Frances Dickens (1810–1848 CE)	194
Rani Lakshmi Bai (1828–1858 CE)	197
Josephine Butler (1828–1906 CE)	202
Isabella Bird (1831–1904 CE)	208
Dr Mary Edwards Walker (1832–1919 CE)	212
Yaa Asantewaa (1840–1921 CE)	217
Edmonia Lewis (1844–1907 CE)	221
Emily Hobhouse (1860–1926 CE)	225
Nellie Bly (1864–1922 CE)	231
Edith Cavell (1865–1915 CE)	236
Edith Wilson (1872–1961 CE)	240

Constance Kopp (1878–1931 CE) — 245

Raden Adjeng Kartini (1879–1904 CE) — 249

Huda Sha'arawi (1879–1947 CE) — 253

Anna Pavlova (1881–1931 CE) — 258

Princess Alice of Battenberg (1885–1969 CE) — 263

Milunka Savić (1888 –1973 CE) — 269

Bessie Coleman (1892–1926 CE) — 273

Dorothy Lawrence (1896 – 1964 CE) — 278

Aloha Wanderwell (1906 – 1996 CE) — 282

Irena Sendler (1910 – 2008 CE) — 286

Noor Inayat Khan (1914 – 1944 CE) — 290

Hedy Lamarr (1914 – 2000 CE) — 294

Édith Piaf (1915 – 1963 CE) — 299

Andrée Borrel (1919 – 1944 CE) — 304

Françoise Gilot (1921–2023 CE) — 308

Truus and Freddie Oversteegen (1923 – 2018 CE) — 312

Reference List — 316

Introduction

When looking back at history, the vast majority of names you come across seem to be male. To me, it seems that when a woman did something amazing, she was overlooked and overshadowed. So, this book tells short stories of many real women who led fascinating lives but who seem to be forgotten in history.

There are warrior queens, spies, activists, and many more. Some who were incredibly inspiring and lived good lives, such as Josephine Butler, and some who had slightly more questionable morals, such as Elizabeth Sugrue, the first female executioner!

Some you may have heard of before, such as Hatshepsut and Queen Anne, but perhaps you do not know very much about their lives, just that they existed. Although the focus in history tends to centre on men, there is much we can learn from the women of the past. So, in this book, I have shed light on just a few women in history who led interesting lives, and from many, we can find inspiration.

Pharaoh Hatshepsut (1507–1458 BCE)

The First Great Woman of Whom We Are Informed

Hatshepsut is relatively well known as the woman who wore a fake beard when she became pharaoh. However, there is much more to Hatshepsut's rule. She had an impressively peaceful foreign policy and spent a lot of her reign building monuments, which we can still appreciate today, 3,000 years later. Hatshepsut is a good example of the success of the ancient Egyptians, and it is interesting to learn more about the female pharaoh and the woman behind the beard.

Hatshepsut was the fifth Pharaoh of the 18th Dynasty of Egypt, and after Sobekneferu, who ruled Egypt from 1806 to 1802 BCE, was the second confirmed female pharaoh. Coming to the throne should have been very easy for Hatshepsut in 1478 BCE, because she was the daughter, sister, and wife of a king, so her bloodline was perfect. She was the only child of Thutmose I and his chief wife, Ahmose, as well as the chief wife of Thutmose II. Thutmose II was the pharaoh after Thutmose I, and was his son from his secondary wife, Mutnofret, making Thutmose II not only Hatshepsut's husband but also her half-brother.

The pair married when Hatshepsut was about 12, and they had a daughter named Neferure, but Hatshepsut could not bear any more children. This led to Thutmose II taking another wife, Iset, with whom he had a son, who he named Thutmose. When this new baby Thutmose was just two, Thutmose II died, making the two-year-old child the new pharaoh, so Hatshepsut ruled jointly with the new Thutmose III while he was too young to rule.

The Egyptians did not make their lineage easy to learn with all the similar names and polygamous relationships. But it just means that due to Hatshepsut's proximity to the throne, being the daughter, wife, and sister of a pharaoh, she had every right to rule. However, she did have to defend her right to rule by claiming that her father had appointed her as his successor. Also, due to the lack of many previous female pharaohs (Sobekneferu had only ruled for four years 300 years previously), Hatshepsut took measures to make herself seem more masculine. She did this by wearing a beard and making sure her images depicted a more masculine form, such as having large muscles. However, in other images, she is shown to be a traditional female regalia, so perhaps she did also like the idea of being a strong female leader and wanted future generations to know how much power a woman could hold.

Hatshepsut feared her bloodline would not be enough to secure her rise to the throne and did not want others to make a claim, so she also used education and religion to strengthen her position. She demonstrated that she should be pharaoh because she established herself as the God's Wife of Amun, and this allowed her to rule as regent for her stepson. Later, Hatshepsut would take the full powers of a pharaoh, as she became the official co-rule of Egypt at around 1473 BCE, rather than ruling as a regent for Thutmose III.

It is possible that Hatshepsut bestowed these powers upon herself because other royals were trying to take the throne for themselves, and by becoming co-ruler, Hatshepsut was saving the throne for when Thutmose III would be old enough to rule as a pharaoh by himself. But it is also possible that Hatshepsut took on this title of pharaoh because she had high ambitions for herself and wanted more power, and waited until she was already established as regent before giving herself the title.

Despite the reign officially belonging to Thutmose III, Hatshepsut had the power and ruled as pharaoh for about 20 years, and these two decades were full of accomplishments. Hatshepsut built a large amount of wealth for her dynasty while in power by re-establishing trade networks. This involved preparing and funding expeditions to Punt, and the expedition team returned with 31 myrrh trees, which they attempted to transplant, something that had never been attempted before. They also returned with frankincense, which Hatshepsut could use as eyeliner, and these expeditions created profitable trading.

With regard to foreign policy, Hatshepsut also sent raiding expeditions to Byblos and the Sinai Peninsula, and sent a military campaign against Nubia and Canaan. Other than these expeditions, Hatshepsut's rule was very peaceful, with more focus on domestic policy and improving Egypt.

Throughout Egypt, Hatshepsut worked with the architect named Ineni to complete many construction projects, which were known for being extremely grand, and much more numerous than during any previous reign. She had monuments constructed at the Temple of Karnak and restored the original Precinct of Mut, which had been destroyed. Unfortunately, this was destroyed again later. Hatshepsut also had twin obelisks erected at the entrance of the temple, and these were the tallest of their time, one is still standing as the tallest surviving ancient obelisk on Earth.

Among other impressive projects, Hatshepsut built the Temple of Pakhet at Beni Hasa, an underground temple cut into rock cliffs, which was later greatly admired by the Greeks, who were known for architecture themselves. But Hatshepsut's masterpiece was a mortuary temple, which are usually made by pharaohs to commemorate their own reign. These were the first grand buildings planned for the Deir el-Bahri, near what we now call the Valley of the Kings.

Hatshepsut died after around 20 years of rule and was buried in the Valley of Kings. There is very little to say what her cause of death was, but after the identification of her mummy, it seems that she may have suffered from diabetes and died of bone cancer in her 50s, which spread through her body. It has also been discovered that Hatshepsut's bone cancer may have been caused by a carcinogenic skin lotion which she applied, unknowingly poisoning herself. This is because other members of her family suffered from skin diseases, so she used this poisonous cream while trying to soothe her itchy, irritated skin.

Hatshepsut had started building herself a tomb when she was the wife of Thutmose II, but when she became pharaoh, she decided she needed a better one.

Hatshepsut refurbished the burial chamber of her father, Thutmose I, and when she died, she was put in this tomb alongside him. Throughout time, her body has been moved to other tombs, such as with her nurse.

Thutmose III ruled for a further 30 years and inherited many of his stepmother's traits, as he was also an ambitious builder and a great warrior. But he prevented scholars from knowing of Hatshepsut's rule by eradicating almost all images of Hatshepsut as a pharaoh on the monuments she had built. This may be because he did not want to support a female leader, or he just wanted a more elegant lineage, from father to son, rather than having another ruler in between. More realistically, Thutmose III was probably angry at Hatshepsut, as he felt that she had usurped his throne, going beyond regent and fully taking on his role as pharaoh, while he was on the side-lines working in the army and doing construction of his own.

Whatever his reasoning, this was a terrible act, because the Egyptians believed the spirit could live beyond the grave, but only if a memory, such as an image or a statue, remained. So by destroying all statues depicting Hatshepsut, Thutmose III was effectively condemning her to endless death.

To sum up Hatshepsut, she ruled a country that was not used to a female ruler, and she did it fantastically. Her sex did not seem to hinder her at all or make her any less popular with the Egyptian people; however, she did choose to be depicted as a male in many contemporary images. Her reign was a peaceful time, and she spent it constructing buildings that would live on thousands of years later for us to admire. Hatshepsut also succeeded in keeping the succession smooth as she ran the country until her husband's son was able to take on the duty himself.

Hatshepsut may not be the first female pharaoh, but she is regarded by historians as one of the most successful pharaohs, and according to Egyptologist James Henry Breasted, she is known as "the first great woman in history of whom we are informed."

Sappho
(630–570 BCE)

The Poetess

Not very much is known about Sappho's personal life, but she is known for being a lyric poet who was extremely popular in ancient Greece. Sappho was so successful that she was praised by the likes of Solon and Plato, the latter even referred to her as the "Tenth Muse". Unfortunately, not a lot of her work survives. Today we mostly have access to fragments of poems, as it is estimated that she wrote 10,000 lines, and just 650 remain. Some claim this is due to Christians destroying her work to suppress the lesbian themes in her poetry, but this is uncertain. Despite the lack of work that remains, Sappho was admired by many of her contemporaries as well as modern-day poets, and she is known as "The Poetess" like Homer was known as "The Poet".

Sappho was born in the main city on the island of Lesbos in Greece to an aristocratic family, so she lived a relatively privileged life. Especially because on Lesbos, women were held in high esteem, and Sappho was popular because of her friendly personality. In the Mediterranean at the time, women were bound by marriage and motherhood, and were only ever taught to read and write to help them run a household more easily.

Even if a woman was competent in artistic skills, it was still extremely rare for her to take these skills anywhere, as any woman with any talent would be perceived as having masculinity that went against nature, so would be treated with suspicion. But due to her works, it is clear that Sappho had some formal education, suggesting that her island of Lesbos was particularly progressive, and Sappho was very fortunate and privileged to live there, as it enabled her to find success and empowerment from her poetry.

From childhood, Sappho learned to play the lyre and compose songs, which must have supported her future career in poetry. Some sources indicate that she married a man called Kerkylas, who died early in their marriage. However, others speculate that this husband was fictional, and made up by a comic poet because the name Kerkylas comes from a word that translates to "penis", so either he was invented, or he just had an incredibly unfortunate name! But whether there was a husband in the picture or not, Sappho is thought to have had a daughter named Cleis, of whom she wrote, "I have a beautiful child whose face is like/ golden flowers, my beloved Cleis." This daughter was named after Sappho's mother.

Other members of Sappho's family are not very well recorded, but she probably had three brothers, named Erigyius, Charaxus, and Larichus. Other than this, Sappho had little family, as her father died when she was just seven and he is not mentioned in any of Sappho's surviving works. At around 600 BCE, Sappho and her family were exiled from Lesbos to Sicily twice due to conflict the family had with the political elites of Lesbos, but allowed to return each time.

It is clear from her works that Sappho did have romantic interests in women, as she wrote with deep feeling and intimacy about lesbian love. Although, she may have simply been a good writer who liked to write about unusual topics. However, the works are extremely personal and detailed about love, desire, and loss, these she felt were the most basic and enduring human emotions. She felt compelled to write about love because she wanted to display her rejection of masculine warfare, as she preferred to focus on beauty and desire, which she believed to be more feminine topics. Once Sappho wrote about being seated opposite a beautiful woman, and she describes her fluster and heartache at this woman's beauty, and this demonstrates her pure, romantic and honest love for women:

…listens nearby to your
sweet replies
and desire-inducing laugh: indeed that
gets my heart pounding in my breast.
For just gazing at you for a second, it is impossible
for me even to talk…

Not only was she proficient in writing so intimately and emotionally, but Sappho also invented a new meter for poetry, known as the Sapphic Meter or Sapphic Stanza, consisting of three lines of eleven beats and a concluding line of five. Solon of Athens, one of the Seven Sages of Greece, once heard someone sing one of Sappho's works and asked to be taught it so that he could "learn it, then die". He thought it so moving that he would desire nothing more after learning the song. Sappho was writing not too long after the works of the Homeric poets, which were epic poems telling stories of the Trojan War in epics such as the Iliad and the Odyssey, but Sappho wrote in a very different style, and of different subjects, such as flowers and garlands.

Instead of writing epics, Sappho wrote short verses on many topics, such as hymns to gods, marriage songs, short tales of myths and legends, and songs about passion and love, for which she is known best.

Sappho's death is a mystery. Menander, the Athenian playwright, claimed that she jumped from the Leucadian cliffs, ending her own life because she was in love with a ferryman named Phaon who did not return her love. The Leucadian cliff was known to be a "lover's leap" because of a story about Aphrodite leaping from it while mourning Adonis. Menander was probably making fun of love, suggesting the irony of a lesbian killing herself for the love of a man.

More recently, historians have rejected the idea of Sappho ending her own life, instead, most believe that Sappho lived for a long time and died of natural causes. It could be argued that Sappho was killed a second time, but in this case, it was her works that were destroyed by Saint Gregory of Nazianus and Pope Gregory VII. They agreed with other Christians in Alexandria, Rome, and Constantinople, who condemned Sappho as "a whore who sang about her own licentiousness". It is sad that these people failed to see the love and beauty in

Sappho's poetry because they were blinded by their close-heartedness, and this has left us with just one or two full works of Sappho, and the rest are just fragments.

Of course, Sappho is known not only as an incredible poet but also as a symbol of love between women, with the English words 'sapphic' and 'lesbian' being derived from Sappho's name and home island. In classical Athenian comedy, Sappho was made into a promiscuous heterosexual woman, and it was not until the Hellenistic period that Sappho was known to be romantically and sexually attracted to women. Some claimed that she was "accused by some of being irregular in her ways and a women-lover", but many ancient authors did not believe this and argued that Sappho had been "slanderously accused" of having sexual relationships with women. Sappho's sexuality is still debated, and some early translators heterosexualised her poetry, and they claimed she was just describing friendly affection rather than romantic love.

In a way, the fact that we know so little of Sappho's life is a credit to her work, it shows that she is respected due to her poetry rather than a tragic back story. Many phrases which she used in her poetry, such as "more golden than gold" became commonly spoken in the Greek language, and in this way, Sappho was remembered and admired long after her death. Even Sappho knew her poems, or at least some lines, would be remembered forever, and she even referred to her poetry as her "immortal daughters". So overall, Sappho's sexuality is irrelevant, because her poems were her pride, not her relationships.

Empress Lü Zhi
(241–180 BCE)

The Murderous Dowager Empress

Zhi was respected greatly, almost as much as she was feared, and for very good reason. She had so much popularity and control over the ministers of China, that she was able to cause the execution of an emperor and have him replaced while she was the dowager empress. Zhi murdered many people who she was threatened by in very violent ways, including mutilating her husband's concubine to create a "human swine". This is one example highlighting Zhi's ruthlessness, as well as her firm grip on control, which she maintained throughout her life as Empress and later as Dowager Empress of China.

However, Zhi and her family were not always in control, as she began her life fleeing to Pei County from her father's enemies. But while there, Zhi's father found success as he had become friends with the county magistrate, making his position much more influential. Once, at an event in Zhi's house, her father met

Liu Bang, who was just a minor patrol officer at the time and was impressed by the young man.

After sitting together throughout their dinner party, Liu Bang had impressed the family so much that Zhi was offered to him in marriage, and their wedding followed soon after. The couple thrived, and Zhi gave birth to a girl and a boy, named Yuan of Lu and Liu Ying respectively; however, both children and Zhi spent a few years living with Zhi's father while Liu Bang was fighting against the Qin Dynasty.

The oppressive and unpopular Qin Dynasty fell in 206 BCE, which was marked by the last Qin emperor surrendering the capital, Xianyang to Liu Bang. However, Xiang Yu, who had rebelled against the Qin Dynasty along with Liu Bang, took a lot of control and split the former Qin Empire into 18 kingdoms. Xiang Yu took control of the Kingdom of Chu, and gave Liu Bang the Kingdom of Han; however, this meant that Liu Bang was deprived of his title in Guanzhong, which he had held previously, and was sent with 30,000 troops and thousands of civilians to Bashu.

Once he arrived there, Liu Bang was quite annoyed that he had not gained more after his efforts against the Qin Dynasty. In retaliation, he ordered to have the gallery roads leading into Bashu destroyed, to prevent attack from the rear and to pretend to Xiang Yu that he would not leave Bashu, but he was planning to rebel. While Xiang Yu was putting down some small rebellions in Qi and Zhao, Liu Bang attacked the Three Qins in Guanzhong, which he believed he had the rights to, and in two battles Liu Bang and the Han forces were victorious. But Liu Bang was still not satisfied, so he also conquered other regions, such as Longxi, Beidi and Shangjun, before inviting his family to join him.

This was a mistake. When Liu Bang took Pengcheng, Chu's capital, Xiang Yu responded by recapturing the city, along with Liu Bang's family. After a long civil war, known as the Chu-Han Contention, Xiang Yu agreed to release Liu Bang's family during a ceasefire at the Treaty of Hong Canal, but he immediately renounced this. So after yet more conflict, at the Battle of Gaixia Liu Bang defeated Xiang Yu, and the latter committed suicide, leaving China unified under Han rule and Liu Bang declared himself emperor, with Zhi as his empress.

To help resolve some instability left over from the civil war, Liu Bang placed Zhi in a position to help with decision-making, and her popularity with the officers enabled Zhi to be successful. But they also feared her, because early in her position of power, Zhi displayed her ruthless behaviour via the deaths of Han Xin and Peng Yue.

In 196 BCE, Liu Bang left the capital to suppress a revolt in Julu, and Zhi believed that Han Xin was involved in the revolt, as he was known to be friendly with the leader of the rebellion. Acting on suspicion only, Zhi invited Han Xin to Changle Palace. As soon as he arrived, Zhi had him arrested and then put to death along with the rest of his family. Then Peng Yue declined to send reinforcements to Liu Bang to help him put down a rebellion after claiming he was ill, making himself another suspect of scheming. So Liu Bang responded by having him arrested, demoted to a commoner and then exiled.

But Zhi believed that her husband was not firm enough with this potential traitor, so she met Peng Yue on his journey. Knowing her reputation, Peng Yue was terrified and begged for his life and asked to go home, so Zhi tricked him by agreeing. But while he was under a false sense of security, Zhi took the opportunity to have him executed on false charges of treason. She then ordered his clan to be put to death and have Peng Yue's body mutilated.

Han Xin and Peng Yue were just the first of Zhi's targets; she was also prepared to harm anyone who she felt threatened by. Liu Bang, like many Emperors of China, had concubines and illegitimate children, including Concubine Qi and her son, Liu Ruyi. This pair became favourites of Liu Bang, and he even planned on making Liu Ruyi the prince and heir, rather than Zhi's son, Liu Ying. Zhi was unsurprisingly not happy about this; in fact, she was furious.

Her husband had deemed Liu Ying too soft-hearted and weak to be a ruler and did not resemble Liu Bang as well as Liu Ruyi did, so Zhi decided to take action. The ministers admired Zhi so were generally on her side in the matter, but Liu did not care, so Zhi had someone speak to the Four Whiteheads of Mount Shang on her behalf. The Four were a group of wise men with opinions that the emperor would listen to, and they spoke to Liu Bang, promising to support and assist Liu Ying if he became emperor. Liu Bang was satisfied with their support (and probably feared to go against them) and told Concubine Qi that he was no longer going to make her son the new prince. Allegedly, he said he wanted to replace Liu Ying, but with the support of the Four, Liu Ying was difficult to unseat.

In 195 BCE, the emperor was succeeded by his and Zhi's son, Liu Ying, who became known as Emperor Hui of Han. Zhi was also honoured with the new title of empress dowager, which gave her a lot more influence than she had previously. Although Zhi was very civil with her deceased husband's concubines during his life, she was extremely resentful of Concubine Qi and her son, due to the dispute over the succession struggle between Liu Ruyi and Liu Ying. So with her new powers, Zhi stripped Qi of her position, had her head shaved, put her in stocks and forced her to do hard labour, such as milling rice.

Then Zhi summoned the 12-year-old Liu Ruyi to have him killed; however, he was temporarily protected because he was too ill to travel long distances. Zhi then detained Liu Ruyi's protectors, so he had no choice but to go to her the next time he was summoned. This time after Liu Ruyi was summoned, the current emperor intercepted his half-brother on his journey, and stayed with him on the way, preventing Zhi from harming the boy in case her own son was harmed too.

Finally, in 194 BCE the emperor went on a hunting trip without Liu Ruyi, as the boy did not want to get out of bed, so Zhi sent an assassin to poison Liu Ruyi with wine. By the end of the hunt, Liu Ruyi was dead. His mother, Concubine Qi, faced a messier death. Zhi had Qi's limbs chopped off; her eyes gouged out and her ears were sliced off; she was forced to drink something that made her mute; and she was thrown into a latrine. There, Qi was known as a "human swine", and when the emperor saw her, he was sick at the sight.

Liu Ying was poorly for a long time and claimed that this disgusting creation of the "human swine" could not have been done by a human. As it was his own mother who had done this, he felt he was not fit to rule, so from then, the emperor indulged himself in carnal pleasures, ignoring state affairs entirely.

Soon after, Zhi hosted a dinner and invited the emperor as well as Liu Fei, the son of the late Liu Bang and Lady Cao, another of his concubines. The emperor honoured Liu Fei as his half-brother at this dinner party, which angered Zhi, so she told her servants to poison Liu Fei. But just before he could take a sip, the emperor realised his mother's intentions and took the drink from Liu Fei, and Zhi thought he would drink it himself, so Zhi knocked the cup from her son's hands. After this incident, Liu Fei feared for his life, so offered to give a commandery from his principality to Zhi's daughter so that he may live, and luckily for him, Zhi accepted this offer, sparing his life.

Soon, a third of Liu Bang's illegitimate sons was targeted by Zhi. This time it was Liu You, who was married to Zhi's niece. Liu You's wife discovered that he was having secret affairs with other women, so she decided to take revenge by telling Zhi that Liu You was plotting a rebellion. Zhi summoned Liu You to her, had him imprisoned, then starved him to death.

Liu Hui was the next target, yet another son of Liu Bang. Zhi forced Liu Hui to marry a member of her family so they could watch over Liu Hui, controlling him and restricting his authority. So the family was not very impressed when they found out he was taking concubines, and they arranged to have his favourite concubine poisoned to death. Liu Hui was distraught by this and feared for his own life, so he eventually committed suicide. In total Zhi caused the deaths of three of her husband's sons, and had attempted to kill a fourth. This highlights how hungry for power Zhi was, as well as her fear of losing it to the family of her deceased husband.

In 192 BCE, Zhi received a letter from Modu, part of the Xiongnu, in which marriage was proposed to her in an extremely mocking and intimidating way, angering Zhi. She then decided to rally an army to destroy the Xiongnu, even considering declaring war, until it was pointed out how much stronger the Xiongnu army was. Instead, Zhi modified her plans and rejected the proposition quite politely.

A year later, Zhi insisted that her son, the emperor, should marry his niece, Zhang Yan. The pair were not able to have any children, and so it is claimed that Zhi encouraged the new empress to adopt eight boys and have their mothers killed, but these boys were possibly born to the emperor's concubines. When the emperor died in 188 BCE, it was one of these sons that succeeded him and became Emperor Qianshao, who allowed Zhi to remain the empress dowager. At some point, Emperor Qianshao found out that his biological mother had been murdered by Zhang Yan, so he decided to avenge his mother when he grew older.

Zhi confined the emperor in his palace to prevent him from acting on his anger after finding out about his parentage. She announced that he was ill with psychosis, isolating him from everyone and Zhi even claimed that he was incapable of ruling and should be replaced. It shows just how much power Zhi had that this was not questioned. The emperor was executed and replaced with his brother, Liu Yi.

A few years later, Zhi died at the age of 61 and was laid to rest in her husband's tomb in Changling, but Zhi's body was desecrated by rebels who raided her tomb. Not long after Zhi's death, her clan members were overthrown and massacred, this event was known as the Lü Clan Disturbance.

It is amazing how Zhi held on to so much power throughout her life. She outlived three emperors since becoming empress but always kept her authority strong, using the respect from ministers and her ruthlessness at dealing with those who she perceived as a threat. Zhi was strong and harsh as a dowager empress, with as much, if not more, power than the emperor. Especially when she revealed the "human swine" to the emperor, leaving him incapable of ruling and so taking on this power herself.

When Zhi did not approve of someone or found them a threat, she was deadly, her grandson is an example of this, as despite being emperor, Zhi was still able to exert her control over the ministers and have him killed because he did not suit her. Not many have managed to cling to such great power for such a long period as Zhi.

Trưng Trắc and Trưng Nhị
(12–43 CE)

Warrior Sisters

The Trưng sisters are Vietnamese national heroines and for a very good reason. Their bravery on the battlefield is portrayed in many images in which the sisters ride elephants into battle with their swords drawn. The older sister, Trắc, was the queen of the independent nation she and her sister took from the Chinese, whereas Nhị was known for her strength as a great warrior. The pair fought for their independence and an end to their suppression with an army of 80,000 people, many of whom were women, and these rebels fought off the invading Chinese forces for three years.

The sisters lived in Nanyue at a time when Vietnam did not exist as a nation yet, and they were born during a very long period of Chinese occupation. This occupation began in 111 BCE when the Chinese Han Dynasty annexed the area during the Han-Nanyue War, then they assigned puppet Vietnamese leaders for each district who would answer to their Chinese government. The Trưng sisters' father was one of these puppet leaders; however, he and many others stood up to the Chinese when they could, and tried to let the Vietnamese people in the area live as if they were not being ruled by the Chinese. So the sisters were given a good education, and taught martial arts, as well as literacy, but most importantly about warfare.

At this time, women in Vietnam were well respected and could be political leaders, judges, traders, and warriors. But eventually, the Chinese regime became more strict and repressive. They replaced the Vietnamese culture of having a matriarchal family system with a patriarchal system, and imposed excessive taxation from the Vietnamese. The Trưng sisters also witnessed the Vietnamese people being treated with cruelty, as those who were uncooperative were imprisoned or executed.

At some point during this time, a neighbour visited their father, potentially his doctor, accompanied by his son, named Thi Sách. Trưng Trắc fell in love with this young man and the pair married soon after this meeting. Thi Sách was deeply furious with the way the Vietnamese were being treated, and the Chinese policy of forcible cultural assimilation, so he plotted with his lords to rebel and he stood up against the unfair taxation. Soon he was executed by the Chinese, and his wife was raped. This was to prevent others from rebelling, and to strike fear into the Vietnamese; however, the death of Thi Sách spurred on Trưng Trắc, as she loved her husband, so instead of going into mourning, she began to spread his ideas of rebellion.

In the year 39, both sisters took back their village from the Chinese. The Chinese administrator of the area only managed to escape back to China by shaving off his long hair, as at the time it was custom for Vietnamese men to shave their heads, whereas the Chinese did not. The sisters then gained support from the villages in Cửu Chân, Nhật Nam and Hợp Phố, eventually recruiting an army of 80,000 people. Many of these were women, including 36 of the generals. The pair continued to gain support by committing acts of bravery, including killing a man-eating tiger, who was terrorising the locals, as well as using their natural charisma and intelligence to their advantage to incite rebellion in as many as possible. But they did not just recruit rebels, the sisters also helped to train the troops so that they could fight against the Chinese.

Eventually, the Trưng sisters led their army into battle upon the backs of elephants, and they took back 65 citadels from the Chinese, liberating Nam Viet.

When this massive feat had been achieved, the rebels accepted Trưng Trắc as queen of an independent state, making her the first woman to be a Vietnamese monarch.

After managing to expel the Chinese from Vietnam, the sisters began to consolidate their leadership. It was clear that Trưng Nhị was a better warrior, and Trưng Trắc excelled at leadership, so took on the role of queen. For her three-year reign, Trưng Trắc was known as "Trưng Vuong", which means "She-King Trưng", and established her royal court in Me-Linh, which was a political centre in the Hong River plain. She aimed to restore the Vietnamese government and remove the unpopular taxes, while also respecting the country's traditions and values, and engaging in battles to solidify their leadership. For three years the sisters, along with their army, fought the Chinese, preventing them from invading, and the Vietnamese people thrived.

However, in the year 43, the Chinese managed to defeat the Vietnamese rebels, partially due to the Vietnamese army lacking supplies and trained soldiers. They launched a massive attack on Nam Việt, and won by allegedly going into battle completely naked! This scared off most of the army of Vietnamese women, and many of the male rebels had already fled as some did not think they could succeed under female leadership. A notable woman who was not scared off by the naked Chinese army was Phung Thi Chinh, who was a heavily pregnant captain protecting Nam Việt and who gave birth on the front line.

She fought the battle with her new-born baby in her arm and a sword in her hand. But tragically, when the fight was lost, rather than die at the hands of the Chinese, Phung Thi Chinh killed herself and her new baby. Many others also committed suicide, one woman charged against the Chinese, screaming and slaying men before killing herself. Others loyally fought to the death in this battle, but the sisters realised that they were defeated, so to protect their honour in Vietnamese tradition, they drowned themselves in the Hát River.

Legend then claims that the bodies of the sisters turned into statues, washed ashore, then were placed in Hanoi's Hai Ba Trưng Temple for worship. However, Chinese sources suggest that they were beheaded by a Chinese military leader. Yet another legend of this battle claims the sisters did not die, but simply vanished into the clouds. After their defeat, the culture and customs of the local people were aggressively sinicised, and their tribal ways were removed so that the Han government could rule them more easily.

The Trưng sisters do symbolise female empowerment, as against all the odds, together they became heroines and queens, uniting thousands of women to fight for their homes. They may not have ruled for a very long time, but they led the first resistance movement against the occupying Chinese after 247 years of domination. Some say that without them, without their inspirational story which encourages future Vietnamese people who fought for independence, Vietnam may not be the country that it is today.

Empress Jingū
(169–269 CE)

Legendary Empress

Jingū was an Empress of Japan, and although her life is shrouded in legend, she probably did exist and was known for establishing Japanese authority in Korea. However, her life is controversial. It seems that there is a lack of evidence and there are contradictory records of her Korean conquest, but despite the mystery, what we do know of Jingū is that she was a very powerful woman. She could strike a fierce image of a warrior empress, as she went into battle dressed as a man wielding a sword, but despite this aggressive image, Jingū was respected and admired for her mercy, as her most successful campaign was completely bloodless.

Jingū was a descendant of a legendary Korean prince named Amenohiboko, so enjoyed the respect of those around her, especially because during this time there was a matriarchal society, so female and male chiefs could rule together.

Jingū married Emperor Chūai, the 14th sovereign of Japan, and was known as the empress consort. While in this role, Jingū would accompany her husband on military campaigns to perform mystical rites of divination, as her ability to communicate with spirits helped to gain the support and popularity of the people.

One example of this was in the year 200 when the emperor was fighting the Kumaso people. A male shaman strummed an instrument to put Jingū into a trance. Then she became a medium used by the spirits to communicate. The spirit inhabiting the empress consort told her husband to stop fighting the Kumaso, instead, to turn his attention to a kingdom called Silla. The spirit claimed that if he agreed to worship the spirit with an offering of a ship and a rice field, then the emperor would find success in Silla. No swords would have to be drawn, but the emperor would become rich from the gold, silver, and jewels that he would find there. But the emperor refused to obey the spirit, which led to his death in a battle against the Kumaso, which he had refused to give up.

Jingū was left to rule as regent, but for a while, she kept her husband's death a secret so that she could obtain the spiritual resources to consolidate her rule. This included entering a ceremonial hall to purify herself, then she spent eight days trying to identify the spirit. When it came to her, the spirit repeated what it told the emperor, so Jingū followed its order and made offerings at the correct shrines, allowing her to quickly complete the campaign over the Kumaso people. According to sources, Jingū fought this battle in a fit of rage because she was distraught at her husband's death. After this, Jingū focussed on her taking of the "promised land", which is believed to be land in the Korean Peninsula, including the kingdoms of Silla and Paekche. This is the area that the spirit had guided her to, where she would be destined to find riches and victory.

Before this invasion however, Jingū went to the counsellors dressed as a man and asked permission for the declaration of war, first stating she had the support of the spirits. Jingū also promised that if she was victorious the counsellors would be credited with the success, and if she was defeated then she would accept blame. With these promises, the counsellors unanimously supported the declaration of war against Silla. Next, Jingū needed to recruit soldiers, which she achieved without difficulty. When the empress assembled the three divisions on the beach, she wore men's clothing and wielded a sword, striking such a formidable figure that she was cheered by her soldiers.

With their full support, Jingū told them: "You must not engage in atrocities; avoid unnecessary killing and spare those who surrender", also promising to reward those who followed her instruction as well as punish those who showed cowardice. It was at this moment when Jingū first felt her baby move inside her womb, but she invoked the spirits to postpone the birth of the child until after her successful return from the campaign.

The campaign was a major success. When the troops landed in Silla, they marched unopposed into the palace of the king, who was so impressed with Jingū's supernatural powers that he surrendered and offered her an annual tribute gift of horses and 100 artisans. Some troops did want to kill the King of Silla, but Jingū did not allow this. Instead, she had the soldiers collect riches and help to fully subjugate Silla with taxation. When Jingū returned to Japan victorious three years later, she had won the full love and support of her people, as she had led a successful bloodless campaign herself.

It is said that during those three years in Silla, Homutawake, her unborn baby son, had remained in her womb to give her time to complete her conquest and return to Japan. But some claim that her pregnancy was symbolic, others that it was three harvests (which amounts to about nine months), rather than three years that she was conquering these areas in Korea.

After returning to Japan, Jingū ascended to the Chrysanthemum Throne as the Empress of Japan and gave birth to her baby. A few years later, the King of Baekje presented Jingū with a seven-branched sword, giving her a very strong image of a fierce warrior empress. After about 68 years of ruling as the 15th Japanese imperial ruler, Jingū died of unknown causes, and her son, now known as Emperor Ōjin, succeeded her.

He was later worshipped as Hachiman, the God of War, perhaps because he remained in his mother's womb while she was at war. However, Jingū's name was removed from the imperial lineage by Emperor Meiji to make the lineage unbroken, as he did not believe she should be a "true" ancestor of those on the throne. It was also argued that she was just ruling as regent for her son.

But despite the controversy over Jingū, and the lack of evidence of her life, in 1881, Empress Jingū became the first woman to be featured on a Japanese banknote. She was also featured on the 1908/14 postage stamps, again the first woman to do so. So although she was mysterious and controversial, Jingū left her mark on Japan and proved that women can be leaders as well as warriors.

If we believe the legend of Jingū, she was greatly loved by her people, as well as respected outside her kingdom for her strong authority, shown by her defeat of the Kumaso people. As well as being an authoritative leader, Jingū was merciful, displayed by her bloodless invasion of Silla.

St Agnes of Rome
(291–304 CE)

The Patron Saint of Girls

Agnes is remembered as a virgin martyr, who later was made a saint for her abundance of faith in Christianity when this faith was punishable by death. She had an abrupt end to her life, but if her story is true, then she truly does have great strength and deserves to be remembered. Agnes faced persecution but always remained loyal and true, not only to the god she believed in but also to herself and her own values.

Agnes was a member of the Roman nobility and part of an early Christian family. Despite just being the age of 12 or 13, Agnes was an extremely beautiful girl so she had many high-ranked suitors asking to marry her. But Agnes refused all of these young men because she had promised God that she would not stain her purity. Whenever a man asked to marry Agnes, she would say "Jesus Christ is my only Spouse", but this constant refusal angered the young men, so they told the authorities of her faith in Christianity, it was regarded as a cult.

By the early 4th century, about 10% of the Roman population were Christians, and the city would not adopt Christianity until 380. Unfortunately for Agnes and other Christians in Rome at this time, the Emperor Diocletian had launched a campaign against the Christian population which did not end until 311 when Diocletian died. This was the worst persecution that Christians have ever faced. It all began because many Christians refused to see the emperor as a god, so in his anger, he decided on a policy of extermination and purged the imperial household of Christians and Christian sympathisers, including his own wife and daughter.

In the year 303, the emperor signed an edict ordering the destruction of Christian churches and books and deprived Christians of their civil rights. A year later, he ordered all Christians to be put to death if they refused to offer a sacrifice. This persecution was extremely bloody but did not hinder the growing numbers of Christians in the city. When Emperor Galerius, who had supported the persecutions as a fanatical anti-Christian, took over he signed an edict allowing the practice of Christianity under his rule. But it was not until Constantine I was emperor that Christianity was actively supported in Rome.

So, at this time, Agnes was in real danger since these men had accused her of practising Christianity. At one point, Procop, the governor's son, tried to win Agnes with gifts and promises, but she still refused, despite his authoritative position. Procop angrily took Agnes to his father, who promised Agnes riches and gifts if she would deny God, but the young girl still refused, even when she was put in chains. Agnes' punishment was to be dragged naked through the streets to a brothel, but she prayed, which caused her hair to grow, covering her body because Agnes was allegedly being protected by an angel. Any man who tried to rape the young girl was struck blind, and one was even struck dead, but Agnes prayed for him and he was revived, securing Agnes' release.

After this incident, Agnes was put on trial and sentenced to death for her crime of being a Christian. She was led out and bound to a stake, but the wood would not burn and the flames would part away from her. As the fire would not engulf Agnes, the officer in charge of the troops drew his sword and beheaded her, although some say that he stabbed her in the throat. Her blood poured to the floor and other Christians soaked it up with cloth. Despite their anger towards

Agnes, it is said that even the Pagans cried to see such a young and beautiful girl die.

Agnes was buried in Rome and a few days after her death, Emerentiana, her sister, was found praying at her tomb. She condemned the Pagans for murdering her sister and then she was stoned to death. Emerentiana was also later canonised along with Agnes. At this tomb, the daughter of Constantine I, Constantina, was said to have been cured of leprosy after praying.

Agnes is usually portrayed holding a lamb, which is not only a symbol of her virginal innocence, but also the Latin word for "lamb" is "agnus", so the image also evokes her name. Agnes was made the patron saint of those seeking chastity and purity, as well as the saint of young girls and rape victims due to the circumstances surrounding her martyrdom. As a saint, Agnes has a feast day, which falls on the 21st of January, on which it is customary to have two lambs brought to be blessed by the Pope.

Agnes' story can be appreciated by many, whether or not they are Christian, because she was treated harshly at such a young age, but kept strong throughout this treatment. Now, she is remembered as a saint to many and is a symbol for purity and chastity, as well as being one of just seven women (excluding the Virgin Mary), who is commemorated by name in the Canon of the Mass. Despite being so young, Agnes was stoic in the face of danger, never once outwardly showing her distress at the unfortunate situation she found herself in; instead, she remained positive and faithful to what she truly believed in.

Hypatia of Alexandria (370–415 CE)

Martyr of Academia

In her time, Hypatia was one of the world's leading scholars, which was a very uncommon position for a woman to be in. So Hypatia is an extremely interesting and noteworthy character in history. She lived during a turbulent time in Alexandria, when there began persecutions of the Jewish community, creating religious conflicts between the Jews and Christians. However, Hypatia was not a member of either of these groups, instead, she was a Pagan who got caught up in the conflict when all she wanted to do was teach and study.

Hypatia was the daughter of Theon, the head of a school called the "Mouseion", which was highly prestigious and exclusive. He was an extremely progressive man and decided to raise his daughter as if she was a boy, by teaching her his trade. This involved tutoring Hypatia in mathematics, astronomy, and philosophy, giving her an excellent education and allowing her to follow in her father's footsteps and teach these subjects. Although nothing is known of Hypatia's mother, she may have had a brother named Epiphanius, as he is referred to by Theon as "my dear son", but he may have just been a favourite pupil.

Of course, Hypatia lived in Alexandria, which was a city in Egypt seen as the philosophical capital of the Greco-Roman world, second only to Athens. However, the city had begun to decline since it was conquered by Caesar in 48 BCE, when he accidentally burned down the library, and although it was later rebuilt, a lot of information was permanently lost. Despite this decline, Alexandria still attracted the best minds of many different disciplines, such as the mathematician, Archimedes. Although previously the city was relatively peaceful, when Constantine the Great became the Roman emperor, he made Christianity the official state religion, which encouraged religious rivalries between Jews, Christians, and Pagans who were all living in the city, and this would later lead to problems for Hypatia.

At this time Hypatia was a respected academic at a university, surpassing her father and most of the other men with her intellect. She was known to fully devote her life to teaching and learning, which meant that she never married and remained celibate, as she did not want to be distracted from her work. But this does not mean she was unattractive and not pursued, as Damascius wrote that she was "exceedingly beautiful and fair of form", leading one man to attempt to court her during her lectures. Hypatia tried to soothe his lust by playing the lyre; however, he was persistent. So when he next attempted to seduce Hypatia, she rejected him by displaying her bloody menstrual rags, proclaiming, "This is what you really love, my young man, but you do not love beauty for its own sake." The man was so traumatised that he immediately ceased his pursuit of Hypatia.

Everyone in Alexandria seemed to love Hypatia and her teaching. When she gave surprise public lectures in the streets of the city, donned in her philosopher's cloak, she would draw very large crowds. Some of her lessons involved teaching the construction of astrolabes (devices that are like analogue calculators that solve astronomical problems), and hydrometers (which are used to find out the relative density of liquids based on the concept of buoyancy); however, she did not invent these.

Mostly, Hypatia lectured about mathematics and philosophy, in particular the philosophy of Neoplatonism, basing her teachings on Plotinus, who founded Neoplatonism, rather than Iamblichus, who was more extreme in his idea of

Neoplatonism. Plotinus taught that Neoplatonism was the idea that there was an ultimate reality beyond the reach of thought and the goal of life is to aim for this reality, which cannot be described because we do not have the mental capacity to fully understand it. Hypatia taught these ideas with more scientific emphasis than her predecessors.

Another legacy of Hypatia, preserved by a student, was the pursuit of "the philosophical state of apatheia—complete liberation from emotions and affections". Despite this teaching, Hypatia was known to be very kind and charismatic as a teacher. Some Christians believed some of Hypatia's teachings to be Pagan; however, she taught many prominent Christians. One of these was Synesius of Cyrene, who later became the Bishop of Ptolemais, and he revered Hypatia. The pair stayed in contact after he finished studying under Hypatia and he used her teachings and ideas throughout his professional and personal life. Hypatia had this good relationship with many of her students who came from all different backgrounds from all over the Mediterranean.

From 382, the Bishop of Alexandria was Theophilus and he was very much against Iamblichean Neoplatonism, so in 391 he demolished the Serapeum, which is where the overtly Pagan Neoplatonism was taught. Hypatia taught a much more moderate variety of Neoplatonism, based on the teachings of Plotinus, so she was not targeted by Theophilus. She also had close relationships with Roman prefects and other political leaders, giving her some political influence. Under the orders of the Roman emperor, Theophilus destroyed all Pagan temples, which incited some feelings of religious tension and division.

But in 412, this tension was increased when Theophilus died and was replaced by Cyril, who began persecuting the Jewish population of Alexandria. Amid this religious divide and persecution, some Jewish extremists massacred Christians who they felt were unfairly trying to take control of the city. Cyril responded by closing the synagogues, confiscating property belonging to Jews, and expelling many Jews from the city. During this persecution, Christians looted the synagogues and homes of the Jewish people. Orestes, the Roman Prefect of Alexandria and friend of Hypatia, was outraged by Cyril inciting this persecution, as although he was a Christian, he did not want Alexandria to be ruled by the church.

When he reported this to the Roman emperor, the violence escalated, a riot broke out and a group of Christian clerics nearly killed Orestes. It was believed that Cyril sent this group, so Orestes responded by having the monk leading the riot publicly tortured to death. Cyril attempted to proclaim this monk as a martyr but failed because he was despised for starting a riot. The feud continued and so Orestes asked Hypatia for advice in this conflict, because she was loved by both Pagans and Christians, and she had the reputation of a wise counsellor.

Cyril disliked that Hypatia was going to be involved in this feud, so tried to discredit her by spreading rumours. He claimed that Hypatia was preventing Orestes from reconciling with Cyril, as well as keeping the prefect from his "true faith", as he knew Hypatia was a Pagan. Because of this, he also claimed that Hypatia took part in satanic rituals. Most knew this was nonsense, as Hypatia had many Christian students who loved her as much as the Pagans. They knew that although she was a Pagan, she tolerated Christianity, as her student's faith did not affect their ability to learn or listen to her teachings. Although a few did dislike some of her mathematical concepts, which they believed went against the teachings of the church.

During an attack on the Jewish community in 415, Hypatia was on the way home from delivering lectures at the university when she was attacked by a mob of Christians. They dragged Hypatia from her carriage into a church, which used to be a Pagan temple, stripped her naked, and then murdered her using shards of broken pottery. They also cut out her eyeballs and tore her body into pieces before dragging her limbs through the town to Cinarion. When there, they set her limbs on fire, which is the traditional treatment of the worst criminals, as their bodies would be cremated to purify the city. After Hypatia's death, the University of Alexandria was sacked and burned, Pagan temples were torn down and there was a mass exodus of intellectuals and artists from Alexandria. Cyril was declared a saint for this.

Hypatia was murdered brutally during a religious dispute, even though she did not care about how others felt about religion, as long as everyone was good to each other. Her death was seen as a tragic loss to the world, as scholars and philosophers saw her as an intelligent woman who gave a lot of input to the scientific and academic world. Nowadays she is a symbol of feminism, as she was seen as one of the greatest minds of her time and not held back by her sex.

After her death, some made Hypatia a symbol of Christian virtue, despite her lack of Christian faith, because they thought she was the basis for the legend of Saint Catherine of Alexandria. But in the Age of Enlightenment, she was seen as the opposite, a symbol in opposition to Christianity, encouraging future Neoplatonists such as Damascus to oppose Christianity. However, this is a shame because Hypatia did not hate Christians or religion at all; she was simply a victim of the religious divide. Other philosophers remembered Hypatia as a martyr for philosophy, and her devotion to the pursuit of learning is still greatly admired.

Liu Chuyu
(446–465 CE)

The Princess with a Harem

This is a story of a princess who knew what she wanted. Not much is known of Chuyu's short life, but what is known is that she was demanding and not afraid to ask for outrageous favours, even from the emperor. Chuyu lived in the Liu Song Dynasty of China and was the daughter of one emperor and sister of the next, so she led a very privileged life. But she could still see when she was treated differently by society because of her sex, so took matters into her own hands and asked for equality.

When Chuyu was young, there was political turmoil in China. In the year 453, Liu Shao assassinated his own father, who was the emperor at the time. This angered many people because one of Confucianism's fundamental rules was to respect one's father. So Liu Shao's brother, who was Chuyu's father, Liu Jun, took advantage of his brother's unpopularity and rose against him. He defeated

Liu Shao and beheaded him, allowing Liu Jun to rise to the throne as Emperor Xiaowu. As the oldest daughter of the emperor, Chuyu was now called Princess Shanyin and was married to He Ji, the son of one of Emperor Xiaowu's officials.

Unfortunately, the reign of Chuyu's father was not very popular because the emperor was seen as very immoral for many reasons. Mostly, people disliked the emperor because he was known to have committed incest with his cousins and sisters, and some say even his own mother. But despite the unpopularity of his personal life, Emperor Xiaowu's reign was quite peaceful.

When Emperor Xiaowu died in 464, Liu Ziye, one of Chuyu's five younger siblings, ascended to the throne and was known as Emperor Qianfei. But he was also regarded as immoral, some even labelling him as a tyrant. Emperor Qianfei seemed to be very suspicious and paranoid, as he executed many of his uncles. He also committed incest as his father did before him, as the emperor hired some of his aunts and cousins to be his concubines. Once, the emperor ordered his female family members to join him at the palace to have sexual intercourse with him, when one aunt refused, he executed her three sons.

One day, Chuyu, who was one of her brother's attendants, complained to Emperor Qianfei, saying that it was unfair that he had more than 10,000 women kept in his palace to have sexual relations with, but she was allowed only one husband. She pointed out that the two of them came from the same parents and so the only difference was that she was a woman and he was a man, making it unfair that this difference meant they were permitted such different pleasures.

The emperor listened to this argument and agreed with her, so he selected 30 young handsome men for her to have in her harem. These men were called Chuyu's "mainshou", literally translating to "prime faces", because they were some of the most attractive men. Chuyu was allowed to have these men as her lovers and the word "mainshou" is now used to describe a woman's male lover, particularly the lovers of honoured women.

Chuyu's brother also honoured her with the improved title of Princess Kuaiji. But the princess was still not content, because despite her harem of attractive men, the man she found most desirable was the mid-level official called Chu Yuan. So Emperor Qianfei gave this man to Chuyu as a lover for 10 days. But Chu Yuan refused to have sexual relations with Chuyu, despite being ordered to do as she asked, so she released him.

In 465, the emperor was assassinated by his attendant and replaced with his uncle, Liu Yu, who became Emperor Ming. This was because the people were tired of Emperor Qianfei's tyrannical method of ruling, by executing those who disagreed, and by keeping his family close and having them as his concubines. The new Emperor Ming condemned Chuyu for her immorality, claiming that she had participated in her brother's immoralities and tyrannical governance, so ordered her to commit suicide at the age of just 18 or 19.

Chuyu had a short life, but seemed ignorant of the political strife and was able to do as she wished. Although her father's and brother's immoralities are well known, it is unclear whether Chuyu was ever one of the emperor's concubines. It seems that she may have been killed for acting on her sexual desires in the same way that most wealthy men did at the time. Whatever anyone thinks of Chuyu's decisions, she was bold, determined, and believed that being a woman should not stop her from doing what she wanted.

Queen Seondeok of Silla (606–647 CE)

The First Queen of Korea

Queen Seondeok knew she was capable to rule a country and persuaded her father to allow it. She was able to use this sort of diplomacy and intelligence throughout her reign to rule very successfully. The period that Seondeok ruled was known as the Three Kingdoms period, which was when the Korean Peninsula was made up of three kingdoms: Silla, where Seondeok ruled, Goguryeo, and Baekje. Seondeok was not afraid to ask for political and military alliances which she was able to manipulate, leading to Silla's dominance in the Korean Peninsula. She also encouraged a cultural Golden Age and peace between religious groups. Seondeok was the first true Queen of Korea, as previously women had only ruled as regents for their sons or as dowager queens.

Seondeok was the middle of three daughters of King Jinpyeong. Her two sisters were Cheonmyeong and Seonhwa, but King Jinpyeong had no legitimate sons, leading to a question of succession. Because he had no sons, King Jinpyeong sent his wife to a Buddhist nunnery and took another queen who he hoped would produce male heirs. But this was done in vain, so with no sons, other than those born to concubines, the king began to look for possible heirs. The Silla social class system was based on the bone rank system, which dictated privileges and obligations based on birth. But in accordance with this, there were very few men who were of high enough rank to be king.

While the king could not have more children, he hoped that one of his daughters would produce him a male heir, so he had Seondeok marry Kim Yongchun, hoping they would produce a son; however, they were unable to conceive. Kim Yongchun was then permitted to retire from being Seondeok's consort; however, he promised to assist her later when she was queen. Seondeok may have married other men during her life, but this is debated, as some claim that she did not allow herself to marry so that she would not create political conflicts.

With his plans to produce a male heir foiled, King Jinpyeong considered passing the crown to his son-in-law, Kim Yongsu, the husband of Princess Cheonmyeong. When Seondeok heard of this, she begged her father to give her a chance to compete for the throne. He agreed to this as a woman had in the past acted as a regent for him.

So King Jinpyeong accepted Seondeok as heir. The reason for this was because of her impressive natural intelligence, shown from a young age. When Seondeok was just seven years old, her father received a box of peony seeds along with a painting of peonies from the Emperor of China. Upon seeing the painting, Seondeok remarked that the flowers were beautiful, but it was a shame they do not smell nice. When asked how she knew this, she stated that if they smelt nice, then there would be butterflies and bees in the painting. This perceptive intelligence is partially what led her father to choose Seondeok as heir.

Although Seondeok was the first Korean reigning queen, most people were open to the prospect of a female monarch due to women in Silla having relatively high statuses. This is because at this time the Confucian model, which placed women in an inferior position, was not yet in place. But women were expected to act in a certain way and run households; however, could influence politics and could be advisors and regents. So, most people happily accepted Seondeok as their leader.

Of course, some officials disagreed with the decision of choosing a female ruler. Ichan Chilsuk and Achan Seokpum planned an uprising to have their queen replaced, but their plan was discovered early. As punishment, Ichan Chilsuk was beheaded in public with the rest of his family, but Achan Seokpum fled to Baekje's border. However, he began to miss his wife so returned to Silla and was arrested straight away, then was executed. So when Seondeok ascended to the throne in 634, she did face some opposition; but she was able to use her intelligence and resourcefulness during a time of political turmoil.

As queen, Seondeok's priority was to her people. One of the first actions she took as ruler was to send royal inspectors throughout her kingdom to oversee the care and needs of the widows, widowers, orphans, poor and elderly, who had no family to support them. She then helped the poor further by announcing a whole year of tax exemption for the peasants, and reduced tax for the middle class, which won the support and love of her people, strengthening her against the opposition of the male aristocracy.

Seondeok encouraged a renaissance in thinking and literature in her reign, and encouraged the Buddhist faith. Like her father, she was interested in Buddhism and became a bhikkuni (ordained nun) after studying Buddhism seriously. To honour this faith, she built many Buddhist temples with the help of the monk, Jajang, who had studied with the Tang Chinese for many years, but not many of these temples survived as they were made of wood. With this knowledge of Buddhism, Seondeok strengthened her position on the throne by endorsing the idea of the monarch being an incarnation of the Buddha.

So, she successfully introduced Seon (Zen) Buddhism into Korea. The Star-Gazing Tower called the Cheomseogndae was built under Seondeok's rule and was the first observatory in the Far East. It could be used as a sundial and was a dedication to science and astronomy, and is still standing today. It is located in Gyeongju and is based on the Chinese theory of "round-heaven, square-earth", with 27 levels of stone because she was the 27th ruler of the Silla Dynasty. This helped to create a Golden Age in Silla, especially when she began to invest in establishing a university plus many schools to encourage learning. Seondeok was also interested in Chinese culture and would send scholars and monks there to study, keeping her ties with the Chinese Tang Dynasty strong.

An interesting story of Seondeok's reign is the Legend of Jigwi; however, there are many versions of the story. It states that there was a man called Jigwi who once saw the queen passing by and became mesmerised by her beauty and fell in love with her. He stopped eating and sleeping because he was so in love with Seondeok and would constantly call out her name. One day Seondeok went to pray at a Buddhist temple and Jigwi called out her name as she passed by, but a guard pushed him aside.

When Seondeok questioned the guard about his actions, the guard explained that Jigwi was infatuated with her. Seondeok was flattered by this and allowed Jigwi to follow her to the temple, this kindness caused Jigwi to dance for joy. While Seondeok was praying in the temple Jigwi had to wait outside, but she took so long that he fell asleep under a pagoda. After praying and exiting the temple, Seondeok saw the man sleeping so asked her attendants to be quiet to not disturb him. To let Jigwi know of her presence, she stopped to place her bracelet on Jigwi's sleeping chest.

When he woke up, he was overjoyed with love and passion, which was so strong that his whole body set aflame and burned down the pagoda. There are other stories of Jigwi, but all tell of an ordinary man who was so in love with the queen, who pitied and was flattered by the young man, that he burst into flames.

Throughout her reign, Seondeok achieved many military successes, which were mostly late in her rule. In the 640s, Baekje was becoming more aggressive towards Silla, so Seondeok sent a diplomat to the King of Goguryeo to ask for help, but he would only help Silla if they gave up some territory to Goguryeo. Seondeok refused, leading to the imprisonment of her diplomat, so Seondeok dispatched a 10,000-man army to rescue the diplomat. As soon as the King of Goguryeo heard of this army he released the diplomat.

Then in 642, the ruler of Baekje led a campaign against Silla, taking 40 fortresses with 10,000 men. Baekje then allied with Goguryeo to block Silla's route to the Tang Chinese. When this crisis struck, Seondeok decided that she needed urgent help and so wrote to the Emperor of Tang to ask for assistance, as they had been long trading partners and had a good cultural exchange. But he was firm and gave her three options: first, he offered to lead a naval campaign to occupy the Baekje; second, he would provide Tang uniforms to help Silla soldiers disguise themselves as Chinese troops; or third, he would send a male royal of Tang descent to serve as King of Silla. He believed that while Silla was led by a woman, it would constantly be threatened.

When Seondeok had first contacted the Tang Emperor to tell him of her ascension to the throne, he refused to acknowledge a female monarch. Seondeok refused to give up her crown so easily, but she still managed to gain Tang support. They formed a joint army to destroy Baekje and Goguryeo, but they were soon defeated by Goguryeo.

Seondeok met with the Buddhist monk Jajang about the crisis, and he advised her to build a nine-storey pagoda. Each storey represented one of Silla's enemies: Japan, China, Wuyue (Shanghai), Tangna, Eungnyu, Mohe (Manchuria), Danguk, Yeojeok, and Yemaek. This was to block foreign invasions and to calm her people. This would be built on top of the Hwangnyongsa, which was also finished in Seondeok's rule and was known as the "Imperial Dragon Temple" because it was built on the spot where a yellow dragon had appeared promising that Silla would destroy all its enemies. Seondeok decided to follow this advice, even though her subjects were worried it would be costly and that they would be taxed harshly. But Seondeok did it anyway, telling the people to tear down her palace to use its bricks if they lacked funds, as she thought this religious building would bring her people together.

The finished building was the tallest temple in East Asia, standing up to 80 metres in height. This pagoda represented the wish of Seondeok and her people to protect their country and to bring the three kingdoms of Korea under one ruler. It was also an offering to the Buddha so that these wishes could be fulfilled. Unfortunately, the Hwangnyongsa temple was destroyed by the Mongols in 1238, but the foundations and some statue bases remain.

Eventually, Seondeok found military success using her intelligence and charisma to manipulate political alliances to gain dominance. She first allied with the kingdom of Goguryeo to destroy Baekje, then with Tang Chinese assistance, was then able to destroy the Goguryeo. Afterwards, she eliminated the threat of Chinese occupation by removing them from the peninsula, and they were never able to reclaim the land. Seondeok kept Silla safe from the Tang Chinese by sending young Hwarang warriors to study martial arts in China, and they became expert fighters who would protect Silla from its neighbouring enemies. This led to Silla controlling all of the Korean Peninsula just a few years after the end of Seondeok's reign.

After these foreign policy successes, Seondeok appointed Bidam, a nobleman, to the position of Sangdaedeung, the highest position in court. But this was a big mistake. In 647, Bidam stated that Seondeok was not capable of ruling, and because he had political influence in court, he was able to create the biggest rebellion in Silla's history. He wanted to replace Seondeok with a male ruler, even if it was a member of the aristocracy rather than royalty, and he was backed by the Tang Dynasty. This situation was made worse by the fact that most of Seondeok's soldiers were in different parts of Silla to defend it from foreign invasions, so could not support Silla against threats from within.

On the night of Bidam's rebellion, a star fell near Seondeok's residence, so Bidam claimed to his superstitious followers that it was a sign of her impending downfall. This made Seondeok very anxious, as her health was deteriorating. One who remained loyal to the queen calmed her by flying a kite with a burning scarecrow attached to it, making the rebels believe the star had risen, discouraging them. This general then went on to suppress the rebellion before executing Bidam and his 30 followers.

Unfortunately, before the rebels had all been executed, Seondeok died of an illness, but some say her death was partly caused by the shock of Bidam's betrayal. She was buried in a tomb on Nangsan, one of the sacred mountains in Gyeongju, and she was succeeded by another female ruler, her cousin, Queen Jindeok.

After her death, legends surrounding Seondeok circulated, in particular two examples of her ability to see or predict the future. In the first story, Seondeok was at the Jade Gate pond and heard a hoard of white frogs croaking all of a sudden during the winter. She thought this meant there was going to be an attack from Baekje at the Woman's Valley, as the croaking sounded like angry soldiers. So she sent her generals to the Woman's Valley, and they ended up capturing 2,000 Baekje soldiers who were trying to attack. The second legend was that Seondeok successfully predicted her own death date and time, almost to the minute.

Seondeok was a popular ruler, which aided her success. Despite what a few thought of her capability of ruling, most of Seondeok's subjects loved her because she cared for the elderly, orphaned, and the poor by limiting taxes, which was not very common of the monarchy at the time. She also paved the path for two more Queens of Silla, Jindeok and Jinseong. Because of Seondeok's military successes, Jindeok was able to facilitate the establishment of unified Silla. Seondeok's reign was prosperous and a Golden Age in art and culture in Korea.

This Golden Age was established because she did not focus only on foreign policy, although she did spend many of her last years dealing with aggressive neighbours. Seondeok also focused on caring for her poorer citizens as well as establishing religious contentment and improving education to create a successful culture.

Empress Wu Zetian
(624–705 CE)

China's Only Female Sovereign

Zetian started as a lowly concubine and ended up becoming China's only female empress regnant. She was an incredibly ambitious woman, as well as extremely intelligent and manipulative, but these traits enabled her to ascend to the throne on her own accord. Some would describe Zetian's reign as a reign of terror, due to her use of secret police and because she would destroy anyone who opposed her. However, others may argue that Zetian was an effective leader who established her own dynasty, then reformed government, the education system, the military, and the taxation system to make it more efficient.

As a ruler she was controversial, and despite her brutality, Zetian was popular with her subjects because she took into account what they wanted, setting up a system so that they could directly voice their opinions to her. It is impossible to know which stories are true because after her reign there was a smear campaign to establish the opinion that women could not be leaders.

Born in Wenshi County to a wealthy family, Zetian was the daughter of a chancellor of the Tang Dynasty. Zetian's father encouraged her to read, write, play music, write poetry, and develop knowledge of politics and government affairs. Such knowledge was very uncommon to learn as a young girl at the time. Zetian's mother was from the powerful Yang family, who Emperor Taizong had stayed with before he became emperor. For this reason, the emperor was generous to the Wu family, providing them with money, grain, land and clothing. On account of her beauty, Zetian became a concubine for Emperor Taizong at the age of just 14, as a fifth-ranked imperial consort.

As the lesser wife of the emperor, Zetian was not particularly favoured. She did have sexual relations with the emperor, but also had other household tasks, such as laundry, and performing music. But Zetian started working her way up the ranks so that she would be noticed by the emperor, she did this by satisfying his particularly unusual sexual fantasies which the other consorts would not do. This made her more popular with Emperor Taizong and he began to call Zetian "Mei-Niang", meaning "beautiful girl". The emperor was not just intrigued by his young consort's beauty, he was also impressed with her bravery and intellect, which he believed to be uncommon among women.

Zetian demonstrated her ruthless authoritativeness to the emperor when he received a horse that no one could tame. The horse was named "Lion Stallion" on account of its massive size and strength; however, no one could ride it. Zetian claimed that she only needed an iron whip, an iron hammer, and a sharp dagger to subordinate the horse. When asked to elaborate, Zetian said that first, she would whip the horse, if that does not make it submit, she would smash its head with the hammer, if it would still not submit, Zetian would slit the horse's throat. This foreshadows her future ruthlessness and bloodthirst, but the emperor was extremely impressed, praising her bravery.

In another incident as the emperor's consort, Zetian was alone with the emperor doing his laundry, when they spoke together about Chinese history. Taizong was very impressed and surprised that his newest concubine could read and write. He was also mesmerised by her beauty and charm, so he stopped her doing the laundry and made her his secretary instead, which meant that she could pursue education. This put Zetian at the heart of state affairs and she was the new favourite of Taizong. But other young men at court were also drawn to Zetian, including the married son of Taizong. The emperor's son's marriage and Zetian's position as the emperor's concubine did not prevent the pair from beginning an affair and falling in love.

When Taizong died, all of his concubines shaved their heads and went to Genye Temple to become nuns, as was the custom. But when his son, Emperor Gaozong, ascended to the throne, he visited the Temple. When he saw Zetian, his former lover, he thought she was even more beautiful, intelligent, and intriguing than before, so he brought her back to be his consort. This gave Zetian a very good position at court; however, she was not the favourite of the new emperor, as this position was held by the "Pure Consort", much to the discontent of Gaozong's wife, Empress Wang.

At the age of just 21, Emperor Gaozong was a very inexperienced ruler and never expected to be emperor, because he had two older brothers who had been disgraced. This inexperience meant that Emperor Gaozong was very easy to manipulate, particularly because he was also often incapacitated by dizzy spells.

Empress Wang was very jealous of the Pure Consort because she was childless whereas the Pure Consort had three children, so she hoped that the arrival of Zetian would divert Gaozong from the Pure Consort. With this in mind, the empress encouraged Zetian to stop shaving her head so that Zetian would be so beautiful that she would get between the emperor and his favourite consort. Zetian was more than willing to oblige. In just a few years of being in this position, Zetian gave birth to two sons. Neither boy was a threat to Empress Wang because Gaozong had already appointed an heir called Li Zhong, who was a child of another consort, but Empress Wang was still jealous.

Then in 654, everything changed when Zetian's newborn daughter was strangled in her crib. Zetian claimed that the empress had murdered the child because she was the last seen in the baby's room, then she took it further and accused Empress Wang and the Pure Consort of using witchcraft. Because of Zetian's accusations, Emperor Gaozong divorced Empress Wang, exiled the Pure Consort, and cut off his heir. This meant that Zetian became the first wife of Emperor Gaozong. More importantly, she was the Empress of China, and her son, Li Hong, was the heir apparent.

Much more recently, chilling accusations have been made about Zetian, as some claim that she killed her own daughter to frame Empress Wang so that she could take her place as empress. But it is more likely that both women were innocent and the baby died of crib death, as the room was probably poorly ventilated leading to carbon monoxide poisoning. The claim that Zetian committed infanticide was probably circulated as a smear campaign by her descendants, portraying the empress as ruthless and scheming to prevent a woman from gaining power in China again.

Once empress, Zetian began eliminating any possible enemies, starting with her husband's previous wife and the Pure Consort. Emperor Gaozong was considering releasing the two women, but when Zetian found out about this, she ordered their deaths herself. For her first killings, these were particularly brutal, as she had their hands and feet chopped off, then they were drowned in a vat of wine. Zetian later claimed that these two women haunted her dreams as ghosts.

In 657, Zetian and her allies began working against the officials who had opposed her, having chancellors falsely implicated in treasonous plots so that they would be demoted. Li Zhong, Emperor Gaozong's firstborn son and previous heir, was exiled and placed under house arrest. From 660, Zetian was the power behind the throne, although many despised her for usurping the previous empress and her wielding of power. She could get away with this because Emperor Gaozong had become so ill that he had a loss of vision and severe headaches, leaving Zetian to control imperial business. This allowed Zetian to make rulings on petitions made by officials, and because of her quick decision-making and her education, she did this job well, so eventually she became the undisputed power behind the throne.

But by 664, Zetian was interfering so much that she began to anger Emperor Gaozong, even though he had allowed her this power in the first place. He was particularly angry when Zetian enlisted the help of a sorcerer to assist her in ruling the country, even though the emperor's previous wife had been deposed for using sorcery. So a chancellor suggested that Zetian should also be replaced as she could no longer be trusted due to this hypocrisy.

As soon as Zetian found out that her position was being discussed, she begged her husband to not depose her, even sweet-talking him so that she could keep her position and influence. This easily turned Emperor Gaozong back to Zetian's side and she quickly and easily returned to power. Within the same year, Zetian had back enough power to order Li Zhong, the previous heir, to commit suicide. Back in this position of influence, Zetian continued to target those who opposed her, as well as promote her own family members to positions of power.

One of Zetian's targets was Lady Helan. In the year 666, Emperor Gaozong wanted to keep this woman in his palace as his concubine, but this angered

Zetian. Because of his wife's anger at the thought of him taking Lady Helan as his concubine, the emperor decided against the decision. But because there had been a chance of Lady Helan gaining some influence with the emperor, Zetian had Lady Helan poisoned. Then, Zetian blamed the murder of Lady Helan on those in high positions who still did not approve of her. These men were executed for the murder.

Many in government agreed that Zetian had upset the balance of nature by wielding her husband's power. At one point, there was an earthquake with a mountain appearing afterwards which was viewed as nature revolting against the power of Zetian. But the empress claimed that the mountain appearing was actually a good omen because it reflected the Buddhist mountain of paradise, Sumeru, so she named the mountain Mount Felicity, claiming it rose to honour her. When a minister disagreed with Zetian about this, she exiled him.

In 674, Emperor Gaozong and Empress Zetian took the titles of Tian Huang and Tian Hou, meaning Emperor and Empress of Heaven, creating their image as divine rulers. But at this time Gaozong's health was deteriorating even further, so although he held the title of emperor, he did not rule. Because of this, his name is attached with the successful campaigns of Korea, reducing it to a vassal state, which Zetian organised herself. With his eyesight deteriorating, Emperor Gaozong required his wife to read reports and government documents to him. So Zetian would pick and choose what she would read to him, before doing whatever she felt was the appropriate response, rather than using his advice.

As she had charge of her husband's Imperial Seal, Zetian's consent was necessary before any document or order received legal validity. This demonstrates that Zetian was truly the power behind the throne at this point, with the emperor as a figurehead. When he could no longer cope with government affairs, the emperor even considered making Zetian his regent to rule officially on his behalf, but this idea was rejected by officials.

Zetian was not opposed to threatening her own sons when they went against her, despite them being heirs to the sick emperor. Li Hong, the heir apparent, was worried about how much power his mother was wielding and disliked how she punished people who had power. He asked Zetian to allow his half-sisters, who were fathered by Gaozong but born to consorts, to be allowed to marry, which she had previously disallowed. Zetian was offended by this request, as she felt that her son was questioning her authority, so she responded by poisoning Li

Hong, her own son and heir apparent. The other sons born to consorts of Emperor Gaozong were then demoted.

Next, Li Xian, the second son of Zetian, began to cause problems. He had heard rumours that he was not Zetian's biological son, but instead the son of Zetian's sister. The empress was furious with this rumour, so met with a sorcerer who was greatly respected by the emperor and empress, who claimed that Li Xian could never be emperor. Zetian believed the sorcerer and questioned Li Xian's position. Later, the sorcerer was assassinated, and Li Xian was believed to have been the culprit, so in 680 Li Xian was accused of treason and assassination, leading to him being deposed and exiled. When Emperor Gaozong died in 683, it was Zetian's third son, Li Zhe, who ascended to the throne as Emperor Zhongzong, with Zetian becoming the empress dowager and regent.

In his will, Emperor Gaozong had included provisions so that his son would ascend immediately to the throne. He had also requested that the new emperor should look to Zetian in any important matter, whether that be military or civil, she should have senior authority. But Emperor Zhongzong would not cooperate. Like his father, he was easy to manipulate, but was manipulated by his wife, Lady Wei, rather than Zetian. Ironically, Zetian could not stand the wife of the emperor having so much power, so she charged her son with treason, and banished the new emperor and empress.

The next emperor would be Zetian's youngest son, Li Dan, who would be known as Emperor Ruizong. To control him, Zetian kept him under house arrest in the Inner Palace, unable to move into the imperial quarters or appear at any imperial events. This meant that Zetian could continue to rule in the place of her son, continuing to do whatever she wanted, including taking a lover, the Buddhist monk called Huaiyi, and showering him with honours. In 686, Zetian did offer to return the imperial power to the emperor, but he declined because he did not believe her and suspected her intentions. In this same year, there was a rebellion and one official told Zetian that it could only be stopped if she gave authority to the emperor, but she accused this official of being complicit and had him executed.

Although she had recently offered to give up her authority to the emperor, Zetian was infuriated by those telling her to do exactly that. Eventually, Zetian's forces did quash the rebellion and the rebel leader was executed.

For the next few years, Zetian avoided future rebellions by using secret police to crush the rebellions before they began, and encouraged people to report on each other. However, the secret police became very powerful, as they would carry out false accusations, tortures, and executions, leading to what some would call a reign of terror. There were public political massacres of officials and members of the Li clan, who threatened Zetian's position on the throne due to being related to the previous Emperor Gaozong.

With all this power, Zetian was able to force Emperor Ruizong's abdication in 690. He was reinstated as a crown prince and took his old name, Li Dan. Then Zetian proclaimed herself Empress Zetian, ruler of China, the first and only woman to sit on the Dragon Throne and reign in her own name and by her own authority. "Wu" is associated with the words for "weapon", and the name "Zetian" means "Ruler of the Heavens".

To begin her official rule, Zetian established her own dynasty which she named the Zhou Dynasty, then labelled her reign as Tianzhou, meaning granted by Heaven. Despite the traditional Chinese order of succession excluding women from ruling, there was not a huge amount of opposition to Zetian's reign because of her network of spies and secret police. To ensure her success, Zetian selected many capable men to serve as officials, choosing men based on their skills rather than family links. In 692, Zetian impressed China by attacking the Tibetan Empire, recapturing four garrisons of western regions that had fallen into the hands of the Tibetan Empire decades before.

However, just four years later, another army was sent against the Tibetan Empire but was defeated. Zetian recast the nine tripod cauldrons, which was the symbol of ultimate power in China, to reinforce her authority, but the Tibetan threat did not cease until 699.

Early in her reign, Zetian damaged relations with her heir who she had previously usurped, Li Dan. This is because Zetian's lady-in-waiting, who hated Li Dan because she had been rejected by him, falsely accused the prince's wife and consort of witchcraft, so Zetian had them killed. Li Dan was very upset by this but did nothing in response as he feared being targeted next. The lady-in-waiting almost falsely accused Li Dan of crimes, but she was informed on first, so was executed. However, Li Dan was still barred from meeting officials and was investigated for treason. This involved having his servants tortured for information, but one, who was very loyal to Li Dan, cut open his own stomach to swear that Li Dan was innocent. This extreme sacrifice convinced Zetian of her son's innocence, so the investigation was dropped.

In 694, Zetian became immersed in mystics and religion, as early in her reign she had elevated the status of Buddhism above Taoism. There was a group of mystics that Zetian was particularly impressed with. This unusual group consisted of a hermit who was more than 350 years old; a Buddhist nun who could predict the future; and a non-Han man who claimed to be 500 years old. Zetian enjoyed the imagery of the mystics, subsequently, she proclaimed herself an incarnation of the Maitreya Buddha, calling herself Empress Shengsen (Holy Spirit).

Statues were built of the Maitreya and sculpted so that they resembled Zetian, implying that she was a divine ruler who could apply any laws she saw fit. But this interest in mysticism did not last long. The next year, Zetian's lover, Huaiyi, was jealous that Zetian had found another lover, so burned down the Imperial Meeting Hall and the Heavenly Hall. Zetian was furious that the mystics did not predict this disaster, therefore the Buddhist nun and her students were arrested and made to be slaves; the hermit committed suicide; the non-Han man fled; and Huaiyi was put to death for his crime. Zetian then ended her fascination with mysticism and instead focused on the affairs of the state.

Despite her problematic rise to power, Zetian was very popular with her subjects because she reformed everything while ensuring that all the ideas came from the people themselves. This was conducted by the installation of a box with four slots: one for men to recommend themselves as officials; one where a citizen could anonymously criticise court decisions; one to report strange omens or plots; and one to file accusations and grievances. This allowed Zetian to have a direct link to her people, which made her popular and efficient.

Her government efficiency was also improved by pressuring officials who were not performing well to resign. She completely restructured government by appointing intellectuals and bureaucrats to high positions and this helped to decrease spending and increase efficiency.

The education system was also improved simply by hiring better teachers, again who were appointed based on their skill set rather than family. Another popular change was the complete change in the taxation system. Zetian created a system that rewarded officials who produced the most crops and taxed their people least, in addition to redistributing the land so that everyone had a fair and equal share. Zetian had shown her military competence in years previously, so it is no surprise that the military was another area that she successfully transformed. Zetian introduced exams that commanders had to take to display that they were competent, intelligent, and could make decisions. The commanders were also personally interviewed and like the government officials, did not gain positions just from having family connections.

But despite all of this work, in 697, Zetian became paranoid and spent too much time with lovers and she became addicted to aphrodisiacs. This was scandalous because she was much older than the lovers she took (even though it was normal for male rulers to have much younger concubines). The secret police had stopped their work, but anyone suspected of disloyalty was banished or executed, so the efficiency of court declined. Zetian's favourite lovers were two brothers called Zhang Yuzhi and Zhang Changzong, who were honoured with dukedoms and asserted a lot of power. Some claim that she liked them because one was particularly handsome and the other allegedly had impressive skills in the bedroom!

Many people were not happy about the Zhang brothers having so much power and influence with the empress. At one point, Zetian's grandson, granddaughter, and grandson-in-law were criticising the brothers, but their conversation was leaked to Zetian. She was furious and ordered the three of them to commit suicide, highlighting that these lovers had gained more power and influence with the empress than her own family members.

By 704, the situation had worsened and everyone hated the influence that the Zhang brothers had and accusations of corruption began to fly. Due to these accusations, Zetian should have removed them from court, but she refused. That year, Zetian became very ill and only allowed the brothers to see her, not even her own sons, leading many to believe that the pair were plotting treason.

Eventually, Zetian's children agreed with court officials to kill the brothers in a coup. Once the murders had taken place, the group surrounded Changsheng Hall, where Zetian was residing, telling her that her lovers had been executed for treason. Then they forced Zetian to yield the throne to her son. Zetian had no choice but to stand down, allowing Emperor Zhongzong to retake the throne and restore the Tang Dynasty. She died a year later.

Scandal seemed to run in Zetian's family because after her death, things did not quiet down. Zhongzong had no real power as he was ruled by his wife, Lady Wei. She used Zetian as a role model to manipulate her husband. Meanwhile, another faction formed around Zetian's other son, the previous Emperor Ruizong, who was supported by his sister, Taiping. In 710, Zhongzong was poisoned by his wife, who hid his body until her son, Chong Mao could be made emperor.

But in a twist, Princess Taiping had Lady Wei and her family murdered, leaving Ruizong to return to the throne. He then abdicated two years later when he saw a comet, so his son, Li Longji succeeded him. Princess Taiping tried to manipulate the new emperor in the way that Zetian was able to manipulate emperors, but Taiping failed at this and committed suicide.

To conclude, Zetian was an extremely controversial figure. Although she was ruthless and cruel, Zetian did reform her country in many beneficial ways. Also, not many leaders took into account the opinions and ideas of their subjects, and not many would choose skill over family ties when choosing government officials, which made her popular for a while.

Zetian was an impressively ambitious woman, going from the position of a fifth-tier consort to becoming an empress in her own right, which was a massive achievement, especially considering that most women born in her position would not have even been able to read.

Pope Joan
(818–857 CE)

The Pope who was a Woman

Joan's story is a legend and it is often debated as to whether she was real or fiction. She is remembered as the only female pope, who was elected to the role for her superior intellect. As pope, she was known as John VIII or John Anglicus. However, many believe that Joan never existed, partially due to the inconsistencies in her story; for example, she is also referred to as Agnes and Gilberta. These inconsistencies have led modern scholars to believe that her story was made up by opponents of the Catholic Church, or even as a story to warn women against trying to wield too much power. Whether real or not, Joan's story has made its impact on the Catholic Church and the papacy.

Joan was an Englishwoman born in the German city of Mainz, where her parents may have migrated. At this time, women had severely limited rights, for example, no woman could appear alone on the streets publicly, or she would be named as a prostitute. So generally, women were confined to their homes, which would have been comparable to a mud hut, with an average lifespan of about 30 to 40 years, as it was a very underprivileged area.

However, there was a monastery called Fulda in Germany, which was a centre of education, exclusively for boys. But it seems that Joan was determined, so dressed as a boy and learned Greek and Latin at this monastery. This was an easier feat than expected, as clergy members normally wore loose fitting clothing, were clean-shaven, and everyone had similar, gaunt figures from malnutrition.

At some point in her early life, Joan fell in love with an English Benedictine monk, so decided to follow this secret lover to Athens, again dressed as a man. While in Athens, Joan acquired great learning, so eventually, she travelled to Rome. Here she discovered that not many could equal her knowledge of the scriptures, so she gained a lot of respect and authority. Because of her superior intellect, Joan became a cardinal, before continuing to work her way up the church ranks. After distinguishing herself as an impressive scholar, Joan was elected Pope John VIII in the year 855. She ruled as pope for over two years and hid her gender under the flowing holy robes.

But in 858, her scandalous secret was revealed when she went into labour and gave birth during a papal procession to the Lateran. Some claim that Joan died during childbirth, but others allege that she was dragged behind a horse from Rome and stoned to death. However, another version of Joan's story claims that she did not die so soon after her exposure. Instead, they argue that she was deposed and confined to do years of penance, then after her death, her son, the Bishop of Ostia, ordered Joan's entombment in his cathedral.

However, most sources suggest that she died on the day of her disgrace. After this event, papal processions avoided a particular street, known as the Street of the Female Pope, where it was believed Joan had fallen into labour.

There are many legends associated with Joan, as after she was revealed to be a woman, it allegedly rained blood in Brescia for three days and nights. In France, there was a plague of locusts, which miraculously drowned in the British Sea, but their bodies were rejected by the water and corrupted the air, causing many to die.

The Vatican then removed Joan from its official lists, as they saw Joan's reign as a disgrace, and crafted rituals to ensure that future popes were male. One ritual involves the pope having to sit on a "dung chair", which had a hole in the seat, like a toilet seat. A cardinal then has to reach up through the hole and establish that the new pope has testicles, before announcing "Duos habet et bene pendentes", which translates to "he has two, and they dangle nicely"; however, many just say "habet" for short.

During this era, many women martyrs were tortured for their religious beliefs, who became saints after cross-dressing as monks. St Eugenia became a monk while disguised as a boy, and was so convincing that she was brought to court on charges of fathering a local woman's child. She proved her innocence by baring her breasts in public. So perhaps the story of Pope Joan is a cautionary tale, warning women to not reach for power or they'll end up exposed and humiliated.

Now Joan is believed to be a myth, as her supposed reign overlaps with Leo IV and Benedict III, but it is possible that she did exist and was removed from church histories. Others claim that she was real, but she was a mistress of Pope John XII who had lots of influence in Rome. To most modern scholars, it seems likely that Joan's story was anti-papal satire popularised by disgruntled monks, early Protestants, and other critics of the Catholic Church.

In the 1500s, the Siena Cathedral featured a bust of Joan among the other popes, but this was protested against so was removed in 1600, after Pope Clement VIII declared the legend of Pope Joan to be untrue. However, many are inspired by Joan, as despite her low status in society as a woman, she worked her way up through the ranks, and gained her position as Pope through hard work and superior intellect.

Murasaki Shikibu (978–1014 CE)

The Lady of the Chronicles

In her writings, Murasaki has taught us a lot about women and court in Japan. Despite her animosity with the other noblewomen, Murasaki and these women helped to develop kana, the first form of the written Japanese language, which was used by women as they were not permitted to learn Chinese. But Murasaki's most notable achievement was writing the first ever novel, *The Tale of Genji*. It took her a decade to write and is double the length of Tolstoy's *War and Peace*. Not only is it the world's oldest novel, but it is perceived as Japan's greatest work of literature.

Murasaki was born during the Heian Era of Japan, into the northern Fujiwara clan, who dominated court politics by strategically marrying off their daughters into the imperial family. But Murasaki was in the middle to lower ranks of the aristocracy at the level of provincial governors, who were typically posted away from court. Not so much is known about Murasaki's childhood, even her real name is unknown. She acquired the name Murasaki Shikibu because Murasaki is the name of the heroine in her novel, and Shikibu reflects her father's position at the Bureau of Rites. What is known of her childhood is that Murasaki lived in her father's household with her father and brother, as Murasaki's mother had died in childbirth while she was young. This left Murasaki in an unusual position, as normally children were raised with their mothers in a separate household from their fathers.

During this time in Japan, there was a strong national culture emerging, as missions to China had ended. Also, Japanese was gradually becoming a written language called kana, which was based on abbreviations of Chinese characters. This written language was mostly used by noblewomen, who wrote for entertainment and used kana as a language of intimacy, whereas the men would write formally in Chinese. This is because Chinese was the language of government, so women were not supposed to know it so that they could be separated from matters of government.

But Murasaki grew up with her brother who was learning Chinese to prepare for a future career in government, so Murasaki would listen to these lessons and learn classical Chinese herself. This allowed her to study Chinese literature with her brother, as well as other subjects, such as music, calligraphy, and Japanese poetry. This access to education was extremely unusual, as women were thought to be incapable of intelligence. However, this learning meant that Murasaki was seen as pretentious and haughty to those around her, preventing her from making any friends, except her sister who died when she was just 20 years old.

Unlike most noblewomen of the time, Murasaki did not marry upon reaching puberty; instead, she stayed in her father's household until she was in her 20s when she married a second cousin in 998. This man was much older than Murasaki and was called Fujiwara no Nobutaka. He dressed very extravagantly and loved to dance. He already had many households and wives by the time he married Murasaki; however, that did not stop him from being extremely flirtatious with the women at court.

Although some sources suggest that Murasaki was resentful of her husband, others claim that she was very happy in this marriage. Not long after her union, Murasaki gave birth to a daughter called Kenshi, but just two years later, her husband died of cholera during an epidemic. But as a married woman, Murasaki could have servants run her household and care for her daughter, giving her plenty of leisure time to read.

When she was widowed, Murasaki was inspired by looking at the moon to write *The Tale of Genji*, to help cope with her grief. This book is known as the greatest work of Japanese literature and the world's oldest novel, with three parts comprised of 1,100 pages and 54 chapters. She also wrote about her feelings of depression and confusion after her husband's death. The early chapters of *The Tale of Genji* may have been written for a private patron, but Murasaki continued writing when she joined court as she needed court patronage so that she could be provided with paper and ink.

Once a chapter was completed, Murasaki would distribute the chapter to her friends, who in turn would copy the pages and pass them on, enabling Murasaki to gain a reputation as an author. *The Tale of Genji* is a story about a prince called Genji and his various love affairs. There is not much action in this, but it does depict a complex society at court, as well as provide the theme of the fragility of life and the sorrow of human existence. Genji is an interesting protagonist, who recognises the inner beauty of each of his lovers, displaying the sensitivity of human emotions. As the novel goes on, the tone gets darker, ending with a gloomy psychological analysis of unrequited love. The heroine of the book is called Murasaki, who lived with Genji and was tormented by the jealous spirit of Genji's former lover.

Soon after her husband's death, Murasaki became a lady-in-waiting at the court of Empress Akiko as a companion-tutor. She probably got this position at court due to her reputation as an author, as she had begun *The Tale of Genji* by this point and it was very popular with courtiers. Many of the other ladies-in-waiting were also talented women, including Izumi Shikibu and Akazome Emon, creating a strong rivalry among the women.

At this time, people at court often turned to artistic endeavours to occupy themselves and to express their emotions through art or poetry. Those who were not able to follow this aesthetic would quickly lose popularity at court, so it was common for the noblewomen to write poems and keep diaries. Murasaki's other two works were *The Diary of Lady Murasaki,* in which she detailed her life at court, and her *Poetic Memoirs,* a collection of 128 poems, some of which appear to be written for a lover, perhaps her husband before his death.

She also wrote of a sister who died, her visit to Echizen province with her father, and poems she wrote for Empress Akiko. These works are important because they reflect the development of Japanese writing during a period when it shifted from an unwritten to a written language through the development of kana.

Murasaki was known to have taught Chinese to Akiko, who was interested in Chinese art. Akiko also caused outrage when she became empress and decorated her screens with Chinese script, which was thought to be unladylike, as only men learned Chinese. Because she did not want to be seen as unladylike, Murasaki made an effort to keep her knowledge of Chinese hidden, so these lessons between the women were held in secret. Murasaki soon earned the nickname "The Lady of the Chronicles" because she taught Akiko literature.

Despite being around other women who wrote, Murasaki was unhappy and withdrawn at court, as she found it too strict and boring. She would exchange poems with the other ladies, but only really had one close friend, finding the other women difficult to get along with. Not only did Murasaki have disdain for the women at court, but she also hated the men, thinking them all drunk and stupid. But there are rumours that Murasaki had a romantic relationship with a statesman, Michinaga at court, but it seems more likely that he pursued her and pressured her strongly.

In 1010, Murasaki wrote in her diary of this man, stating "you have neither read my book, nor won my love". Once, Michinaga snuck into Murasaki's room to steal a chapter of *The Tale of Genji* and made sexual advances. However, Murasaki needed Michinaga's patronage to write, so she often just put up with these inappropriate advances.

Murasaki may have entered a convent a few years before her death because her writings suggested that she sensed the violent changes that were coming to her upper-class life. Although Murasaki struggled to fit in with other ladies at court, she was very popular as an author and is remembered as the first ever novelist, as well as the author of Japan's greatest work of literature. Not only did she create a novel in *The Tale of Genji*, but her writings in her diary also have given us insight into the life of a Japanese noblewoman. We do not even know Murasaki's true name, yet by creating the novel, she made something that would last over a millennium beyond her death.

Empress Matilda
(1102–1167 CE)

The Lady of England and Normandy

Despite Mary I being officially crowned as the first female monarch of England, Matilda by rights should have been, but she was never officially crowned. Instead of being called a queen, Matilda is known as an empress due to her marriage to the Holy Roman Emperor, but also because at that point when there had never been a female monarch in England, a queen was regarded as beneath a king, so empress seemed more fitting. Much of Matilda's life was filled with fighting for the throne in the conflict known as "The Anarchy" after her crown was snatched before she even had it in her grasp in a treacherous coup.

Matilda was the daughter of King Henry I of England, who had one other legitimate child, William Adelin. Matilda also had roughly 22 illegitimate siblings, but spent most of her early life with her mother, learning to read and to study religious morals. But at the age of just six or seven, King Henry V of the

Romans proposed that Matilda marry him. This was seen as a great match for Matilda, as Henry V ruled a prestigious dynasty in Europe and would be a powerful ally against France. So Matilda left England in 1110 to live in Germany with her betrothed, where she was taught about German culture, manners and government until she was ready to marry Henry in 1114 and be crowned Queen of the Romans. At this point, Matilda had her own household and began to have a role in government.

Not long after the marriage, political conflict broke out when Henry V arrested the chancellor and some German princes. This led to rebellions and opposition from the Church, including the excommunication of Henry V. To settle matters with the pope, Henry and Matilda travelled over the Alps to Italy in 1116. By this time, Matilda was playing an important role in the imperial government, sponsoring royal grants, dealing with petitioners, and taking part in ceremonies. When they arrived in Italy, the pair established their control over North Italy and then advanced on Rome. The pope fled as soon as he saw the army.

In the pope's absence, Henry and Matilda were crowned at St Peter's Basilica as the Holy Roman Emperor and Empress. It was from this point that Matilda began calling herself empress. In 1118, Henry left Matilda as regent to govern Italy, while he crossed the Alps to put down rebellions in Germany, so Matilda used this opportunity to gain experience of government. There continued to be unrest in 1122 when Henry and Matilda travelled to the Rhine together, but Henry was suffering from cancer and died in 1125. As Matilda was childless, she had no reason to stay in Europe, therefore she travelled back to her father so that he could arrange a new marriage to benefit England.

In 1120, a few years before Matilda returned to her father, there was a disaster in England known as the White Ship disaster. This involved the ship, containing 300 passengers including nobles and Prince William, England's heir, foundering due to excess drinking and overcrowding. Tragically, all but two passengers died. This left uncertainty as to who would ascend to the English throne, as William was the only legitimate son to Henry I, who did not want to choose an illegitimate son as heir, despite having many, such as Robert of Gloucester.

To produce a new heir, Henry I took a beautiful young wife called Adeliza, but they did not conceive any children. There were other possible male options, such as Stephen of Blois, but Henry wanted his own child to secure the dynasty.

So when Matilda's husband died and she was no longer committed to the Holy Roman Empire, she became the king's first choice of heir, declaring that she was the rightful successor if he should not have another legitimate son. At Westminster, on Christmas Day 1126, the barons gathered to recognise Matilda as the heir; however, many did not approve of this.

Henry quickly started looking for a new husband for his widowed daughter, so that she could produce a son to secure the dynasty. In 1127, he chose Geoffrey the Count of Anjou, whose alliance would secure the southern borders of Normandy. Unfortunately, Matilda thought this offer was insulting because Geoffrey was a mere count, whereas Matilda had previously been married to an emperor, therefore she felt as though her status had been diminished. What made matters more frustrating for Matilda, was that Geoffrey was only in his early teens at the time of the betrothal and she was 25.

However, Matilda knew that this alliance would be beneficial to her country, so in 1128 the couple was married. The marriage was not only despised by Matilda, but also by many of the barons who thought Matilda should not be married out of England without their consent, especially as she was now the heir. As expected, Geoffrey and Matilda did not get on at all, instead, they rowed constantly, including having disputes about Matilda's dowry and Geoffrey's claim to England.

In a rage, Matilda fled her husband, returning to Normandy, but she quickly reconciled with Geoffrey when Henry told her to do so. To relieve Matilda's worry about her status in England, Henry had the council give another oath of allegiance to Matilda as heir.

Despite being childless in her first marriage, Matilda gave birth to a son who she named Henry in 1133. Very soon later, Matilda gave birth to another son, Geoffrey, which delighted Matilda's father, who was pleased to see his dynasty being secured. However, the birth of Geoffrey almost killed Matilda. At this point, Matilda's relationship with her father started to deteriorate.

When Henry I visited the young family, he loved to play with his grandsons, but would quarrel with his daughter about her dowry. This is because Henry had not given Matilda and Geoffrey their castles in Normandy which was promised in her dowry, so the couple worried they lacked support from Henry and others in England. Although Matilda and Geoffrey had been married for a while, Henry still refused to give the castles or have Norman nobility swear allegiance to Matilda. This is because although Henry wanted Matilda to be recognised as his heir, he was afraid that Geoffrey would take power in Normandy straight away. So when a rebellion broke out in Normandy, Geoffrey and Matilda gave the rebels military support, much to Henry's fury.

Sadly, before this dispute had been resolved in 1135, Henry died of food poisoning. Some say that on his death bed he reaffirmed Matilda as his heir, leaving her all his land, but others claim he renounced this. At this time, Matilda was in Anjou and pregnant with William, her third son. So when she received the news that her father had died, she could not travel to England to consolidate her power. But she did send troops to march to southern Normandy to seize castles that were part of Matilda's dowry which they had never received. Stephen of Blois on the other hand travelled straight to England and took power himself, gaining the backing of the English Church, and he was crowned King Stephen.

Stephen had pledged his allegiance to Matilda previously, but his brother, Henry of Blois, claimed that Henry I had renounced Matilda as his heir on his deathbed. Stephen made sure to have his coronation before Matilda could do anything about it, as he knew Matilda expected to ascend to the throne herself. Most of the barons supported Stephen because they assumed that if a woman could not sit as a judge or lead an army into a battle, then she could not rule. In addition to this, they did not want a woman to rule who was married to a foreigner, particularly as Normans thought of Angevins as barbarians, and believed Geoffrey would end up ruling England.

To top it off, Norman law stated that all property and rights should be handed over to men. Matilda was furious at this treachery, not only from Stephen, but from all those who had sworn an oath to her while her father was alive. But Matilda could not travel while she was pregnant, especially because of how difficult her previous birth had been. So Stephen proclaiming himself as king triggered the civil war known as "The Anarchy", a fight for the throne between Stephen and Matilda.

Geoffrey began to invade Normandy in the name of his wife immediately, while Matilda began to gain support in England. From the beginning of the Anarchy, Robert of Gloucester declared his support for his half-sister. Once in England, Matilda's forces were led by Robert and his allies, who fought with Stephen's forces for a long time. With Geoffrey in Normandy and Robert in England, King David of the Scots invaded the north of England, declaring his support for his niece, Matilda. However, his army was defeated at the Battle of the Standard in Northallerton.

Eventually, in the Battle of Lincoln, Stephen was captured and the clergy declared Matilda as "the Lady of England and Normandy" before her coronation. But despite having a lot of support after her success in Lincoln, once in London for her coronation, many still supported Stephen. This was because they thought that the authority and command that Matilda tried to assert was unnatural for a woman, coming across as arrogance. Also, Stephen had been popular because he had promised the people of London more self-government, whereas Matilda had imposed a tax. So the city rose against Matilda when she arrived for her coronation, and she was forced to flee to Oxford.

After more fighting, Robert was captured and negotiations were held to come to a peace settlement, as both Stephen and Robert were held prisoner. But Stephen's wife, Queen Matilda, refused to compromise with Empress Matilda. Eventually, it was agreed that both Robert and Stephen would be released, Stephen was then reaffirmed as king in another coronation. Robert on the other hand went to Normandy to help Geoffrey; eventually, by 1144, the pair conquered Normandy in Matilda's name, as Stephen no longer held a single Norman stronghold.

Despite this success, this left Matilda alone in Oxford. Her isolation enabled Stephen to storm into the town and he besieged the castle, planning to wait Matilda out. Eventually, in December, Matilda escaped by abseiling from a window in the castle with a few knights wearing white for camouflage. They crossed the icy water, then made their way on foot past the enemy army, all the way to Wallingford.

In 1147, Matilda's oldest son, Henry, was beginning to assume more of a role in the government of family lands with his father. He was summoned to England so that his presence would increase support for Matilda's cause, but at this point, Matilda had returned to Normandy, while her son took up the struggle for the crown. At one point, Henry decided it would be a good idea to take England for himself in a campaign, so travelled to England with a small mercenary army, but he could not pay his men. The young man asked Matilda for money to pay for his campaign, but she refused as she did not approve of the escapade and neither did Robert, who thought that the young Henry was being impatient and naive. In the end, Stephen paid Henry to leave.

By 1150, Henry had matured a little, so was handed the government of the duchy of Normandy from his father. While Matilda was in Normandy, Henry had intervened in England, so eventually, an agreement was decided upon in the

Treaty of Winchester in 1153. Henry agreed to recognise Stephen as king for the rest of his life, but became Stephen's adopted son and heir, with Eustace, Stephen's real son, being disinherited. Eustace was not happy with this treaty, so travelled to Cambridge to plan a further campaign, but he died the next month. Finally, Stephen died, and Henry became King Henry II of England after a 19-year civil war.

Matilda spent the rest of her life in Normandy, constantly involved in Henry II's reign, including mediating between her son and his opponents, such as the Archbishop of Canterbury and the King of France. She also gave him advice on policy matters and governed Normandy herself, as the de facto ruler recognised by France, and did not remarry once Geoffrey had died. Matilda herself died in 1167. She had become deeply religious by the end of her life, so her wealth was given to the Church and she was buried under the high altar at the abbey of Bec-Hellouin. Her tomb reads "Great by birth, greater by marriage, greatest in her offspring, here lies the daughter, wife and mother of Henry."

Although it is a shame that Matilda was never able to rule in her own right, it seems that England was not quite ready for a female monarch, and would not be for centuries, until Queen Mary took the throne in 1553. Many would argue that Matilda was successful because her son was able to rule as King Henry II, so her family continued to wield power. In addition, although she was not the official monarch at this time, Matilda did have an incredibly important role in helping her son rule England, as did Henry II's wife, Eleanor of Aquitaine, another incredibly powerful woman. Matilda displayed incredible determination as well as courage in her fight for her throne and her son's inheritance.

Hōjō Masako
(1156–1225 CE)

The Nun Shogun

Masako assumed great power; not only was she the wife of Yoritomo, the first Shogun of Japan, but she also wielded the power of the shogun herself. Throughout her life, Masako suffered great losses, including the deaths of all her children, leaving her suicidal, but she pushed through her pain for the good of her country. Masako was also responsible for the ousting of her own son and father when they became corrupted by the power that they held.

Masako was the oldest daughter of the Hōjō clan leader, Tokimasa of the Izu province; however, was raised by ladies-in-waiting and nannies because her parents were just teenagers when Masako was born. As a child, Masako was described as a tomboy, spending her time riding horses, hunting, and fishing with her 14 siblings. But Masako's childhood was not always so idyllic because she was born during the civil war known as the Hōgen Rebellion of 1156. This was a dispute about the succession, as the cloistered emperor and emperor were warring over who would be the next emperor in the succession. The Hōjō clan wisely stayed out of this conflict, despite being descended from the Taira clan, who was related to the Imperial family. This conflict would lead to the Minamoto-Taira rivalry.

This rivalry became relevant during the 1159 Heiji Rebellion. The Taira clan defeated the Minamoto clan with the support of the emperor, so they exiled the 13-year-old son of the leader of the Minamoto clan, from the capital. The boy, named Yoritomo, became a prisoner under the watch of Tokimasa, Masako's father, but Masako did not meet this guest for a few years.

One day, Masako's younger sister described an odd dream, in which she held the sun and moon in her hands. At this time, it was common practice for a person to sell their dreams if the dream had bad luck to protect the dreamer; however, this dream was one that would bring good luck. So Masako tricked her sister by telling her that it was an unlucky dream, even though she knew otherwise, and offered to buy it. Falling for the trick, Masako's sister agreed to sell the dream and exchanged it for a Kosode kimono.

Soon after this, Masako came across some good luck when she met Tokimasa's prisoner, Yoritomo. The pair spent a lot of time together while Tokimasa was away and they fell in love. But when Tokimasa found out, he worried about what the ruling Taira clan would think, so he tried to quickly marry Masako to a member of the Taira clan. Just before this wedding went ahead, Masako ran away from her family and trekked over a mountain to escape to Yoritomo, who she married in 1177 at the age of 21. The couple took refuge in the mountains of Izu under the protection of the warrior monks, who prevented anyone from reaching the couple.

Around this time, Imperial Prince Mochihito called on Minamoto members to overthrow the Taira, because he felt they had denied him the throne, but Yoritomo did not respond. In 1180, Mochihito sent out a bid to Minamoto leaders and monasteries that the Taira had offended for support. But the Tairi acted quickly to try to capture him, so Mochihito was forced to flee with a small Minamoto force to the River Uji, where the Tairi caught up with them.

The Battle of Uji took place mostly on the bridge across the river, so Minamoto warriors smashed the planks to prevent the Taira from crossing and allowing their escape. But this was done in vain because Mochihito was captured and then executed. This failure from the Minomoto force scared Yoritomo. He thought the Taira may target him next because he was also a Minomoto. So Yoritomo took up arms for self-protection with the support of Tokimasa and Masako. This triggered the Genpei War, the final war between the Minamoto and Taira clans.

By 1185, Yoritomo had wiped out the Taira by execution or by forcing them to drown themselves, making Yoritomo the undisputed leader of Japan. In 1192, the cloistered emperor named Yoritomo the first shogun. The Shogunate was a warrior government governed by a military general, the shogun, on behalf of the emperor. So Yoritomo was effectively a military dictator and the most powerful man in Japan. He shared this power with his wife, who had helped him to found the Kamakura Shogunate.

Although they were childhood sweethearts and ruled together, Masako and Yoritomo had a troubled relationship. This is mostly due to Yoritomo's interest in other women; however, at this time it was quite normal for a married man to have multiple lovers. But Masako would not stand for this, especially when she was pregnant. In one incident, Masako had the home of one of these lovers destroyed due to her jealousy. Some of Yoritomo's other lovers were run out of the region in shame by Masako, but Yoritomo continued to have affairs, despite the danger his lovers faced.

Once Yoritomo was pursuing a dancer, who was not romantically interested in the Shogun, but he persisted. She infuriated Yoritomo by publicly announcing her disdain of him in a poem. Masako thought that this was brilliant, so took this dancer under her wing and helped her escape Yoritomo's wrath.

It was relatively normal for wives to seek revenge on the women their husbands were interested in, and this is referred to as "unwanari-uchi", literally translating to "strike of the after-wife". Masako reacted harshly to these women because she was defending her status as Yoritomo's main wife, as well as protecting her son's right to succession.

The couple had a few children, but custom dictated that they be raised by foster families, so many believed they were unfit for ruling the warrior government. Despite not raising her children, Masako seemed to be close with her daughter, Ohime, who suffered from severe depression following the execution of her husband. Masako tried to help Ohime by organising grand memorials for her husband, but at the age of 20, Ohime died. Masako grieved so deeply for her daughter that she wanted to kill herself, but Yoritomo stopped Masako by saying that her death would only make Ohime's afterlife worse.

In 1199, Yoritomo died when he was thrown from his horse, so Masako's son, Yoriie, succeeded him. Some believed that Yoritomo had been assassinated, perhaps by a jealous Masako. They believed, that Masako had detached her spirit from her body and haunted her husband to death. But Masako was distraught about Yoritomo's death, despite his infidelity, and upon his death, she said "With Ohime and Yoritomo gone, this is the end for me, but if I die, young Yoriie will lose both parents. I cannot abandon my children."

Again Masako wanted to die and only the love for her children kept her going. As was the norm at the time, Masako shaved her head and became a Buddhist nun after being widowed, but remained very much involved in political affairs and she did not join a monastery or nunnery. Masako first was pulled back into politics when her son began killing people and seizing their properties, overcome with his newly found power. He even made plans to kill a governor, so Masako decided to intervene and stood in front of the governor's house, claiming that if he was to kill the governor, he had to kill her too. She then mediated between the two men.

At one point, a murder attempt was made on Yoriie and Masako, but the Shogun was incompetent at dealing with the assassins. So Masako stepped in, took control of the shogunate, then killed the assassins. As Yoriie was only 18, Tokimasa proclaimed himself regent. Masako then set up a council of elders, called the "shukuro" to moderate the power of the shogun, which infuriated Yoriie. Masako, Tokimasa, and Yoshitoki (Masaka's brother) were on this council of regents, but Yoriie disliked and resented his mother's family, favouring his wife's family, the Hiki clan.

This became a problem when Masako overheard Yoriie and his father-in-law plotting to kill Tokimasa. She immediately reported this to Tokimasa, who had Yoriie's father-in-law executed. Masaka then ordered Yoriie, who was severely unwell at the time, to abdicate to the Izu Province, where he was murdered on Tokimasa's orders in 1204, which Masako was not aware of. Tokimasa then had Yoriie's heir executed during the murders and purges of the Hiki clan, as the heir's mother was a Hiki. Masako did not seem to approve of this murder, so sent Yoriie's other children into priesthood to protect them.

Masako's other son, Sanetomo, then became shogun, but could not exercise his own power because Tokimasa was wielding the power as regent. To ensure he did not have to share the power, Tokimasa transferred the shogun from Masako's residence to his own, despite Sanetomo being close to his mother.

Sanetomo was more interested in culture than his brother had been, so tried to unite with the Imperial court, but the samurais complained about this.

In 1203, Masako found out that Tokimasa and his second wife were scheming to drive out Sanetomo as shogun and replace him with their son-in-law. Soon after, there was an unsuccessful assassination attempt on Sanetomo, in which Tokimasa was implicated. So Masako and Yoshitoki immediately ordered Tokimasa to step down and go into priesthood or they would rebel, so he abdicated as regent in 1205. He spent the rest of his days in a monastery, where he shaved his head and became a monk, dying a decade later.

Yoshitoki became the new regent and he enabled Masako to exercise indirect power. She became the negotiator with the court and could work towards the creation of an advisory council. In 1218 she was given the important role of asking the cloistered emperor to have one of his sons made heir, as Sanetomo was childless, but this was refused.

In 1219, Sanetomo was assassinated by his nephew, due to the samurai being discontent with his relationship with the Imperial court. He died with no heirs, leading to a succession problem. Masako was extremely devastated by her son's death and claimed she was suicidal at this time of her life as now all her children were dead. But Masako and Yoshitoki had to quickly decide on a new shogun. They chose a great-grandson of Yoritomo, a baby called Yoritsune. As he was still a baby and the Minamoto line was extinguished, Masaka became the guardian of the new shogun.

Yoritsune was just a puppet shogun, with Masako dominating government, and she was known as the "Ama Shogun", meaning "Nun Shogun". Because of her guardianship, Masako acted as the de facto shogun and overseer until her death. She continued to consolidate rule under the advisory council, manage the relationships and connections between imperial and aristocratic families, and administer judgements and post-war rewards. Masako is recognised as a source of power that enabled the Hōjō clan to dominate the Kamakura Shogunate until the downfall of the government in 1333.

There were many times when Masako was able to strengthen the Shogunate, such as in 1221, when the cloistered emperor tried to restore power to the emperor, rebelling against the shogun. He raised an army and called on all of Japan to conquer the Shogunate, which caused the samurai to shake with fear because they were in awe of the Imperial court. Masako responded by rallying the Shogunate samurai and made a powerful speech in which she spoke through tears. In this speech, she asked the samurai to be grateful and to remember the kindness, "higher than a mountain and deeper than the sea", of the first shogun, her husband.

This speech successfully calmed the samurai. Yoshitoki and his eldest son then attacked the Imperial court with 190,000 samurai and exiled the cloistered emperor in what is known as the Jōkyū War or the Jōkyū Disturbance. Just a few years later, the regent, Yoshitoki, died of a sudden illness. His second wife took this opportunity to support an attempt to topple the Hōjō government in favour of her Miura clan. So Masako rushed to negotiate and successfully put down the Miura before installing Yoshitoki's son as the new regent; however, she died just a year later in 1225.

Masako is remembered as the "Nun Shogun", which is a suitable legacy for her successful leadership. Unlike her father and son, Masako was not hungry for power; instead, she wielded it when there was no one else who could, and ruled using the support and advice of her brother and council of advisors. With strong leadership skills and powerful public speaking, Masako gained the trust and support of her subjects, leading her to be remembered as a powerful and successful woman. Not only was she a great leader, but Masako was also a dedicated wife and a compassionate mother.

So although never a shogun in her own right, Masako had all the qualities of a brilliant ruler and used these qualities, as well as the support of her friends, to create a peaceful rule.

Queen Tamar the Great (1166–1213 CE)

King of Kings

Tamar was Georgia's first female monarch and known as a king, or "mepe" because of the lack of grammatical genders in the language. Many call her Tamar the Great, as she reigned during a Golden Age in Georgia. Although many did not believe that she could rule successfully, Tamar improved Georgia by expanding its borders further than they had ever been before, in addition to encouraging a cultural Golden Age. She encouraged learning, building and she significantly improved the economy, allowing everyone to live comfortably. With the help of her noble's council, forward-thinking father and constantly supportive husband, Tamar became one of Georgia's greatest medieval monarchs and known as a "King of Kings".

    Tamar was the only daughter of King George III of Georgia, who ruled during the Bagrationi Dynasty. Her parents chose the Hebrew name "Tamar" because Biblical names were favoured by this dynasty, and they claimed to be descendants of David, the second King of Israel. During Tamar's childhood, George III faced rebellious groups of nobles who wanted to replace him with his nephew, Demna, who did have a valid claim to the throne. George III defeated the rebels and replaced them with unranked individuals, preventing the dynastic gentry from attempting to usurp him again.

But George III did not just replace the rebels, he also punished them harshly, some were driven out of Georgia and others were killed. Demna was treated most harshly, he was castrated and blinded before being carted off to prison where he died due to the mutilation.

After the rebellion was dealt with, in 1178, George III crowned Tamar as co-ruler in front of all the Georgian senior aristocracy and clergy. During this ceremony, George III proclaimed "it matters not if a lion is male or female", because he foresaw difficulty for Tamar after his death, as he feared that she would not be accepted as ruler on account of her sex. From this point, Tamar was included in government decisions so that she could learn how to efficiently rule Georgia, which cemented her as the legitimate heir.

This pre-emptive crowning of the heir was not done by previous rulers of Georgia, such as Demetrius I and David IV, who had left the succession unclear. Unlike his ancestors, George III made sure the succession was clear so that his daughter would have a smooth ascension to the throne.

Father and daughter ruled together until George died in 1184. Tamar was then crowned for the second time in Gelati Cathedral in Kutaisi at the insistence of the nobility before she began her life as the sole ruler. Although George III had left his daughter a relatively strong kingdom, Tamar still faced a great deal of opposition, as, despite her father's best efforts, many still did not want a female ruler, as there had not been one before. The nobles also opposed Tamar because of her father's repressive policies towards the nobility since Demna's rebellion. Due to the opposition, Tamar had no choice but to make important concessions to the nobility, as she feared facing a rebellion. She was forced to replace her father's appointees of serfs and foreigners, who had helped him crush the nobility so that the aristocracy were in the centre of power again. Two who were particularly influential to Tamar were her aunt Rusudan and the Catholicos Mikel, who helped to legitimise Tamar's succession. However, Tamar was also pressured into making Mikel the chancellor, placing him at the top of both the clerical and secular hierarchies.

Although Tamar was forced to replace her father's men, one who did keep his position was the treasurer, Qutlu Arslan. But he attempted to control Tamar. He led a group of nobles and wealthy citizens to create a new council, the karavi, whose members would alone deliberate and decide policy, including appointing government ministers and enacting laws. This would seriously limit the royal authority and was an attempt at feudal constitutionalism. Although up to this point Tamar had allowed herself to be pressured by those around her, this was a demand that she would not concede to, so Tamar had Qutlu Arslan arrested.

Others who had supported Qutlu Arslan were pardoned by Tamar, which displays the mercy she showed throughout her rule. The catholicos Mikel also made trouble for Tamar, as since the reign of David IV the catholicos was also the prime minister of Georgia, so he had enormous power. Tamar tried to restrict him by summoning a synod in 1185 to overthrow him, but the synod would not oppose Mikel. This meant that Tamar was often restricted by Mikel due to his huge influence.

Early in Tamar's reign, the nobles aimed to have Tamar married so that she could produce an heir. They also expected Tamar's new husband to become the head of the army. Therefore, every faction strove to have their candidate selected to marry Tamar so that they could have more influence at court. Eventually, Mikel and Rusudan approved a man named Yuri to be Tamar's husband, which the feudal court agreed to. Yuri was a Rus prince, whose father had been assassinated, so he was living as a fugitive in the North Caucasus, and in 1185 he was brought to Georgia to marry Tamar.

At first, Yuri was valuable to Tamar as a successful military commander who would lead Tamar's troops into battle, whereas previously Tamar had only led them partway. He was an attractive man and an able soldier, but unfortunately a difficult person. As time went on, Yuri became more assertive, threatening Tamar's rights as ruler, but she was also becoming more confident in herself.

Tamar began appointing her supporters to important roles, such as Anton Gnolistavisdze as chancellor. This gave her the confidence to gain the noble council's permission to annul her marriage to Yuri based on his sodomy and addiction to drunkenness. Tamar was granted this, and Yuri was sent away to Constantinople. In the same year, Catholicos Mikel died, leaving Tamar free to make her own decisions now that both Yuri and Mikel were gone.

Tamar knew she needed to marry again, as she had no children with Yuri, but this time she would choose her own husband. Before she did this, Tamar took the time to fill the top positions with her own men, including the interior minister and commander-in-chief. Two who became particularly important advisors and military commanders were the Mkhargrdzeli brothers, who were promoted due to their loyalty to Tamar. Eventually, Tamar decided to marry David Soslan, an Alan prince and military commander, who became Tamar's biggest supporter, unlike her previous husband, who had just wanted her power for himself.

David was an acceptable match because he was distantly related to Tamar and was raised at the Georgian court in Tbilisi. David held the position of king consort and was present in art, on charters, and on coins because of the necessity of male aspects of kingship. But although he shared the throne and derived some power from his wife, he was a subordinate ruler and always supported Tamar in every decision she made. During their marriage, Tamar and David had two children, a son, Lasha-Giorgi, and daughter, Rusudan, both of whom became future monarchs of Georgia.

In 1187, Saladin and his Muslim forces had retaken Jerusalem from the Christian crusaders. This threatened Georgia as it was a Christian nation, so when she saw that Muslim power was on the rise, Tamar realised she needed to ensure peace. So Tamar sent two diplomatic missions to Saladin to secure the safety of Georgia's Monastery of the Cross, and its exemption from taxation in exchange for peace between Georgia and Saladin's state. Although Tamar had successfully kept peace with Saladin, there were others making trouble.

Tamar's first husband, Yuri, showed up in Turkish Erzurum, planning to take power for himself. He was brought across the border by Georgians who supported him and they crowned him as king at the royal palace of Geguti. Diplomacy had worked for Tamar in the past, so she sent negotiators to Yuri. But this was not enough, and she had to send her loyalist army to defeat Yuri and the rebels. When they surrendered, Tamar proved herself to be merciful by sending her former husband back to Constantinople, removing the lands and titles from the other rebels, and allowing them all to keep their lives.

In 1192, Tamar gave birth to her first child, the future George IV. To celebrate the birth, David launched two military campaigns in which he captured the city of Bardavi (the old capital of Albania) and Erzurum. But many did not approve of this violent celebration. In Baghdad, a jihad (holy war) was declared of all Muslims against Georgia, led by Abu Bakr, a Muslim ruler in Azerbaijan. He quickly occupied Georgia's ally, the Muslim state of Shirvan. Meanwhile,

Yuri pledged his loyalty to Abu Bakr. This time Yuri was defeated by a Georgian duke and vanished from historical records.

At the Battle of Shamkor in 1195, David faced the Muslim army under Abu Bakr. David was victorious in this battle, so the Georgian army marched on Ganja, capturing the city and creating a Georgian vassal. In response, Abu Bakr poisoned the leader of this vassal state and recaptured the Ganja. But the Georgian army continued to march south, capturing the important trading city of Nakhichevan, leading Abu Bakr to drink himself to death.

By this point, Georgia was at its greatest territorial expanse, which some found threatening, such as the Seljuk Sultan. The Sultan attacked Erzurum and sent a rude letter to Tamar, in which he called her a "simpleton of a queen", demanding Georgia's surrender. The Sultan stated that if Tamar converted to Islam, he would make her his wife; if she refused, Tamar would be his concubine.

In response to this disturbing insult, Tamar assembled her Georgian army. David then led the army to victory at the Battle of Basiani in 1202. Just four years later, Georgian forces occupied Erzurum and Kars, further expanding Georgia's already huge area of influence.

Unfortunately, David died in 1207, but the expeditions continued to the southeast, further expanding Georgia's borders. However, there were some setbacks without David as the military commander. For example, in 1209, the Sultan of Ardabil sacked Ani (the former capital of Armenia), slaughtering the Armenians as he did so. Georgian forces continued into Iran and the cities of Tabriz and Qazvin offered tribute to Tamar. The loot from this Iranian expedition helped pay to rebuild Ani, but the tragic loss of life could not be repaid.

In 1204, Constantinople had been sacked by the Fourth Crusade, so the Byzantine Empire disintegrated into a land grab. But there were two surviving family members of the Byzantine Emperor, who was overthrown in 1185. These were Alexios and David, who were being raised in Tamar's court in Georgia as they were her nephews. So when the Byzantine Empire was disintegrating, Tamar decided to help her nephews recapture some of their family's land. The Georgian forces enabled Alexios and David to capture Trebizond and the Black Sea coast up to Sinope. Alexios soon became Alexios I of the Empire of Trebizond, which survived as a Byzantine successor state. Because of the help Tamar gave, the new Empire of Trebizond was close with Georgia, expanding Tamar's zone of influence. After this, Georgia became the strongest Christian state in the whole East Mediterranean area.

Tamar spent her reign strengthening Georgia's power and she gained support in Georgia by reviving the expansionist foreign policy of her ancestors. She cleverly took advantage of the decline of other major powers in the region, with the help of her husband and the noble council because of their military skills, rather than having a dictatorial leadership. By the end of her reign, Georgia was at the peak of its power in the Middle Ages. Although Tamar made use of those around her, it was Tamar's influence that kept the dynastic princes from fragmenting the state.

Under Tamar's rule, Georgia was threatened by invasion from several Muslim rulers, and Georgia's victory over them at the time was attributed both to the will of God and to the piety of Tamar. Her success at expanding Georgia is highlighted by some addressing her as "The Queen of Abkhazians, Kartvels, Rans, Kakhs and Armenias, Shirvan-Shakhine and Shakh-in Shakhine, the sovereign of the East and West". This quote demonstrates Tamar's influence and power over a massive number of people.

Not only did Tamar expand her territories and found success in military matters, but she also encouraged a Golden Age in culture. The locals began to identify with the Byzantine West rather than the Islamic East and there were architectural developments throughout the country. Tamar was involved in the construction of many of Georgia's domed cathedrals, churches, and the monastery of the caves at Vardzia. There was also a flourishing in science, learning, and literature, as Georgia's national epic poem, *The Knight in Panther's Skin* was produced during her reign and dedicated to Tamar.

In addition to this cultural change, the economy and trade flourished under Tamar's reign. Georgia found wealth from the flourishing trade epicentres and this brought in commerce. Tribute taxes and war spoils also helped increase Georgia's wealth, so living conditions were high. It was reported that peasants lived like nobles, nobles like princes, and princes like kings.

Tamar's death is shrouded in mystery, as her burial place is unknown. Some claim she is in Jerusalem. However, others believe that she is not dead, just sleeping in a cave in the Caucasus. Like the legends of Arthur of Camelot, they believe that one day she will wake up and leave the cave, bringing with her the dawn of a new Golden Age for Georgia. Due to her impressive achievements in all areas of ruling, Tamar is known as a "King of the Kings" and is considered one of the greatest of medieval Georgia's monarchs.

She was also declared a saint by the Georgian Orthodox Church, but others think of her as a warrior queen, despite not fighting in battles. Although she faced initial resistance towards her reign, Tamar proved herself to be a competent and merciful ruler, who was loved by her people.

Queen Isabella (1295–1358 CE)

The She-Wolf of France

Isabella had an extremely eventful life. She took her first steps into the world of government at the age of just 12 and developed strong diplomatic skills from this, so later acted as ambassador to France before taking matters of the English crown into her own hands. She was known to be a beautiful Queen of England and ruled as a regent for three years; however, her reign, although diplomatically successful, was unpopular, corrupt, and tyrannical. In plays and literature, Isabella is portrayed as a beautiful but cruel and manipulative woman.

Isabella was born in Paris as the only surviving daughter of Philip IV, also known as Philip the Fair of France, and Joan I of Navarre, who died when Isabella was young. She had three brothers who would all become Kings of France: Louis, Philip, and Charles. At the time, this royal family ruled the most powerful state in western Europe, since Philip had built up centralised royal power in France, but the family was constantly short of money, due to their engagement in conflicts to expand French authority. Growing up as a French princess, Isabella was given a good education and taught to read, which led to her having a lifelong love of books. But at the age of just 12, Isabella was sent to England to become the wife of King Edward II.

This marriage was arranged to resolve conflicts between France and England over England's possession of Gascony and claims to Anjou, Normandy, and Aquitaine. When Isabella arrived in England, she brought a vast wardrobe, including dresses of velvet, taffeta, and cloth, along with furs and over 72 headdresses and coifs, as well as two gold crowns, gold and silver dinnerware, and 419 yards of linen, displaying her wealth and French power. Unlike traditional kings, Edward was not obsessed with war, but instead loved music, poetry, and crafts, although some accused him of being cowardly and light-minded.

Edward was also notorious for being very generous to his favourite, the Earl of Cornwall, Piers Gaveston, an English nobleman who was believed to be the lover of Edward. The pair were so inseparable that during Edward and Isabella's wedding feast, Edward sat with Piers rather than his new wife. Edward even presented Piers with Isabella's jewellery, which he wore in public. After Isabella complained of this to her father, Philip intervened so that his daughter would be treated more like a queen. Although personally Isabella did not like Piers, she built a working relationship with him as he was the king's favourite. But the barons would not follow suit, as they were angry that Piers had so much influence over the king.

Opposition began to build up against Piers and his influence with the king. This opposition was led by Thomas of Lancaster, who was secretly funded by Philip of France. Eventually, this opposition forced Edward to exile Piers to Ireland. Meanwhile, Isabella was gaining respect and was being assigned lands and patronage. She used her royal French links to gain authority while learning how the English court works so that she could assert herself as queen. As soon as Philip stopped supporting the barons' opposition of Piers, the king's favourite returned to England. However, Edward, Isabella, and Piers lived together quite comfortably, with Isabella building up her support, such as the Beaumont family, who originated in France.

But in 1311, Isabella's relationship with her husband began to change. Edward failed in a campaign against Scotland, in which Isabella barely escaped capture, so the barons rose against their king again, due to his incompetence in Scotland. Therefore, the king was coerced to sign the Ordinances of 1311. This promised action against Piers, due to his influence being too great. While Edward and Piers were fighting the barons, Piers became stranded at Scarborough Castle and was executed.

Edward quickly found a new favourite in Hugh Despenser, who was also believed to have a sexual relationship with the king. But the barons opposed him in the same way that they had opposed Piers, and Isabella also could not tolerate Hugh. In 1313, Isabella and Edward travelled to Paris to gain French support against the barons. During this visit, there was an incident in which Isabella was injured. Her tent caught fire, but fortunately, she was saved by her husband when he lifted her and rushed her out of the tent, both of them naked. Other than this, Edward and Isabella were successful in Paris, as they received assurance of French support against the English barons.

So when the couple returned to London, celebrations ensued; however, at these celebrations, Isabella noticed that Norman knights were carrying purses that she had gifted to her sisters-in-law in France. She deduced from this that her sisters-in-law were having affairs with the knights, so Isabella informed her father. This resulted in the Tour de Nesle Affair, in which the sisters-in-law were imprisoned for adultery, and uncovering this scandal diminished Isabella's popularity in France.

There were also difficulties in England at this time. Edward was again trying to quash the Scots but was defeated at the Battle of Bannockburn in 1314. This terrible defeat was embarrassing and the barons fully blamed Edward for the failure. This enabled Thomas of Lancaster to take increased authority, which was a problem for Isabella, as Thomas opposed the queen. He cut off Isabella's funds and harassed her household. Eventually, Edward and Hugh again increased their authority but did not improve life for Isabella. They appointed a housekeeper for the queen who spied on Isabella and censored her correspondences.

Allegedly, Hugh even contacted the pope asking him to annul the marriage between Edward and Isabella. Despite their marriage seeming disastrous at this point, Isabella gave birth to two children, Edward and John, around this time. Despite the birth of heirs, matters were worsening for the country because the Great Famine of 1315 to 1317 brought about widespread death and financial difficulties.

The situation was made even worse for Edward when a man called John Deydras appeared in Oxford, claiming that he was switched with Edward at birth, so he was the rightful king. Eventually, he was executed, but not before the rumours had spread. Isabella was anxious about the difficulties they were facing as a country, so took up more time in government, attended council meetings, and acquired increased lands. Because of her increased influence, in 1319, the war leader for the King of Scotland tried to capture Isabella at York, and she only just escaped.

In 1321, the Lancastrians moved against Hugh, sending troops to London and demanding his exile. A baron with strong French links asked Isabella to intervene to prevent war, so she fell down to her knees and begged Edward to exile Hugh. Edward obliged, but quickly arranged for Hugh's return. Soon after, Isabella went on a pilgrimage to Canterbury, stopping at Leeds Castle, which was held by Edward's opponents. The baroness of the castle refused Isabella's admittance, so fighting broke out between Isabella's guards and the garrison, which began the Despenser War. Leeds Castle was placed under siege and Edward mobilised his faction and gave Isabella the Great Seal, so she assumed control of the royal chancery from the Tower of London.

Eventually, Thomas of Lancaster was executed, leaving Edward and the Despensers victorious against the barons. Once they assumed power, the pair ruled harshly, punishing the barons with confiscation of land, large-scale imprisonment, executions, and punishment of extended family members, including women and the elderly. This ruthlessness concerned Isabella, as some of those being persecuted were her friends, so her relationship with Hugh deteriorated, as did her influence with the king.

Hugh went out of his way to reduce Isabella's power, and her ability to see Edward. He would refuse to pay money owed to her, would not return her castles at Marlborough and Devizes, and he even tried to assault her.

Hugh's treatment of Isabella was affecting her marriage severely. But the relationship crumbled in the early 1320s when Edward and Isabella went on a campaign against Scotland. While Edward was raising men, Isabella was sent to Tynemouth Priory. Soon, Scottish troops began to march south, leaving Isabella to fear for her safety and the safety of her unborn baby, as she was three months pregnant at the time. So Isabella wrote to her husband, requesting assistance, and Edward offered to send Hugh to protect her. But Isabella hated Hugh, so refused this offer and asked for friendlier protectors.

Instead, Edward sent no one to protect his wife and ran to safety from the Scots with Hugh, leaving Isabella cut off from the south by the Scottish army. When Isabella realised that no one was coming to save her, she and her household commandeered a ship to escape the fighting, resulting in the deaths of two of Isabella's ladies-in-waiting. The escape was precarious, so once they arrived in York, Isabella was furious with Edward for abandoning her to the Scots, as well as angry at Hugh for convincing Edward to retreat rather than send help. Isabella was so angry that she went on a ten-month pilgrimage around England by herself in 1322. When she returned, she visited her husband but refused to take a loyalty oath to the Despensers, so was removed from granting royal patronage.

As the Duke of Aquitaine and King of England, Edward owed homage to the King of France for his lands in Gascony. But when Charles IV, Isabella's brother, took up the French throne, Edward did not want to leave England to pay homage to him in fear that the barons would rise, creating tensions between the two kings. Feeling disrespected, Charles attacked the English-held Montpezat, leading to the War of Saint-Sardos in 1324. Charles took the whole of Aquitaine from English control, but Edward still would not travel to France because he feared assassination plots. Throughout the conflict with France, Isabella was treated like an enemy because of her French blood.

Around this time, a famous magician had reportedly been hired to kill Edward and Hugh using necromancy. In addition to this, there were criminal gangs all over the country, leaving Edward's position weak, and he needed to resolve the conflict with France. To do this, the pope suggested that Isabella should travel to France as an ambassador. By this time, Isabella had lost any loyalty she had to her husband, as he had confiscated her lands, taken over her household, imprisoned her French staff, and had her youngest children taken from her and placed in Hugh's household. So Isabella agreed to go to France as an ambassador, but she had more radical motives.

Isabella reached Paris in 1325 and quickly came to a truce in Gascony, under which Prince Edward, England's heir, would give homage on his father's behalf. But once this was completed, Isabella would not return to England. Instead, she imposed an ultimatum. Isabella stated that she would only return to England with Prince Edward if the Despensers were removed from court, and if she would be allowed to resume her position as queen and have her lands restored to her.

Edward refused, so Isabella publicly defied her husband by having his enemies gather at the French court.

Isabella dressed as a widow, claiming that Hugh had destroyed her marriage with Edward, so she assembled a court in exile. It was at this time that she began her affair with Roger Mortimer. He was an exile who had been imprisoned in the Tower of London but escaped to France through a hole in the wall of his cell. The King of France was embarrassed by his sister's adultery, so withdrew some support when others began complaining of her scandalous behaviour.

Next, Isabella and Mortimer had Prince Edward betrothed to Philippa of Hainault in exchange for a large dowry. This combined with a loan from Charles was used to raise a mercenary army. Isabella and Mortimer had formed a plan to depose Edward and Hugh, so shared this plan with the Scots, then returned to England in 1326 with their army. They all marched through England unopposed, as many men in Edward's army deserted to join Isabella. During this campaign, Isabella took back her daughters, Eleanor and Joan, from Hugh's household. Then she went on to depose Edward, which resulted in the first ever abdication of an English king. Prince Edward was then crowned as King Edward III in 1327, with Isabella as his regent in control of the Great Seal.

Edward and Hugh were punished harshly. A huge crowd gathered to witness Hugh's execution. He was dragged from a horse, stripped, then had Biblical verses scrawled on his skin. Hugh was then dragged into the city and presented to the new dowager queen. He was then was hanged as a thief, then castrated, drawn, and quartered as a traitor, with his quarters dispersed throughout England.

Edward was not executed but instead held in the custody of Henry of Lancaster. But Isabella did not want to leave her husband alive, as she feared a counter-coup. So first, the jailers threw dung and dead animals into his prison, so that he would contract a disease and die "naturally". But this did not work, so instead he was killed with a red-hot poker, which was inserted into his anus so there were no visible signs of harm on his body, making it appear as though he was not murdered. Other sources suggested he was strangled to death; and some claim that Isabella would not have murdered her husband, because she still sent him gifts while he was imprisoned and showed sadness at the news of his death.

A regency council was set up to rule England in Edward's name until he came of age, but although Isabella and Mortimer were not members of this council, they held power. With their new authority, Isabella and Mortimer accumulated huge wealth, granting themselves so much money so that Isabella had the largest income anyone has had, except for kings. During her regime, Isabella faced foreign policy difficulties. There was a war in Scotland that had been left unresolved and was becoming expensive, so Isabella decided to end this conflict with diplomacy.

Initially, Edward opposed his mother, but eventually, he allowed the Treaty of Northampton, which involved the marriage of Princess Joan and David Bruce, who was the heir apparent to the Scottish throne. Edward also agreed to renounce his claims on Scottish lands, in exchange for the promise of Scottish military aid against any enemy except the French, as well as financial compensation for the raids across northern England. Although Isabella gained compensation from the Scottish, the earls who lost Scottish estates did not receive any. So although strategically successful, the treaty was not popular at all.

There was also the situation of England's lands in France to resolve. So Isabella reopened negotiations in Paris, resulting in a peace treaty under which the bulk of Gascony, minus the Agenais, would be returned to England in exchange for a 50,000-mark penalty. This was not popular in England because of the Agenais clause; however, it was an example of Isabella using diplomacy rather than expensive wars.

Discontent with the Scottish and French treaties, Henry of Lancaster broke with Isabella and Mortimer. He was angry about the Treaty of Northampton so refused to attend court and mobilised support amongst the commons of London. Fearing an uprising, Isabella tried to gain local support by pursuing Edward's claim to the French throne, as he was the only grandson of Philip of France. In pursuit of this, Isabella sent advisors to France to demand official recognition of this claim (which Edward III would take years later, beginning the Hundred Years' War between England and France), but this simply turned the French against Isabella.

In response to the tension from France, Isabella proposed the marriage of her son, John, to the Castilian royal family, gaining support against potential French aggression. By 1328, Lancaster had mobilised his army against Isabella and Mortimer, as he was still dissatisfied with their regime. When taking Lancaster's strongholds of Leicester and Bedford, Isabella herself rode into battle on a warhorse wearing armour. At the same time, Edward marched north, so Lancaster surrendered and was penalised with a fine so large that his power was crippled. To those who supported him, Isabella was merciful, but some fled to France.

Unfortunately, there was still discontent in England, which led to conspiracies, including one which aimed to restore Edward II, who some claimed was still alive. The Archbishop of Canterbury was involved in this, so was arrested when the conspiracy was broken up.

By 1329, Edward was becoming frustrated with Mortimer, so he assembled support against him from the nobles and the church, including the pope, for a potential coup. The final straw was when Mortimer declared that his word had priority over the king's, encouraging Edward to act. He launched the coup and had Mortimer arrested. Isabella begged for her son to be merciful, falling to the ground and exclaiming "fair son, have pity on gentle Mortimer". Her cries were in vain, as Mortimer was put on trial for treason and executed. The only mercy was that he was given a kinder death, as he avoided being quartered and disembowelled. On the other hand, Isabella was treated as an innocent bystander. Once Edward was 18 and had full authority, Isabella lost her regency and was put under house arrest at Windsor Castle until 1332.

Isabella was then was moved to Castle Rising. It is reported that Isabella suffered from occasional fits of madness at this time, which was probably a nervous breakdown after the death of her lover. Once Isabella was released from house arrest, she lived very comfortably. Although she had to surrender her lands when she fell from power, she could still live as a traditional dowager queen, with no influence over government, however, she did negotiate with France on her son's orders after her house arrest. Isabella had a yearly income of £4,000 by 1337 and lived a very expensive lifestyle, with grooms, minstrels, and huntsmen.

At this time in her life, Isabella became close to her daughter, Joan, after she left her unfaithful husband, King David of Scotland. Isabella also remained close with Mortimer's children and adored her own grandchildren, her favourite being Edward the Black Prince. Eventually, King Edward forgave his mother and visited Isabella a few times a year.

In her old age, Isabella grew interested in religion and eventually took the nun's habit of the Poor Clares before her death at Hertford Castle. Isabella was buried in her wedding dress with Edward II's heart placed on her chest in her casket. Every year, on the anniversary of her death, her son would order Isabella's tomb to be dressed in cloth of gold and have masses said for her soul.

All through her life, Isabella proved herself to be a strong woman. Most notably, she led an army in a coup, causing the first abdication of a King of England. Although some claim that her coup swapped one tyrant for another, she did create peace treaties that ended wars quickly and diplomatically. Her skills in negotiation and diplomacy were also put to good use while she was living as a dowager queen.

Despite scheming and being corrupted by wealth and power throughout her regency, Isabella lived in comfort after Edward consolidated his authority. This was lucky considering her lover's fate; perhaps Edward felt merciful towards his mother, or he valued her skills as a diplomat and an ambassador.

Christine de Pizan
(1364–1430 CE)

Woman of Letters

Christine was a French Renaissance writer in the French court of King Charles VI, as well as the first European woman of letters, meaning that she was the first European woman to earn a living by writing professionally. As an author and a poet, Christine gave herself the responsibility to write in support of women, giving a voice to those who did not have one yet. She also wrote documents advising how kings should rule, about the morality of war, and a beautiful poem to Joan of Arc. But Christine's life was not always so idealistic, she suffered greatly at the loss of her husband and the financial difficulties that followed when she became the head of her family.

Christine was born in Venice, but at a young age moved to the French court with her father, who was a physician who had been asked to become the astrologer of King Charles V of France, so, despite her Italian heritage, Christine was very nationalistic for France. As a young girl, Christine had a comfortable childhood and her father ensured that she was educated in many subjects, including Greek and Latin, as well as having access to an extensive library. However, Christine's mother disapproved of this education, as she felt that Christine should remember her place and concentrate on women's work. But this did not stop Christine from reading all about science and philosophy.

But Christine's childhood quickly came to an end when she was married to the royal secretary, Etienne du Catel, at the age of just 15. Although this was an arranged marriage, and she was so young, they were happy together and Etienne, a nobleman and scholar, encouraged Christine to read and write to educate herself, which was very unusual at the time. Together the couple had three children, one of whom became a nun at the Dominican Abbey in Poissy to be a companion to the king's daughter, Marie.

In 1389, Christine's comfortable life changed completely. In a short space of time, her husband and father both died, leaving Christine in a very difficult position. Her father's death destroyed the family's link with the French monarchy, and Etienne's death gave Christine severe financial issues, especially because the family was in debt. Christine did receive offers to join the royal courts of England and Milan, but she was determined to stay in France.

To support her mother, children, and niece, Christine first asked for the money her husband should have been paid, had he not been killed in the plague abroad, but Christine was ignored by those in charge. As she did not want to remarry, Christine knew she had to work hard to earn money for her family's survival. This was breaking traditional roles because women had no legal rights and were considered a man's property. But Christine was educated so decided to make a living through writing, and pull herself out of debt.

To do this, Christine began writing love ballads of lost love written to the memory of her husband, which was popular with wealthy patrons in the court. Although these works were traditional, they lacked misogynistic themes, such as the idea of a damsel in distress who needed a knight to save her. This is displayed in one of her first works, *Alone am I, alone I wish to be*: "Alone am I, to feed myself with weeping / Alone am I, suffering or at rest / Alone am I, and this pleases me the best."

Before Christine could establish herself as a professional writer, she earned her money by transcribing and illustrating other authors' works, making herself known in the profession. When she began writing books, unlike many other writers, she ensured that she would not be financially bound to just one patron, but instead had many. Christine would gain patrons by dedicating ballads to many at court, including the French Queen Isabeau of Bavaria, Louis I of Orléans, and Marie of Berry. At the time, bookmaking was cheap so not just royals, but the nobles could also afford libraries.

However, there was political turmoil in the French court due to King Charles VI's constant mental breakdowns. Because of this, the king was often absent from court, leaving his wife, Queen Isabeau, to govern. This was similar to Blanche of Castile's situation, who governed as a regent for her son in the 1200s. With these powerful women in mind, Christine published books expressing the virtue of women, referencing Queen Blanche and dedicating these works to Queen Isabeau.

In 1400, Christine wrote a book called *Letter of Othea to Hector*, as Christine believed that France was founded by the descents of the Trojans. Hector in the book is tutored by the Goddess of Wisdom, Othéa, in statecraft and politics. This was dedicated to Louis of Orléans, the king's brother, because he was very powerful. She also produced a luxury edition which was heavily illustrated and produced further editions, including editions with customised prologues for patrons, such as Philip the Bold, Jean of Berry, and Henry IV of England.

Christine instigated the controversy known as the "Querelle du Roman de la Rose" in 1402. It began because Jean de Meun wrote a book called *Romance of the Rose*, which was a satirical book about courtly love, in which it critically depicted women as nothing more than seducers. Christine did not like this notion and critiqued Jean de Meun, questioning his literary merits in her own book, *The Tale of the Rose*. In this book, Christine claimed that Jean de Meun's views were misogynistic, vulgar, immoral and slanderous. After some debate, Christine published *Letters on the Debate of the Rose*, in which she belittles her own writing style, employing a rhetoric strategy by writing against the grain of her meaning, known as antiphrasis.

Around this time, Christine also published her dream allegory called *The Book of the Path of Long Study*. This was a first-person narrative in which she travelled with the priestess Cumaean Sibyl and witnessed a debate between the four allegories: Wealth, Nobility, Chivalry, and Wisdom. Her conclusion to this book states that justice could be brought to Earth by a monarch who has all the necessary qualities.

To further show her support for the king, Christine wrote a story about the life of Charles V, portraying him as the perfect leader in a book called *Book of the Deeds and Good Morals of the Wise King Charles V*. This was commissioned by Philip the Bold, but when he died, Christine gave this book to Jean of Berry, so he would become a new royal patron, as Christine's goal was to have as many patrons as possible in the French court to continue her success.

It was just a few years later in 1405 when Christine began writing a lot more about women and their virtues, something which was completely unheard of at the time. First, Christine wrote *The Book of the City of Ladies*, which included three women named Reason, Justice, and Rectitude, who, together with the narrator, built a symbolic city in which women are celebrated and defended. The book describes various powerful women from the past, such as Queen Zenobia, focusing on the intellectual skills of these women. Also the book included women who ruled, honoured their parents, guarded their chastity, were faithful to their husbands, and became martyrs for their faith, as these were the virtues that Christine valued.

Normally, people just focused on the men of the past, but Christine gave light to these women's accomplishments, putting them on the same level as men. Not only this, but Christine wrote about women's contributions to society, and all from a female perspective. The ladies Reason, Justice, and Rectitude, which are the three virtues Christine found most important to women's success, gave voice to women through their conversation, particularly Reason, who stated that negative stereotypes of women are caused by women not being included in the conversation.

The quote "for you know that any evil spoken of women so generally only hurts those who say it, not women themselves" in *The Book of the City of Ladies* concisely demonstrates this point. Christine also wrote, "There Adam slept, and God formed the body of woman from one of his ribs, signifying that she should stand at his side as a companion and never lie at his feet like a slave, and also that he should love her as his own flesh." This argues that men and women may be different, but both are equal and should love and respect each other equally.

After writing *The Book of the City of Ladies*, Christine wanted to rest but felt that Reason, Justice, and Rectitude would not allow it until she completed her work, so she wrote *The Book of the Three Virtues*. This book is a practical guide for women, explaining how to take care of themselves, their homes, and their husband's lands and business affairs. It was inspired by Christine's feelings of helplessness after her husband had died, when she had been unable to navigate the financial world of men as a recent widow.

Christine believed that a woman's success depends on her ability to mediate by speaking and writing effectively, so sought out other women to collaborate in this work. This included the illustrator known as Anastasia, who Christine described as the most talented of her day. In her literature about women, Christine wrote about many topics, including women's oppression, their lack of education, the different expected social behaviours, how to combat this misogynistic society, and her visions of an equal world.

Christine dedicated these books to the dauphine, Margaret of Nevers, to expose the princess to powerful women who she would be inspired by. The dauphin on the other hand was given three works by Christine. These were to promote wise and effective government and analysed the customs and governments of late medieval European societies. She argued for hereditary monarchs and wrote to the dauphin about the duties of a king as a military leader, describing the role of the military in society. In this, Christine shows that she was interested and engaged with political issues of her time. The largest political upheaval that Christine would have experienced was caused by Charles VI's insanity, leading to a civil war, facilitating the invasion and occupation of France by the English.

During the civil war, Christine was commissioned to write a treatise on military warfare. So in 1410, Christine published her manual on chivalry called *The Book of Feats of Arms and of Chivalry.* She earned a lot of money for this book, partly because she wrote it in French rather than Latin, so that more people could read it, making the book more accessible. In the book, Christine discussed the just war theory, and referenced classical writers on military warfare, such as Vegetius, Frontinus, and Valerius Maximus. Many matters related to warfare were also discussed, including capital punishment, payment of troops, and treatment of prisoners of war.

Christine also argued about the morality of war, as she acknowledged that they were a proper execution of justice, but that many atrocities are committed during conflicts, such as rapes, killings, and arsons. So Christine suggested that the right to wage war should be limited to sovereign kings, as they were responsible for the welfare of their subjects. Just a few years after Christine made this point, the royal court published an edict prohibiting nobles from raising an army.

Christine directly addressed the dauphin, Louis of Guyenne, in her works, encouraging him to continue the quest for peace in France during the civil war. To encourage him further, she wrote of a utopian version of a just ruler, who would take advice and deserved respect because he would administer justice and live by example. This utopian ruler would be available to his subjects and avoid anger and cruelty. He should also act liberally and be clement and truthful. These traits are what Christine expected from a Christian prince.

In 1414, Christine gave Queen Isabeau a decorated collection of her works, which contained 30 of Christine's writings and 130 of her miniatures. Queen Isabeau asked for this collection, and the opening page of the book portrayed Queen Isabeau being presented with the book by Christine, demonstrating her links with the French royalty.

A few years later, France was defeated by England in the 1418 Battle of Agincourt during the Hundred Years War. This left Christine distraught and she published a book called *Letter Concerning the Prison of Human Life* especially for women, to console them for those they lost in the battle. Unlike her usual descriptions of symbolic cities and utopian princes, Christine did not write of hope and peace, but instead about how the soul was trapped in the body and imprisoned in Hell. She then moved to the Dominican Convent of Poissy because of the civil war and the occupation of Paris by the English.

Christine became less active at this time, but her final work was after Charles VII's coronation and Joan of Arc's military victory over the English. Delighted by such a strong, contemporary female warrior, Christine wrote a poem called "The Tale of Joan of Arc", a lyrical and joyous outburst expressing her renewed optimism in France. Her admiration of Joan of Arc is clear in this verse:

We've never heard
About a marvel quite so great,
For all the heroes who have lived
In history can't measure up
In bravery against the Maid.

Christine suggested that Joan was a fulfilment of prophecies made by Merlin, Cumaean Sibyl, and Saint Bede, to help Charles VII fulfil predictions of Charlemagne. Before Joan of Arc was executed by the English, Christine died, never living to see the end of the civil war.

Christine's works remained very popular after her death, as they were printed in French, English, Portuguese, and Dutch in the 15th century. Anne of France was particularly inspired by *The Book of Three Virtues,* and Christine's advice to princesses was translated and circulated among royal families of France and Portugal. *The Book of the City of Ladies* was acknowledged by 16th century French female writers, including Anne de Beaujeu, Gabrielle de Bourbon, Marguerite de Navarre, and Georgette de Montenay.

In 1470, Jean V de Bueil reproduced Christine's detailed accounts of the armies and material needed to defend a castle or town against a siege. *The Book of Feats of Arms and of Chivalry* was translated into English for Henry VII in 1489. Another powerful woman, Queen Elizabeth I of England, kept copies of *The Book of the City of Ladies, Letter of Othea to Hector,* and *The Book of Feats of Arms and of Chivalry* in her library, as well as tapestries with scenes from *The Book of the City of Ladies.*

In her life, Christine had to work hard for the financial stability of her family, which was not usually expected for women at the time, but she managed it superbly by becoming the first European woman of letters. Through writing, Christine did what she could to make the world better, by calling for equality between the sexes, limiting war, and advising future kings to be effective and respectable.

In 1949, Simone de Beauvoir wrote that *The Tale of the Rose* was "the first time we see a woman take up her pen in defence of her sex", which was brave during a time when women were not supposed to behave in this way. Christine lived when women were not allowed to have a voice or be independent, but she managed both in the most eloquent way possible.

Agnes Waterhouse
(1503–1566 CE)

England's First Executed Witch

As the first woman executed for witchcraft in England, Agnes was an unfortunate woman, and lived most of her life in poverty, probably as a healer. According to the stories, Agnes used her familiar, a cat named Sathan, to commit many killings, which led to her being accused of witchcraft, along with her sister and daughter. Now it seems very unlikely that Agnes was a real witch who murdered people with her cat, instead, she is seen as a symbol for all the women who were treated unfairly in the justice system because of their gender.

Agnes' childhood is quite undocumented and uncertain, but it is known that she lived in a small English village called Hatfield Peverel with her grandmother, Mother Eve, and her sister, Elizabeth Francis. They also lived with Mother Eve's familiar, which is a witch's supernatural entity, in the form of a white-spotted cat, named Sathan. When Agnes and Elizabeth were children, Mother Eve taught

Elizabeth about witchcraft and how to use Sathan, and encouraged her to renounce God. When Mother Eve died, she left Sathan to Elizabeth, but both of her granddaughters ended up living in poverty after their grandmother's death.

Elizabeth had to resort to begging for food and became romantically involved with a wealthy man called Andrew Byles for his money. By this point, Sathan had told Elizabeth that he would get her anything she wanted in exchange for a drop of her blood. So Elizabeth told the cat that she wanted to marry Andrew so her poverty would end, and Sathan promised that this would happen. However, Sathan decreed that to become his wife, Elizabeth would first have to allow Andrew to abuse her. This resulted in Elizabeth falling pregnant, yet Andrew refused to marry her, despite what the cat promised. So Elizabeth took potions so that she would miscarry the baby, before taking her revenge on Andrew by ordering Sathan to murder him.

Elizabeth used Sathan to do her bidding frequently, which left her with a red spot on her body where she would prick herself to give Sathan drops of blood. Eventually, Elizabeth married and gave birth to a baby. But the husband and wife would row constantly and the house was filled with swearing and cursing throughout the days. After suffering abuse from her husband, Elizabeth willed Sathan to murder her six-month-old baby, then caused her husband to lose all feeling in his legs so that he became lame. Whether she intended this harsh revenge or not, Elizabeth became afraid of the cat's power, so she decided to give Sathan to Agnes in exchange for a freshly baked cake.

At this point in her life, Agnes was probably a popular member of the community, as she was known as Mother Waterhouse, so was likely to have been a healer. When she received Sathan from her sister, she also received instructions on how to use him and care for him. Firstly, Agnes asked Sathan to kill one of her pigs to see what he was capable of; when the cat did this successfully, Agnes rewarded him with a drop of blood and a chicken. From that point, Sathan taught Agnes witchcraft, so she could use it to punish those in the village who offended her.

Once, Father Kersey offended Agnes, so she took Sathan in her lap, and willed him to kill three of Father Kersey's pigs, and the cat obliged. Then she fell out with Widow Gooday, so Agnes willed Sathan to drown the widow's cow, again he did so. Throughout this, Agnes kept Sathan in a pot lined with wool. When Agnes needed the wool, she prayed and Sathan turned into a toad.

Agnes was widowed, apparently because she asked Sathan to kill her husband. But she was left with an 18-year-old daughter named Joan. Agnes had been poor throughout her life, but during her childhood, she could go to the Benedictine priory in the village, seeking charity, such as bread and milk, from the monks. But in 1536, King Henry VIII began the Dissolution of the Monasteries during the English Reformation, so the priory was closed. This meant that Agnes was no longer able to go to the monks for support.

During the Reformation, the English people were legally obliged to pray in English rather than Latin, as the Protestants thought everyone should pray in their mother tongue. But perhaps due to her Catholic upbringing, or because Sathan forced her to, Agnes continued to pray in Latin, so the other villagers suspected Agnes was a witch. Agnes seemed to know of this danger, as she tried to protect Joan from Sathan by keeping the familiar a secret from her daughter.

Despite this, Joan was naturally fascinated by Sathan. Although she did not learn witchcraft from him, she did treat Sathan as a pet, exercising him when Agnes was out of the house. Joan believed that Agnes would soon teach her witchcraft and how to use Sathan.

One day, Joan was begging for food and saw a young girl who lived near them, called Agnes Brown, who was eating some cheese and bread. Joan asked the girl for food, as she was starving, but Agnes Brown refused. This angered Joan, so she asked Sathan to frighten Agnes Brown. But Sathan was cunning and knew of Joan's naivety, so the toad asked Joan what she would give him in return. She promised him a red cock, but Sathan refused, claiming that he would only follow her order if she gave him her body and soul.

This scared Joan so much that she agreed, so that she could to be rid of Sathan. He then promptly transformed from a toad into a dog with horns; in this form, he haunted Agnes Brown.

According to 12-year-old Agnes Brown, Sathan turned up at her house and asked for some cheese, which she refused. So Sathan came back with a key for her milkhouse and took the cheese for himself. After this, Sathan returned to threaten Agnes Brown with a knife. When the young girl asked who his "dame" was, he wagged his head at Agnes Waterhouse's home, displaying to Agnes Brown that she was the one to blame. She quickly alerted the authorities of the incident, accusing Agnes of having a demon, which she described as having the face of an ape, a short tail, and horns.

In 1566, a trial took place in Chelmsford which was attended by Sir Gilbert Gerard, the queen's attorney, and John Southcote, justice of the queen's bench, meaning that the case was of great significance. The trial was recorded in a pamphlet called *The examination and confession of certaine wytches at Chensforde in the Countie of Essex before the Quenes Maiesties Judges the XXVI daye of July anno 1566*. The first to be examined in this trial was Elizabeth, who confessed to having a familiar in the shape of a white-spotted cat, who was given to her by her grandmother and taught her witchcraft.

Elizabeth said she kept the cat for 15 years before giving it to Agnes. She claimed that the cat spoke to her in a hollow voice and would do anything for her in exchange for a drop of blood. Elizabeth then confessed that she had used the cat to steal sheep and kill people, including the wealthy Andrew Byles, who would not marry her when she became pregnant with his child.

Then Elizabeth admitted that the cat informed her on what herbs to drink to terminate her pregnancy, and willed the cat to kill her baby daughter and make her husband lame. Despite this incriminating evidence, Elizabeth escaped the death sentence by giving evidence against Agnes.

Next, 18-year-old Joan was put on trial. She explained how the toad agreed to help her if she gave up her soul, which caused the toad to haunt Agnes Brown, but this time in the form of a horned dog. Joan claimed not to use the supernatural powers of the cat much, instead, she was just playing a trick on Agnes Brown. But her confession of Sathan being a familiar helped to convict Elizabeth and Agnes, so Joan was acquitted of her charges of using sorcery.

At first, Agnes denied using Sathan to harm her neighbours and killing livestock, as well as bringing about the death of her husband. She did admit to being taught witchcraft by her sister and killing one of her own pigs, but she denied killing anyone using witchcraft. Agnes was accused of hurting Agnes Brown and a neighbour named Wardol, who only lived after being targeted by Sathan because of the strength of his faith. She was also accused of causing illness to a man called William Fynne, who died of this illness. When Agnes Brown told the court that Sathan had named Agnes as his dame, Agnes was found guilty of witchcraft under the 1563 Witchcraft Act.

Just days later, Agnes was taken to the gallows, where she confessed to her crimes and begged forgiveness from God before she was hanged to death. Joan and Elizabeth were not executed at this time. Elizabeth was jailed a few times after Agnes' death before she was eventually executed by hanging for causing the death of a woman called Alice Poole a few years later. However, Joan's fate remains uncertain.

Over time, Agnes has been remembered not only as the first witch executed in England, but also as a symbol of the unfair way women were treated throughout history. Based on nothing but the word of a 12-year-old child, Agnes was killed for a crime that she probably did not commit. Many other women, and some men, have suffered a similar unjust fate, found guilty from a false witness or an incriminating mark on their skin for many decades, as the last execution for witchcraft in England was in 1684.

Gráinne O'Malley (1530–1603 CE)

Powerful by Land and by Sea

Gráinne was a formidable woman who would not allow herself or her family to be disrespected. Although she was a pirate who plundered vessels and raided coastal regions, Gráinne also used diplomacy to get what she wanted. She was active in many rebellions against the English, who were trying to control her country and reduce her power, but was willing to work for them too when it was advantageous to her family. Gráinne is famous for meeting with Queen Elizabeth I and refusing to bow to the queen, who she saw as her equal, but still treated Elizabeth with respect, and the two powerful women were able to come to an arrangement after negotiating together.

Gráinne was born in Ireland while Henry VIII was King of England and Lord of Ireland, during a time when Irish lords were semi-autonomous and left to their own devices. But the Tudor conquest of Ireland was close. Gráinne's father was the Lord of the O'Malley dynasty, a seafaring family of Connacht, who built castles facing the sea to protect their territory. But there was a tradition of the Irish nobility to foster their children to other families, so Gráinne may have not grown up with her family. Despite having a half-brother, Gráinne was considered the legal retainer of the family land and seafaring activities, enabling her to gain wealth as her family taxed anyone who fished off their costs, including fishermen from England.

Before Henry VIII proclaimed himself as King of Ireland, a system of clientship existed, in which different families would align themselves together. The families cemented their alliance with military aid, marriage, and fosterage, creating a hierarchical society. However, when England began to rule Ireland, they introduced measures to establish a centralised system of government to Anglicise the population. A surrender and regrant policy was used during Queen Elizabeth I's reign, which involved the Irish lords being guaranteed their land if they cooperated with the English crown officials in Ireland, to help make Ireland into a client state of England. But this led to violence from the Irish lords who did not want to be ruled by England.

The O'Malleys earned their living from the land and sea, they traded raw materials for goods, ferried Scottish mercenaries, fished, plundered, engaged in opportunistic piracy, and levied a toll on shipping in their waters, so they could exist as an independent clan. These activities were punishable by hanging under Queen Elizabeth, but piracy and plundering were part of the seafaring life for many coastal clans.

In addition to the surrender and regrant policy, the English also used a divide and conquer method to take over Ireland, as they did not have the money to send an army to conquer Ireland by force. Instead, they used the feuding between Irish lords to their advantage, replacing them with those who promised to be loyal to the queen and to adopt English law.

As a young girl, Gráinne was fascinated by the sea and wanted to go with her father on a trading expedition to Spain. But he said that she could not go because her long hair would get caught in the ship's ropes, so Gráinne simply cut off her hair. From this incident Gráinne received the nickname "Gráinne Mhaol", translating to "Bald Gráinne". This story displays her determination to be at sea from a young age. Not much else is known about her childhood, apart from that she had a formal education and learned to speak Latin.

When Gráinne was just 16 in 1546, she was married to the heir to the O'Flaherty title, which was a good match. At this time, the law stated that wives could retain control of any personal property they brought to the marriage and were entitled to acquire additional property independently. This property was not just limited to material items, it included troops, ships, and other goods. In her personal property, Gráinne owned galleys and men. She also assumed the mantle of chieftainship of the O'Flahertys, because her husband was both bad-tempered and inept. Together the couple had three children, Eóghan, Méadhbh, and Murchadh. Gráinne was very close with her daughter, Méadhbh, but would eventually be betrayed by Murchadh, who beat his sister and would not listen to his mother on account of her sex. Eventually, Gráinne would cut off all ties with him.

After 20 years of marriage, Gráinne was left widowed after her husband was killed in an ambush while hunting. Gráinne returned to her lands and established a residence on Clare Island, as she was unable to inherit O'Flaherty land. Around this time, Gráinne led a raid on the Cock's Castle in Lough Corrib, and due to her courage and success, it became known as Hen's Castle. After her husband's death, she also took a shipwrecked sailor as her lover for a while, but he was murdered by the MacMahon clan, so she attacked the MacMahon garrison at Doona Castle to avenge her lover. After taking the garrison for herself, Gráinne killed those who murdered her lover, leaving her with the nickname "Dark Lady of Doona".

In another incident, a lord stole property from Gráinne, then fled to a church for sanctuary. Gráinne waited the lord out, saying that he would either starve or surrender. Instead, the thief dug a tunnel and escaped. Afterwards, the hermit who took care of the church broke his vow of silence to scold Gráinne for trying to harm someone seeking sanctuary. While she was unmarried, Gráinne was able to survive by the land and sea because of her ownership of three galleys and some smaller boats, giving her the reputation as the pirate Queen of Connacht. Gráinne often raided areas on the coast a short distance from her residence, levied tolls on passing ships and plundered vessels.

Gráinne justified these actions by claiming that she had to commit piracy to maintain herself and her people. However, she also acted dramatically in response to feeling disrespected. Once, Gráinne was refused hospitality by Lord Howth, so in response to this insult, Gráinne kidnapped his heir and demanded as a ransom that Lord Howth set an extra place at the table during each mealtime for an unexpected visitor at Howth Castle, and this unusual ransom was accepted.

In 1566, Gráinne married Richard of the Bourke clan. The couple had a child called Tibbot, who was born on a galley while it was being attacked by Algerian corsairs. Allegedly, within an hour of giving birth to Tibbot, Gráinne rose from her birth bed to turn the tide of the battle. But this marriage may have only lasted a year, perhaps due to the marriage contract only lasting a year. However, another story claims that Richard returned home one day to see his clothes packed and the doors locked, with Gráinne dismissing him from a window. Others suggest that the couple lived as man and wife until his death.

Together, Gráinne and Richard plundered and raided others, their exploits eventually becoming known to the English, who could no longer ignore Gráinne. So in 1574, the English besieged Rockfleet Castle; however, within two weeks, Gráinne turned her defence into an attack, with the English having to make a hasty retreat.

The province was visited by Lord Deputy Sir Henry Sidney in 1575, as he was planning to introduce a new taxation system, known as the composition, but he was unsuccessful. So he summoned all of the lords to a meeting, which included Gráinne, who offered her services to Henry Sidney, including the use of three galleys and 2,000 fighting men, but he did not require these services. However, Henry Sidney did sail with Gráinne to inspect the seaward defences. Gráinne also engaged in the surrender and regrant process, but Gráinne was mostly at sea and Dublin was a week's march from Gráinne, enabling her to defy the English, as their control was weak.

Within weeks of meeting Henry Sidney, Gráinne was captured while she was plundering Desmond. She was then used as a bargaining chip as a demonstration of Desmond's loyalty to the English, so she was transferred to Dublin in chains and not released until 1579. Just a year later, Gráinne and her husband gathered 2,000 men who pressured the English to have Richard ennobled, as long as he promised to rule by English law, pay rent to the Crown, and lodge and feed 200 soldiers for 42 days per annum.

In 1582, the pair moved to Lough Mask Castle, and with their new influence after Richard's ennoblement, they were able to invade others on the pretext of collecting rent. But this did not last long, because Richard died of natural causes just a year later. Gráinne received a third of his property, as was the custom, then gathered her followers and dwelled with her fleet as a wealthy and independent woman.

In 1584, Sir Richard Bingham was appointed as the new governor of Connacht. He believed that the best way to control the Irish was by sword. So he deprived Gráinne of her income by confiscating her cattle and ships, as he thought she was a source of trouble. At the age of 56, Gráinne was captured by Bingham and barely escaped the death sentence. After her release, Gráinne's influence, wealth, and lands were diminished until she was on the brink of poverty. So, with no other obvious options, Gráinne confided to Queen Elizabeth I, requesting the freedom to fight for her queen, which would enable Gráinne to continue her life at sea, free from Bingham's control.

The Bourkes were attacked by Bingham, as they would not attend Bingham's meetings, so the Bourkes rebelled with the O'Malleys. At one point, Bingham ordered Eóghan, Gráinne's son, to give up his lands, but Eóghan refused. For this refusal, Eóhan was killed, which angered Gráinne, so she rebelled fiercely against Bingham. Eventually, she was exiled for three months due to her fleet being damaged by Bingham. By 1587, the Bourke rebellion collapsed and Bingham was sent to Flanders to deal with rebellions there. In his absence, Gráinne travelled to Dublin to receive a pardon for all her past offenses and the offenses of her children.

Soon, Bingham returned to Ireland because of the Spanish Armada of 1588, as it was feared that the Spanish would land in Ireland. While back in Ireland, Bingham encouraged his troops to persecute the Irish rebels, so the Bourkes and English officials presented a list of charges against Bingham, as he was hated due to his brutality. Unfortunately, in 1590 he was acquitted of these charges, so continued to try to limit Gráinne's influence over the land she owned. While Gráinne was at sea, Bingham devastated her lands. To Gráinne's anger, her son, Murchadh, sided with Bingham, so Gráinne burned her son's town and stole cattle and goods.

Gráinne's other son, Tibbot, initiated a rising against Bingham, but this encouraged Bingham to plunder Gráinne's lands and have her ships destroyed in response. Eventually, Tibbot submitted and was imprisoned and charged with treason due to being implicated in the rebellion. Having lost so much already and afraid to lose her son, Gráinne appealed to Elizabeth in 1593, requesting the return of her property in return for allegiance. After complaining to Lord Burghley about her situation, Gráinne was sent the 18 Articles of Interrogatory.

In this, Gráinne had to explain her circumstances and other aspects of her life, such as her family background and connections. Gráinne portrayed herself as a woman suffering from age and poverty, who had to plunder to maintain herself. In contrast to this, Bingham claimed he had enough evidence to have Gráinne hanged. However, Elizabeth agreed to hear Gráinne's petition and to investigate.

Gráinne's journey to London was dangerous, as the seas around Ireland were patrolled by English warships, and Gráinne was a notorious rebel who would be seen as a great prize. Eventually, Gráinne sailed down the Thames and sought an audience with the queen. Elizabeth could have easily had Gráinne thrown into the Tower of London and have her executed as soon as she arrived, but the Irish pirate woman intrigued Elizabeth, so she agreed to listen. This meeting was significant as it was the first time that the Queen of England had met with a pirate Queen of Ireland.

Gráinne refused to bow to Elizabeth as she did not recognise her as the Queen of Ireland, but both women were civil and dressed in fine gowns for the meeting. However, Gráinne did keep a dagger on her for safety, which worried those around Elizabeth, but not the queen herself. One incident that highlighted the difference between the two women and two cultures, was when Gráinne sneezed and a noblewoman handed her a lace handkerchief, so Gráinne proceeded to blow her nose and throw the handkerchief into the fire. This shocked everyone at court, but Gráinne argued it was because, in Ireland, a used handkerchief is considered dirty and must be destroyed.

Despite the cultural differences, the two women communicated for a long time in Latin, their only common language, and eventually, they came to an agreement.

Gráinne claimed that her previous immoral actions were to protect her family and people, portraying herself as a victim of Bingham. Elizabeth listened with pity and admiration as she heard of Gráinne's difficulties at the hands of the English, so she agreed to free Tibbot and restore most of Gráinne's land to her. Unfortunately, when Tibbot left the prison, he was so crippled from the torture that he could barely walk. Elizabeth trusted that Gráinne would remain a dutiful subject, so agreed that if Gráinne would not support the Irish lords' rebellions, then she would remove Bingham from his position.

Although at the time this seemed like a successful meeting, several of Gráinne's demands were not met, such as the return of cattle and land, and

Elizabeth eventually even sent Bingham back to Ireland. Despite Elizabeth breaking this agreement, when the Nine Years' War broke out in 1593, in which the Irish fought against English rule, Gráinne did not fight for Irish independence, and mostly stayed out of the conflict. However, Gráinne was not happy about having troops on her land throughout this war, so in 1595 she wrote to Lord Burghley complaining of this. In 1603, Gráinne died at Rockfleet Castle in the same year of Elizabeth's death and was buried on Clare Island.

It is a shame that Elizabeth did not follow through with the agreements the two women made, as they could have made a good team, both determined and strong women with power in a world controlled by men. Gráinne was always fierce and strong, and is remembered as a woman who would avenge herself if she was disrespected. The O'Malley clan motto was "Powerful by land and by sea", which aptly describes this particular seafaring leader. Despite suffering from persecution and poverty, Gráinne remained fierce and determined, even willing to travel to her enemy to get what she deserved.

Lady Katherine Grey (1540–1568 CE)

The Would-Be Queen of England

Everyone knows about Lady Jane Grey, the tragic victim of the Tudor era, who was forced onto the throne for just nine days before her execution. But not many people know of her younger sister, Katherine, who also spent her life dangerously close to the throne of England. After losing her older sister, Katherine made some bad decisions, perhaps due to her youth and impulsivity, but this created a dangerous enemy in Queen Elizabeth I. Katherine spent most of her short life imprisoned because she dared to marry a man she loved.

Katherine was born near Leicester and grew up with two sisters, Jane and Mary. As the second child, Katherine's parents were disappointed that she was not born a boy; however, she ended up being treated much better than Jane. Perhaps this was because Katherine was the most beautiful and charming of the three sisters, whereas Jane was intelligent and Mary was kind. Katherine's maternal grandparents were Charles Brandon and Mary Tudor (King Henry VIII's sister), so she was a great-niece of Henry VIII. This meant that throughout their lives, the Grey sisters were close to the throne, because, after Henry VIII's own children, Edward, Mary, and Elizabeth, the Grey sisters were next in line, as Henry's other nieces and nephews had been excluded from the succession.

So Katherine was brought up at court firmly Protestant and received an education like most well-born women of the time. This included the learning of Latin, Greek, French, and music. But in 1553, when Edward VI was on his deathbed, Katherine's world completely changed. Edward did not want his half-sister, Mary, to succeed him due to her Catholicism, so he removed his sisters from the succession, making Lady Jane Grey his heir. This quickly made Jane, Katherine, and Mary very attractive to the noblemen at court, who knew Edward would not produce offspring to succeed him instead, so in 1553, both Jane and Katherine were married, and Mary was betrothed in a large ceremony. Katherine's new husband was Lord Herbert and although Katherine was just 13 when they married, she left her family home to live with her husband. However, due to her young age and his ill health, it is unlikely that the pair consummated their marriage.

In this same year, Edward VI died and Jane was expected to succeed to the throne. However, she famously only ruled for nine days and was never crowned, instead Mary took the throne herself, supported by the public, and sent Jane to the Tower of London. Just a year later, Jane was executed along with her father after the failed Wyatt's rebellion, which attempted to replace Queen Mary with Jane. Just before her death, Jane gave Katherine a parting gift of her Greek Testament with a letter telling Katherine to stay faithful and to trust in God.

Because of the Grey family's fall from grace, Lord Herbert wanted to distance himself from Katherine, so received an annulment from Archbishop Cranmer in 1554 as the marriage was not consummated. Fortunately for Katherine, Queen Mary pardoned the rest of the Grey family, but she did confiscate their lands and money, so they were penniless. But the queen pitied them, so invited Katherine and her sister, Mary, to be her ladies-in-waiting in her Privy Chamber, and later, they were maids-of-honour at Queen Mary's wedding. At this point, the queen's half-sister, Elizabeth, was still illegitimate, so Katherine was the heir apparent. Mary even thought of adopting both of the remaining Grey sisters to make their positions as heirs even more secure.

Another of the queen's ladies was Jane Seymour, who Katherine became good friends with, as they probably shared a room at court. When Katherine was new to court, she even confided to Jane that she wanted to reconcile with Lord Herbert, her childhood husband, but these wishes changed in 1558. An influenza epidemic broke out and Jane was affected badly, so was sent to her family home with Katherine to keep her company. While there, Jane introduced Katherine to her brother, Edward Seymour and the pair quickly fell in love throughout the summer.

Jane encouraged their relationship, sending messages between the two; however, others were concerned about the relationship due to Katherine's position at court. When Edward's mother found out, she ordered her son to forget about Katherine, but he refused. The young couple even talked of marriage; however, being so close to the throne, Katherine needed royal assent before she could marry. This proved difficult for Katherine, as Queen Mary had fallen ill and was dying, so Katherine did not find the opportunity to ask for permission to marry Edward.

When Queen Mary died in 1558, Elizabeth took the throne, which Katherine seemed satisfied with, considering her sister's fate. As Elizabeth had no heir or husband, Katherine was the next logical heir to the throne; however, Elizabeth did not like Katherine and preferred Mary, Queen of Scots to be her heir. Elizabeth was possibly jealous of Katherine, who was a younger lady and known to be the beauty of court, with her long Tudor-red hair and fair complexion, resembling her royal grandmother.

But whatever her reasoning, Elizabeth demoted Katherine from the Privy Chamber, leading Katherine to complain to the Spanish ambassador about her treatment. Although Elizabeth did not like Katherine, she did appreciate that she was the next logical heir due to her coming from a Protestant family, unlike Mary, Queen of Scots, so she also contemplated adopting Katherine as her own child to be the undisputed official heir.

But Katherine's position changed when she married Edward in 1560 without royal assent at a secret ceremony at Edward's house, with Jane as her sole witness. This was kept as a secret between the three of them, and Edward gave his new bride documents to prove their marriage so that if he died, she could inherit his property. But soon, Elizabeth sent Edward away on a tour across Europe with Cecil for the benefit of his education. Not long after, Jane died of tuberculosis and Katherine somehow lost the documents proving her marriage, meaning that there was absolutely no way to prove that Katherine and Edward were married.

This became a huge problem for Katherine when she found out that she was pregnant. Without anyone to turn to, Katherine concealed her marriage and her pregnancy until she was eight months pregnant and on progress with the court to Ipswich. At that point, she knew that she could not hide her pregnancy for much longer, so she confided in Bess of Hardwick. Katherine told Bess everything and asked her to speak to the queen for her, as Katherine knew that Elizabeth would be furious. But Bess would not listen and did not want to be implicated in the scandal.

So Katherine turned to her late sister's brother-in-law, Robert Dudley. He was probably not the best person to tell, as he was very close to Elizabeth, some believing them to be lovers. But Katherine went to his room in the middle of the night explaining her predicament, but his chamber had a room adjoining it to the queen's chambers, so he feared that Elizabeth would hear the commotion and catch him with a heavily pregnant woman in his chambers, so he told Katherine to leave. The next day, Robert told Elizabeth everything.

Elizabeth was furious. Not only was this not acceptable for someone so close to the throne, but also this damaged Anglo-Scottish relations as Elizabeth was arranging a marriage between Katherine and the Earl of Arran. Elizabeth also feared that if Katherine had a son, then people may rebel to support Katherine as queen so that her son, who would have an excellent claim to the throne, would eventually become king. This paranoia was probably partly provoked by a book being written at this time arguing for Katherine's claim to the throne over Elizabeth.

So Elizabeth felt there was no choice but to have Katherine imprisoned in the Tower of London. She then recalled Edward back to England and imprisoned him too, as Elizabeth thought that this marriage was a conspiracy against her. But the Lieutenant of the Tower pitied the separated couple and allowed secret visits between the two. In 1562, Elizabeth launched an inquisition into Katherine's marriage, but of course, the documents were missing and Jane, the sole witness, was dead. So the Archbishop of Canterbury annulled the marriage, meaning that any children they produced would be illegitimate and therefore would not be able to ascend to the throne.

Katherine gave birth to two children in the Tower, Edward and Thomas. When the second was born as a result of the secret meetings between Katherine and Edward in the Tower, Elizabeth was furious, so hauled Edward to the Star Chamber to answer for his sins of "deflowering a virgin of the royal blood", and he was fined £15,000. These charges were based on the Act of Succession of 1536, which made it a crime to marry a member of the royal family without the sovereign's consent. As it was clear that Katherine could not be stopped from seeing her lover even when imprisoned in the Tower, Elizabeth ordered the permanent separation of Katherine and her husband.

Katherine was taken away from the Tower with her younger son, Thomas, but Edward and her older son were taken elsewhere. For a while, Katherine was moved from place to place with a new jailer each time, but eventually, she remained in Ingatestone Hall. Katherine constantly pled with Elizabeth for mercy, but she was refused, so fell into despair that damaged her health. Katherine was not allowed to have any written contact with her husband and she was so depressed that the doctors could do nothing to improve her health. Katherine died at the age of just 27 from starving herself due to her intense sadness.

On her deathbed, Katherine wrote to Elizabeth, begging her forgiveness and a pardon for Edward; she then wrote to Edward to declare her love for him before her death. After Edward died 50 years later, the couple was buried together in Salisbury Cathedral.

Life could have been very different for Katherine if the politics of the time were not so sporadic. Perhaps if Jane had succeeded as queen, Katherine would have been part of the most powerful family in England. Or maybe she would have been able to have the life she wanted as she would not have been a threat simply by existing. It is impossible to tell. Perhaps if Katherine had been less impulsive and had asked permission before her marriage, she could have become the next Queen of England; however, it was not to be.

Without her family around her, Katherine did not have much guidance on how to act, and it should be remembered that she was just a young girl making silly mistakes. But her desire to live as she pleased was dangerous and her crime of marrying the man she loved set her on a road of misery to an early death.

Countess Elizabeth Báthory (1560–1614 CE)

The Blood Countess

After a difficult upbringing with unusual relatives, Elizabeth grew up to be just like the antagonist of a horror film. She tortured and murdered hundreds of young girls in some very gruesome and disturbing ways. More recently, she has been labelled by Guinness World Records as the most prolific female serial killer, and her gruesome crimes resulted in the nicknames of "Blood Countess" and "Countess Dracula". The tales associated with Elizabeth have led people to believe that she helped to inspire Bram Stoker's *Dracula*, but there is no evidence to support these claims; however, her torture and murder methods do suggest that she had monster-like qualities.

Elizabeth was raised as a Calvinist Protestant and spent her childhood at Ecsed Castle, in Hungary, and was the daughter of Baron George VI Báthory of the Ecsed branch of the family. Her family was extremely powerful and wealthy, so Elizabeth had a comfortable childhood with a good education of Latin, Greek, Hungarian and German. But Elizabeth suffered from epileptic seizures, possibly due to the inbreeding of her parents. At this time, symptoms of epilepsy were diagnosed as falling sickness, which was treated by rubbing the blood of a non-sufferer on her lips or giving her a mixture of a non-sufferer's blood and a piece of a skull when an episode ended. So perhaps Elizabeth's future atrocities were motivated by the desire to cure her sickness.

When she was a young girl, Elizabeth was a witness to her parents' cruelty, as she observed many brutal punishments executed by the family's officers, and she was trained to be cruel herself. In addition to this, Elizabeth was taught about Satanism and witchcraft by her uncle, and sadomasochism (the act of gaining pleasure, which is often sexual, by inflicting pain on others) by her aunt, who was rumoured to have had an incestuous relationship with Elizabeth. So throughout her childhood, Elizabeth had the comfortable upbringing of a Hungarian noblewoman but was a witness to all sorts of disturbing behaviour.

By the age of 10, Elizabeth was betrothed to Ferenc Nádasdy, but at the age of 13, she allegedly gave birth to a child fathered by a peasant boy. The Báthory family paid a local woman to take the baby away and hide it from sight. But Ferenc found out and responded by castrating the father of the baby, and had him torn to pieces by dogs as punishment for impregnating Elizabeth. However, the validity of this story is disputed as it is sourced from peasant gossip.

At the age of 15, Elizabeth married the 19-year-old Ferenc, who was of lower social standing to Elizabeth, so she refused to change her last name; instead, he took the name of Báthory. It was a huge celebration, as 4,500 guests were at the wedding and as a gift from her new husband's family, Elizabeth received 17 adjacent villages and the Castle of Csejte, in which Ferenc had built a torture chamber.

In 1578, Ferenc became the chief commander of Hungarian troops, so was away a lot to lead them to war against the Ottomans, so Elizabeth managed the estates and took lovers in his absence. She had a lot of responsibility at this time, as she had to support the Hungarian and Slovak people in her villages and provide them with medical care. During the Long War from 1593 to 1606, Elizabeth was responsible for protecting her people from the Ottomans, which was difficult because her estates were on the route to Vienna, so they were at risk of being plundered by Ottoman troops.

On many occasions, Elizabeth took it upon herself to help destitute women, such as one whose husband had been captured by the Ottomans, and one whose daughter had been raped and impregnated. During this period, Elizabeth gave birth to at least four children: Anna, Orsolya, Katalin, András, and Pál. However, they were cared for by a governess rather than Elizabeth herself.

In 1601, Ferenc became ill with debilitating pains in his legs, which he never recovered from. Two years later, he became permanently disabled and then died by 1604. Elizabeth became crueller after her husband's death, so perhaps Ferenc restrained his wife's bloodthirst; however, some believe that he schooled her in techniques of torture. On his deathbed, Ferenc left Elizabeth and their children to the care of György Thurzó.

It was around this time when rumours began to spread of Elizabeth's atrocities, but as the victims were peasants, these rumours were ignored. It is believed that Elizabeth committed acts of brutality with her late husband as well as her former nurse, Ilona Joo, and the local witch, Dorotta Szentes. A Lutheran minister made public complaints from about 1602 at the court in Vienna, but the Hungarian authorities did not respond until gentry girls, who were sent to Elizabeth to learn courtly etiquette, became victims.

King Matthias II assigned György to investigate. By 1610, he had collected 52 witness statements, and testimonies from more than 300 witnesses in 1611. These testimonies claimed that Elizabeth abducted and murdered peasant girls aged 10 to 14, then began killing the daughters of lesser gentry. There were also reports of Elizabeth abducting children and severely harming them as well as the servants in her household. She kept her servants chained up at night so tightly that their hands would turn blue and spurt blood; the servants were also beaten so loudly that her neighbours would throw clay pots at the walls in protest.

The other victims had their lips and tongues stitched together; knives, candles, and teeth were used to lacerate their genitals; they would be burned and their hands mutilated; Elizabeth bit chunks of flesh from their faces, arms, and breasts; one girl was forced to cook and eat her own flesh and make it into sausages to serve to guests; many were starved to death or forced to stand in cold water until they died; they would be covered in honey then left outside to be eaten by ants; pins would be stabbed into the fingernails; the girls would be whipped with stinging nettles or forced to sit on stinging nettles.

The intimate nature of some of these torture methods suggests a sexual motivation. Elizabeth was also rumoured to have bathed in virgins' blood to keep herself youthful, some believe this tale inspired some aspects of Bram Stoker's *Dracula*.

Elizabeth was arrested with four of her servants, who were accused of being her accomplices when the investigator suddenly entered the room. György claimed to have caught Elizabeth red-handed, as when he entered, one girl was dead in the room and another was being tortured; however, other sources argue that Elizabeth was just having dinner when she was arrested. Most witnesses testified that they had heard accusations from others but didn't see it themselves. Under torture, the servants denied their culpability in the murders but admitted to burying multiple victims, shifting blame to Elizabeth and each other, as well as implicating a dead servant. This resulted in the accomplices receiving death sentences for 80 counts of murder. They had their fingers torn off with tongs, then their bodies were tossed into a fire.

Originally, they planned to move Elizabeth to a nunnery, but as the rumours spread, it was agreed that she should be kept under house arrest; however, György wrote that Elizabeth was locked in a bricked room with slits for air and food. A large debt owed by King Matthias to Elizabeth was cancelled by her family in exchange for permitting them to manage her captivity. Elizabeth escaped the death sentence because it would cause too much scandal and disgrace, so King Matthias reluctantly agreed to keep her alive to protect the nobility.

After a few years under house arrest, Elizabeth complained one night to her bodyguard that she had cold hands, so he suggested that she should go for a lie down, but Elizabeth never woke up. Initially, Elizabeth was buried in the church of Csejte, but the villagers were in an uproar, so she was moved to her family crypt in Ecsed.

Some believe that Elizabeth was completely innocent and the victim of a politically motivated conspiracy due to her wealth and land in Hungary. However, this argument is disputed by the evidence of 300 witnesses, and the bodies of dead and dying girls found in the castle, although some claim that the physical evidence may have been exaggerated. The highest number of victims cited during the trial was 650; this number comes from a servant girl named Susannah and if it is true, it makes Elizabeth the most prolific female serial killer in the world.

If the stories are true, then the atrocities that Elizabeth committed could be the basis of a horror story. Not only would this mean that she was a very disturbed individual, but also demonstrates the unjustness of how nothing was done until the gentry girls became victims, as no one seemed to care when the servants and peasants were tortured and killed. To summarise Elizabeth, she was a sadistic woman who got away with the torture and murder of countless girls because of an elitist system that did not care for the poor.

Mary Frith
(1584–1659 CE)

The Roaring Girl

Mary is admirable in the way that she defied social norms and did what she wanted despite what others may have thought. She is remembered for wearing men's clothing, smoking, and swearing. These traits were all seen as very masculine, but many seemed to enjoy this image and she became famous for being in plays and singing crude songs. But this led to Mary being incarcerated many times; she seemed to be penalised more for her unfeminine attire than her actual crimes.

Mary was born to a shoemaker and a housewife in London; however, she was orphaned at a young age, so may have lived with her uncle, who was a minister. As a child, Mary was a tomboy and grew up to be a tall and imposing woman who smoked a pipe and swore profusely, which only men did at the time. From the age of about 16, Mary began to steal purses and grew in notoriety for this, as she had four burns on her hand, which was a common punishment for thieves.

Dissatisfied with Mary's unfeminine behaviour, Mary's uncle in 1609 tricked his niece onto a ship to New England to be reformed, luring her by saying the ship would take her to a wrestling match. When she was on board and realised she had been tricked, Mary jumped off the boat, refused to leave London, and would not see her uncle ever again. After this, Mary joined a group of pickpockets and gained the name "Moll Cutpurse". Moll was a common nickname for Mary; however, was also a name given to women of a disreputable character. The name Cutpurse came from Mary's reputation as a thief, as she would cut purses and take the contents.

Mary was also named "the roaring girl", which came from the London trend of "roaring boys", who were aggressive men of lower social classes who made fun of the courtly style of the upper class. Mary herself was known to have a brilliant sense of humour. On one occasion, Mary was the victim of a prankster who partially filled her pipe with gunpowder, and Mary found the consequences as funny as everyone else did, she had a loud and infectious laugh.

In her 20s Mary began wearing men's clothing. She wore baggy breeches and a doublet, which was a type of jacket. She may have worn these clothes to attract attention while her accomplices stole from her crowds, or simply to enhance her act as an entertainer. Mary became known for her comedic, musical performances in taverns where she would dance, sing, and play her lute without a license while dressed in male clothing. She would also perform in tobacco shops and playhouses, where she would distract the audience and accomplices would take their purses.

In the 1600s, two plays were written about Mary due to her growing notoriety. One was entitled *The Madde Pranckes of Mery Mall of the Bankside* by John Day, the other was *The Roaring Girl,* by Thomas Middleton. These plays focused on Mary wearing men's clothing, showing her as having improper qualities. However, *The Roaring Girl* also displayed Mary as being virtuous, as there is a scene in which she attacks a man for assuming that all women are prostitutes. She also displays chastity in this play by refusing to marry, despite the real Mary marrying in 1614.

One line in *The Roaring Girl* that is spoken by Mary is "I please myself and care not else who loves me", highlighting Mary's strong character. Not only did Mary have plays written about her, but she also performed on stage herself at the

Fortune Theatre in *Amends for Ladies*, always dressed in men's clothing. She would sing songs, play the lute, and make obscene banter. This was a strong contrast to the other female characters, who discussed their roles as wives and maids, whereas Mary's character displayed the qualities women should not hold. After performing in *The Roaring Girl*, Mary spent time in Bridewell correction house, as her performance was seen as far too immodest.

Not only was Mary a performer on stage, but she also spent much of her life performing. One day, a showman named William Banks bet Mary £20 that she could not ride a horse from Charing Cross to Shoreditch dressed as a man. Of course, Mary took on this bet in a dramatic style. Mary rode a performing show horse and won the bet, flying a banner and blowing a trumpet as she rode. This caused a riot in the streets because some of the crowd wanted her pulled from her horse, but others were cheering her on. Mary seemed to thrive in this attention and loved her image. She even set up mirrors around her house so that she could look at herself whenever she wanted. In her home, Mary also had three full-time maids, as well as parrots and she bred mastiffs, who had their own beds with sheets and blankets.

Her bravado and the way she dressed left Mary in constant trouble with authorities. In 1611, Mary was sent to Bridewell for being dressed indecently on Christmas Day, as she had been in St Paul's Cathedral with her petticoat tucked up in the fashion of a man. She was also accused of being involved in prostitution. Mary admitted to flaunting her male attire, blaspheming and swearing, being a drunkard, and keeping lewd and dissolute company, including cutpurses, but denied being involved in prostitution, despite being pressured by the interrogators. They thought this of her because, at the time, prostitutes often disguised themselves as men to be less noticeable to the authorities on the streets, also women would disguise themselves like this to visit or elope with their lovers, making the style suspicious.

Mary yet again had to do penance for "evil living" the next year. At St Paul's Cross, she was ordered to wear nothing but a white sheet during the Sunday sermon so that she would be shamed. But Mary put on a performance, weeping loudly and wailing in mockery of this; it was later found that she was drunk at the time and was not at all shamed, so Mary herself claimed that the punishment was pointless.

In 1614, Mary married Lewknor Markham, probably not because they were in love, but rather because Mary needed a counterargument when those speaking against her referred to her as a "spinster". The father of Mary's new husband was a prolific author who wrote *The English Hus-wife*, which was a guide to being a model woman. The couple did not live together, Lewknor was not included in Mary's will, and during one court case, Mary admitted to not knowing how long she had been married, so the relationship was not romantic. It was around this time when Mary established a brokerage of stolen goods in her house in Fleet Street, which was benefitted by her being a married woman, shielding Mary from the law.

This business involved thieves bringing Mary their stolen goods, which she would pay for, then sell the goods back to those who had been robbed. This practice was permitted by the local authorities and it was known as fencing. But unlike most fences, Mary gained a reputation of being generous, as she would return items to victims free of charge if they appealed to her sufficiently. This career was a much less dangerous one than being a pickpocket as she had been in the past, so Mary spent much less time in prison.

But by the 1620s, Mary changed her career path and began working as a pimp, even using her own house as a brothel. She would find young women for men, and respectable male lovers for middle-class married women. Once a wife confessed on her deathbed that she had been unfaithful with men who had been provided by Mary. If any of the male prostitutes Mary provided impregnated a woman, Mary would convince him to provide money and support to the child. Despite working in the sex industry, Mary was completely uninterested in sex herself, but because of her clothing choices, she was deemed as sexually riotous and uncontrolled.

After living as a pickpocket, a fence, and a pimp, during the 1640s, Mary became a highwaywoman, which involved stopping travellers and holding them at gunpoint to steal their belongings. She did this during the English Civil War, which began in 1642. Mary was a committed royalist, so at one point held up General Fairfax, who was a parliamentarian, shot his servants' horses, then robbed him of 250 gold coins, after allegedly shooting him too. This crime led to Mary being arrested and she narrowly escaped the gallows by paying a bribe of £2,000. Instead, she was taken to the mental asylum, Bethlem Hospital, and treated for insanity, eventually deemed cured and released in 1644.

Eventually, Mary died of dropsy, which is the build-up of fluid in the body's tissue. According to her wishes, Mary was buried face down, backside uppermost, in a final defiant gesture to the world. This burial seems fitting for a person like Mary, who was constantly defied by the society she lived in, so would defy society in return. Mary provided for herself and did what she wanted to do when she wanted it, whether society deemed it acceptable or not.

Mary's life was not the easiest, and she was could be immoral, but she was true to herself and did not take life too seriously. Whether she meant to or not, Mary defied the strict and unfair gender roles of the time and this gave her the freedom to behave in the way she desired.

Artemisia Gentileschi (1593–1653 CE)

The Painter of Powerful Women

Perhaps the most successful female artist of her time, Artemisia was not a stranger to misfortune and tragedy, but as an artist, she was able to portray these in her paintings. As she was illiterate throughout her early life, Artemisia expressed her pain, caused by the death of her mother and the trauma of being sexually assaulted, in her paintings. Living in Rome, Florence, and Naples, Artemisia was among some of the best and most influential artists of the time and ended up becoming one of the best herself, as she was the first woman to gain membership to the Academy of the Arts of Drawing.

Born in Rome, Artemisia was the only daughter of Orazio Gentileschi. He was a very successful painter from Pisa, who took his inspiration from Caravaggio, later influencing his daughter in this same style. In 1605, Artemisia's mother died, and it was around this time that she began to find comfort in painting. Unlike her four younger brothers, who were trained in art with her, Artemisia was very enthusiastic about visiting her father's studio and demonstrated impressive talent. She was taught by Orazio, who strongly influenced her artistic style, teaching her from a young age about drawing, mixing colour, and painting.

By the time she was 17, Artemisia had completed her first signed and dated painting called *Susanna and the Elders,* which depicts the biblical story of Susanna. For a long time, this was attributed to her father; however, the naturalistic subject is subtly different in style to Orazio's, and this is what gained her respect and recognition.

Many believe that the two men in *Susanna and the Elders* depict Artemisia's tutor, Agostino Tassi, and his friend, Cosimo Quorli. This is because around the time of this painting, these men would leer at Artemisia. Agostino, a landscape painter, had been hired by Artemisia's father to be her tutor, but one day, he viciously attacked and raped her with Cosimo involved. Artemisia clawed at his face as he held her down. After the incident, she threw a knife at him, but he shielded himself. Artemisia felt betrayed, not only by her tutor, but also by her one female friend, Tuzia.

Since the death of her mother, Artemisia was surrounded by her father, brothers and male artists, so when a woman called Tuzia rented the upstairs apartment of Artemisia's family home, the two women became friends. However, Tuzia left Artemisia alone with Agostino and when he attacked Artemisia, she called out to Tuzia for help, as her friend was just upstairs at the time. Tuzia ignored these cries and pretended to know nothing of the incident.

After this happened, Artemisia continued to have sexual relations with Agostino, as he promised that he would marry her, which would secure her dignity and future. But nine months later, the pair were still not married, so Artemisia's father pressed charges, which he was only able to do because his daughter was a virgin before the rape. He also accused the tutor of stealing from their home.

A seven-month trial ensued, which revealed Agostino's plan to murder his wife, his sexual relations with his sister-in-law, and his plans to steal paintings from Orazio. During this trial, Artemisia was tortured with thumbscrews to verify her accusations. Eventually, Agostino was found guilty and exiled from Rome. However, this was not enforced because he had protection from the pope due to his art.

Despite Agostino being sentenced to exile, it was Artemisia who fled Rome, and she married Pierantonio di Vincenzo Stiattesi, a less-known Florentine artist. The couple moved to Florence together and Artemisia was able to flourish in her artistic career. She became popular with the House of Medici and became an important part of court and the culture of the city. In 1616, Artemisia's popularity led her to be the first woman to gain membership to the Academy of the Arts of Drawing.

Her family life thrived too, with the couple having five children; however, only one, named Prudentia after Artemisia's deceased mother, survived to adulthood. Artemisia also had a passionate affair with a nobleman called Francesco Maria Maringhi, and Pierantonio seemed aware of this and may have tolerated the affair for financial gain. In 1615, while heavily pregnant, Artemisia was asked by Michelangelo Buonarroti the Younger, to paint a ceiling with other Florentine artists in celebration of his relative, the famous Italian sculptor, Michelangelo. Artemisia was assigned to paint the virtue of *Allegory of Inclination.*

She painted this in the form of a nude woman holding a compass, and like much of her work, the subject resembles Artemisia. The fact that Artemisia was paid thrice as much as any other artist involved in the project displays her success at establishing herself as an independent artist. This enabled her to be respected by many artists and influential people of the time, including Galileo Galilei. She also took the opportunity, while in Florence, to learn to read and write and became familiar with musicals and theatrical performances.

By 1620, rumours were spreading of Artemisia's love affair, and the family were building financial and legal issues, so they moved back to Rome. This was a stressful time for Artemisia, as her son, Cristofano, died; her father moved away to Genoa; and she had to reduce contact with her lover. Luckily, Rome offered many opportunities for Artemisia to meet other painters and new patrons, easing her money problems.

During this period, Artemisia became associated with Cassiano dal Pozzo, a humanist and collector of arts, who helped her to forge relationships with other artists and patrons. Then, to search for even richer commissions, Artemisia moved to Venice for a while in the late 1620s, highlighting her proactivity in improving her reputation and spreading her influence. Eventually, in 1630, Artemisia moved to Naples, where she was already well-known as an artist, so was able to run a successful studio until her death. It was here where she began to paint in cathedrals for the first time, as well as collaborating with other artists more frequently.

As Artemisia grew in fame, she was often invited to London to the court of King Charles I; however, she always declined until 1638, when her father lived there and was growing ill. Charles was known for his love of art and was often critiqued for spending too much money on extravagant art. He wanted to meet Artemisia because she intrigued him and he already had three of her works in the Royal Collection. When Artemisia visited her father, Orazio was the court painter and was decorating the ceiling of the queen's house in Greenwich, which is now displayed at Marlborough House.

Father and daughter worked on this piece together, but Artemisia did not take to living in rainy England as she was used to the much warmer climate in Italy, so she began planning her return as soon as she arrived in England. When the English Civil War began in 1642, Artemisia left England, but died just a few years later, perhaps in the plague which swept through Naples, killing off many Neapolitan artists.

Artemisia was perhaps the most successful female painter of her time, and 94% of her works featured women as protagonists or as equal to the men in the painting. She intentionally removed stereotypically female traits, such as sensitivity, timidness and weakness, replacing them with courageous, rebellious and powerful women. Not only were her subjects strong and bold, but Artemisia's brush strokes were equally so, and the strength and certainty of her brushstrokes were seen as unwomanly.

Artemisia may have painted in this way because she wanted to portray women as strong and defiant; however, she may have just been taught to paint in this way by her father. Some of her paintings, such as *Judith Slaying Holofernes,* are about violence and could refer to her rape. Many suggest that she used the fame from the rape trial to sell her art; however, others argue that the incident simply influenced her art and the violent themes portray her desire for revenge against her rapist.

For example, *Judith Slaying Holofernes* depicts two women murdering Holofernes; the one who is holding the knife resembles Artemisia, whereas the dying man resembles Agostino and he is held down on the mattress, much like she was. These violent and historical scenes are unique to Artemisia as a female artist, as most women during this time specialised in life and portraiture.

Throughout her life, Artemisia suffered greatly, from losing her mother and children, to being raped and tortured. But she portrayed these sufferings beautifully in her art. Not only was she an incredible artist, but she was also renowned for painting strong female characters, unlike other artists at the time, and massively inspired future artists, as well as the ones around her.

Artemisia once said: "I will show Your Illustrious Lordship what a woman can do", demonstrating her confidence that her sex did not make her any less worthy, much like most of her subjects in her works, who were not timid, feeble and weak, but strong, fierce and confident women.

Queen Anne
(1665–1714 CE)

The First Monarch of the United Kingdom

Queen Anne of England seems to be the least known of England's female monarchs, so it seems only right to shed some light on her reign and her life. This is especially true because Anne is remembered unfairly, due to memoirs published after her death by an ex-friend, portraying her as unintelligent and boring. But really, Anne was very involved in the politics of her country and presided over an important time of British history, as she was involved in unifying England and Scotland to create the United Kingdom.

Anne was born to James, the brother and heir presumptive of King Charles II, who was ruling at the time of her birth. As a young girl, Anne lived in France for two years to have her eyes treated, as she suffered from an eye condition causing excessive watering known as defluxion, which caused her bad eyesight throughout her life. During this time, Anne learned French perfectly, which would later prove useful when speaking to foreign diplomats and ambassadors.

In 1670, Anne returned to England, not long after the death of her mother. As Anne's only sibling was an older sister, Mary, their father remarried so that he may still produce a male heir. But his choice of wife would be controversial, as he married the 15-year-old Maria Beatrice of Modena, who was a Catholic princess, demonstrating that James' true faith was Catholic, rather than following the Church of England. This was not acceptable to King Charles or much of the public, so Charles ordered that Anne and Mary would be raised as Anglicans.

As well as being educated on the teachings of the Anglican church, Anne's education was suitable for a domestic lady, as she was not expected to ever become the monarch. However, learning about the teachings of the church did give Anne a strong loyalty to the Church of England. As a royal child, Anne was raised away from her parents, as was the tradition of the time, so she grew up with Colonel Edward and Lady Frances Villiers; however, it seems that Anne's father was loving and Anne got on well with her stepmother. It was in 1617 when Anne met Sarah Jennings, who would become a close friend and strong advisor in the future. However, at this meeting, Sarah found Anne boring and uneducated but pursued the friendship to secure a good position in the future.

In 1677, Anne's sister married William of Orange; however, Anne could not attend the wedding because she was suffering from smallpox, so was confined to her room. Anne herself was married in 1683 to Prince George of Denmark, who was a drunkard and extremely boring, both when drunk and sober. However, he was a handsome and loyal husband, so eventually, the pair would fall in love and become completely devoted to each other. They often travelled together to Hampton Court Palace to enjoy its clean country air and the hunting grounds.

Soon later, in 1685, the king died, leaving James, Anne's father, as King James II. Due to his faith, James was not popular, as he was giving military and administrative offices to Catholics, which deeply concerned Anne and Mary. Anne was particularly distressed when she gave birth to a baby, and James tried to have the baby baptised into the Catholic faith, causing Anne to burst into tears, claiming that "The Church of Rome is wicked and dangerous". From that point, she became estranged from her father and stepmother. Sadly, the baby did not survive infancy. 1687 was a particularly difficult year for Anne, who miscarried, then lost two daughters to smallpox within a few months.

Around this time, James and Maria were finding more success than Anne when it came to producing heirs, as they had a baby boy, making a Catholic succession in England more likely. However, many, including Anne and Mary, did not believe that the baby was truly born to James and Maria, as neither sister attended the birth. Eventually, this baby would become known as "The Old Pretender" when he attempted to gain support as king in Scotland with French support years later.

This baby was worrying to those who did not want a Catholic England, which was most of the country, so in 1688, Mary and her husband, William, led the Glorious Revolution. William invaded England and quickly deposed James, who fled to France. During this conflict, Anne sided with her sister and brother-in-law, which she was advised to do by Sarah Jennings. She even wrote to William, stating that she approved of the action he had taken. In 1689, a Convention Parliament assembled which declared that James had abdicated when he fled, so the thrones of England and Ireland were vacant. It was then declared that William and Mary would rule as joint monarchs of the realms and a new succession was declared. This succession meant that unless Mary and William had children, Anne was the heir to the throne.

But despite Anne supporting her sister to become queen, their relationship was not good. Mary and William rewarded many of their supporters; however, refused to grant Anne the use of Richmond Palace and opposed the decision to give Anne a parliamentary allowance. Mary feared that Anne's financial independence would weaken their influence over her, which would mean she could create a rival faction. The sisters' relationship only grew worse when Mary dismissed Sarah's husband from his offices, as it was believed he was conspiring to put James back on the throne, despite his previous loyalty to the Glorious Revolution.

When Anne showed support for Sarah by taking her to a social event at the palace, Mary responded by stripping Anne of her guard of honour, forbidding courtiers from visiting her and civic authorities were instructed to ignore the princess. The arguments over Anne's finances, status and choice of friends led to Anne being estranged from Mary. The last time the pair saw each other was after Anne had given birth to a baby who had died within minutes. Instead of comforting her sister, Mary berated Anne for her friendship with Sarah.

Throughout her life, Anne suffered from her poor health. She had constant miscarriages and out of her 17 pregnancies, only one child lived, but he died at the age of just 11 from hydrocephalus. Anne also suffered from gout, leaving her unable to walk through much of her life, and causing her to gain an incredible amount of weight. Anne also suffered from crippling shyness, which she was forced to overcome after ascending to the throne.

In 1694, Mary died of smallpox, leaving William to reign by himself with Anne as his heir apparent. The pair were reconciled as William restored Anne's honours, allowed her to live in St James' Palace, gave her Mary's jewels, and restored Sarah's husband to his offices. But Anne was still excluded from government and was not made regent.

Eventually, William died in 1702, making Anne the Queen of England, Scotland, and Ireland. During her coronation ceremony, Anne had to be carried on a chair with a low back so her ladies could hold her train, due to her gout. In court, Anne had to be carried in a sedan chair or use a wheelchair, giving her a sedentary lifestyle. But despite her physical shortcomings, Anne was very popular.

In her first speech, she said "As I know my heart to be entirely English", distancing herself from her Dutch predecessor. Unlike her sister, Anne did not share her power with her husband; however, she did give him control of the Royal Navy as Lord High Admiral, and the control of the army went to Sarah's husband. As well as this, Sarah was honoured with the roles of Groom of the Stool, Mistress of the Robes, and Keeper of the Privy Purse, giving her a lot of power and influence over the queen.

Clearly, with all these roles bestowed on her, Sarah was still a good and loyal friend of Anne. The pair were inseparable. They even gave each other fake names, Mrs Freeman and Mrs Morley, in their letters as fun nicknames so that they seemed more like equals.

But around the year 1704, Sarah's cousin, Abigail Hill, was invited to the queen's household. By this point, Sarah had become more frequently absent from court, so Abigail began to replace Sarah as the new favourite. Anne even attended Abigail's private marriage to Samuel Masham in 1707. Perhaps Anne's growing confidence and Sarah being absent from court meant that Anne grew to resent Sarah's strong temper and desire for influence, enjoying Abigail's gentle character and lack of scheming.

Sarah was furious that her cousin had supplanted her, so travelled to court with a poem suggesting that there was a lesbian relationship between Anne and Abigail, leading to a furious argument between Anne and Sarah. In the middle of St Paul's Cathedral, the pair argued about the matter, eventually, Sarah shouted at Anne to be quiet, so Anne responded by stripping Sarah of her titles and dismissing her from court.

Later, Sarah threatened to release letters Anne had written decades before to Sarah, which stated "If I writ whole volumes I could never express how well I love you… Unimaginably, passionately, affectionately yours." But at this time, strong emotional language was often used to describe platonic relationships, so this quote may have just been a declaration of amicable love to a best friend.

The relationship between Anne and Sarah crumbled further in 1708 when Anne was devastated by the death of her husband. While Anne was grieving, Sarah insisted that she should leave Kensington for St James' Palace, which Anne did not want to do. Sarah also removed a painting of Anne's late husband from her bedchamber, refusing to return the portrait, as she claimed it was natural to avoid looking at items that reminded the widow of the person they loved. After this, Sarah and Anne had a final argument in 1710, when Anne told Sarah that anything she wanted to say should instead be put in a letter.

Just months into Anne's reign, the War of the Spanish Succession broke out, which England was involved in due to their aim to limit French power. Instead of using England's traditional naval power, they had a series of on-land military victories, won by the Duke of Marlborough. His military successes included the Battle of Blenheim in 1704. When Anne received this message, she was playing dominoes at Windsor and the message came on the back of a tavern bill. The queen cried with delight at the English success against France.

After this, there were further victories at Ramillies, Oudenarde, and Malplaquet, all within the space of five years. Eventually, under the 1713 Treaty of Utrecht, France recognised Anne's title and exiled her Catholic half-brother from France, who had been gaining support as England's true monarch.

Anne was also successful in other areas of foreign policy. In 1707, the United Kingdom of Great Britain was created when England and Scotland were unified under the Acts of Union. This meant Anne was now known as the Queen of Great Britain and Ireland. The treaty meant that both Parliaments agreed to dissolve themselves and form a Union Parliament, which would sit at Westminster from 1707 under a common flag with a common coinage. But Scotland would be able to retain its established church and legal and educational systems. This union was a huge success for Anne, as she had hoped for it since her coronation, as

England and Scotland had been ruled by the same monarch since James I's reign, over a century previously.

From the beginning, Anne advocated the union, claiming to Parliament that it was "very necessary". This became more urgent in 1704 when Scotland passed the Act of Security, allowing them to ignore the Act of Settlement, so they would name their own successor when Anne died, assuming she would produce no heirs. England responded with the Alien Act of 1705, which threatened any Scots who were living in England. This would only be changed if the Scottish repealed the Act of Security or united with England, so Scotland took the latter option. From that point, Anne spent three months agreeing on a treaty, which eventually led to the unification of England and Scotland in 1707, which created Europe's largest free trade area.

Another important development during Anne's reign was the development of a two-party system. The Tories supported the Anglican Church, favouring the interest of the country gentry, while the Whigs supported commercial interests and Protestant Dissenters. As Anne was Anglican, she favoured the Tories and was heavily involved with politics. She was even the last British sovereign to veto a parliamentary bill, the Scottish Militia Bill 1708, which aimed to raise Scottish troops to defend against Anne's Catholic half-brother, who at the time was trying to land in Scotland with French assistance to establish himself as king.

Anne would not give her royal assent for this because she feared the militia would be disloyal and support her half-brother. Instead, the invasion fleet never landed, as it was chased away by British ships. Other than this veto, there was an absence of constitutional conflict between monarch and Parliament, as she chose her ministers and exercised her prerogatives wisely.

Not only was Anne's reign characterised by political and military successes, but there were also great scientific and artistic contributions at this time. Anne herself was a patron of the arts, including theatre, poetry, and music, as she subsidised the German-born Baroque composer, Handel, with £200 a year. Also, in the year 1705, Anne knighted Isaac Newton, acknowledging his contributions to physics, including his theory of gravity and laws of motion. During Anne's reign, Sir Christopher Wren built St Paul's Cathedral, an extremely notable achievement in architecture, as was the construction of Blenheim Palace and Castle Howard, both constructed by John Vanbrugh. Writers also flourished under Anne's reign, such as Daniel Defoe, Alexander Pope, and Jonathan Swift.

By 1713, Anne was no longer able to walk and spent the rest of the year feverish and unconscious for long periods, leading to rumours that she would soon die. The doctors blamed her failing health on the emotional strain of matters of state, yet Anne did continue to attend two late night cabinet meetings to determine a new Lord Treasurer, but the third meeting was cancelled as she was too ill to attend. This displayed just how sick the queen was, as she attended more cabinet meetings than any of her predecessors or successors.

In July 1714, Anne suffered from a stroke, rendering her mute; just two days later, Anne died. Her doctor wrote: "I believe sleep was never more welcome to a weary traveller than death was to her." She was probably in great pain before her death because the doctors treated her with bleeding, blistering hot irons, and garlic on her feet. Anne was buried beside her husband and many children in the Henry VII Chapel at Westminster Abbey, in a square coffin due to how large she had become.

With no surviving heir, Anne was the last monarch of the House of Stuart. Under the Act of Settlement 1701, which excluded all Catholics from the throne, Anne was succeeded by her second cousin, George I of the House of Hanover. Overall, Anne had an important and successful reign, presiding over the creation of the United Kingdom, as well as many cultural, military, and political developments. It seems unfair that Anne did not receive the respect of the other Queens of England, as she is seen as less charismatic and intelligent; however, this is due to Sarah slandering Anne in her memoirs published after Anne's death, allowing her to take the last word, tainting Anne's legacy for years.

Nanny of the Maroons (1686–1755 CE)

Leader of the Liberated

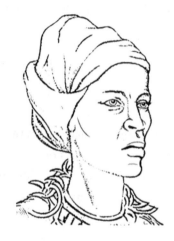

Most stories of Queen Nanny derive from oral history, with little textual evidence, so there are many variations of her life. But what is known, is that she was respected as a formidable political, military, and religious leader of the Maroons, who were a community of escaped slaves in Jamaica. Nanny was beloved by her people as she protected them from the British colonisers, successfully using guerrilla warfare, long-range communication, and Obeah powers against their enemy's superior weaponry.

As well as defending from attackers, Nanny also organised raids on plantations to liberate the slaves who lived there, freeing an estimated 1,000 slaves in her lifetime. Not only did she rescue these slaves and protect her community, but she also kept alive stories and music from Africa, instilling pride into her people.

Not very much is known about Nanny's childhood, as many claim that she travelled from Africa to Jamaica as a free woman, even owning slaves herself. However, it is more likely that she was born to the Akan people in modern-day Ghana, perhaps with royal African blood, and was taken to Jamaica as a slave with her brothers, Quao and Cudjoe. Some think that she managed to escape slavery by jumping from the ship which brought her to Jamaica while it was offshore. But it is more likely that she was sold and worked as a slave on a plantation that grew sugarcane, and the work would have been under severe conditions.

While slaving, Nanny, described as a small, wiry woman, with piercing eyes, was influenced and inspired by slave leaders and Maroons, who were living free in the mountains. Eventually, Nanny and her brothers fled the plantation to the Blue Mountains area. This was a massive risk, as capture would have resulted in either severe punishment or death. So while in hiding, the siblings agreed to split up and organise Maroon communities across Jamaica.

The Maroons are descendants of West Africans, mostly people from the Akan, like Nanny, but many originated from other places in Africa, such as Nigeria, the Congo, and Madagascar. Most of them were transported in the Transatlantic slave trade and managed to flee from the plantations and form their own communities in the hills of the island. Most of the Maroon communities were formed in 1655, after the invasion of Jamaica by the British after the Anglo-Spanish War. The British managed to take over Spanish Jamaica, so when the Spanish left, they freed their slaves, who joined Maroon communities.

The new British colonisers wanted to enslave these people themselves, so there was constant fighting between the British and the Maroons. The two main branches of Maroons were the Leeward Maroons in the west, led by Cudjoe, and the Windward Maroons on the east of the island, who Nanny led with Quao.

As a community, Nanny and the Maroons were peaceful. To survive, they raised animals, hunted, and grew crops. They would also send traders to nearby market towns to exchange food for weapons and cloth, which was similar to how a typical Asante society in Africa functioned. Nanny and the Maroons also led slave rebellions to free slaves from plantations. This involved raiding and damaging lands and buildings held by plantation owners. During these raids, Nanny encouraged her people to take weapons and food, and lead the newly freed slaves to join their community.

Nanny was particularly skilled at organising these raids, and during 30 years of leadership, she freed more than 1,000 slaves and helped them resettle in her Maroon community. One of these Maroons, named Adou, is thought to be Nanny's husband, although the couple had no children that are known of.

But these raids embarrassed the British settlers. They were losing slaves, equipment, and crops due to the Maroon raiders, so demanded that the authorities act. So the British set up hunting parties, made up of British soldiers, militiamen, and mercenaries, who would scour the Jamaican jungles to search for the Maroons. Many members of these groups were known as "Black Shots", who were free members of the black community who worked with the colonisers to fight the Maroons.

By 1720, Nanny was leading the Windward Maroons, who named their area Nanny Town. It was a strategic place to settle, as it overlooked the Stony River, making a surprise attack from the British nearly impossible. There was also just one path in and out of the community, which was too narrow for more than one person to walk side by side, forcing any attackers to be funnelled into Nanny Town single-filed, making them easy to fend off. Not only were they protected by their location, Nanny also developed a long-range communication capability, using a cow horn called an *abeng*. This was used by Maroon lookouts to communicate over great distances, and the messages were not understood by the British, who had no such means of communication.

In addition to this clever tactic, Nanny ensured that her people were superior in camouflage. They could disguise themselves as trees by covering themselves with branches and leaves, even slowing their breathing so that they could get close to the enemy. This was part of Nanny's guerrilla warfare tactics, cleverly using surprise and their familiarity of the terrain to fight the British, who had superior weaponry.

Another method Nanny used, was to order the Maroons to never kill all of the attackers; instead, they would allow a few to flee to their base and recount the story of their terrifying defeat, improving the Maroons' reputation as ferocious warriors.

These battle tactics were used during the First Maroon War, which was fought between the Maroons and the British from 1728 until 1734. Nanny Town was attacked by British forces who were trying to stop the raids on the plantations. On a few occasions, the British were able to capture Nanny Town but were unable to hold it. In 1733, Nanny sent 300 Maroons from Nanny Town across the island to unite with Cudjoe. But he refused the proposed alliance, despite the Windward Maroons having just completed one of the longest marches in Jamaican history. Around this time, a British captain attacked Nanny Town, claiming to have found the huts in which he believed the Maroons to be sleeping, and fired upon them, claiming that they were all slain; however, the vast majority of the Maroons had fled to Rio Grande.

In 1739, Cudjoe signed a treaty with the British, who then offered a less favourable treaty to the Windward Maroons. Quao quickly signed this agreement, which stated that the Maroons would be granted 500 acres of land in Portland, but they could no longer harbour any runaway slaves. Instead, they would catch the slaves for bounty, and the Maroons were obliged to fight for the British in the case of attack from the French or Spanish.

Although this ended the First Maroon War, Nanny was furious at Quao for signing this treaty, as she disagreed with the principle of peace with the British, as she knew it would mean a new form of subjugation. As she had liberated so many slaves in the past, it must have been crushing for Nanny to act as an unofficial police force for the British, becoming an obstacle to the freedom and independence of other slaves in Jamaica. However, it did mean that the Windward Maroons finally could live in peace in their new land, which was named New Nanny Town, later changed to Moore Town.

Nanny's incredible leadership skills in the First Maroon War were partially attributed to her Obeah powers, as she was seen as a religious figure as well as a political and military leader. Obeah is an African developed religion and is associated with good and bad magic, charms, luck, and mysticism. So these supernatural powers enabled Nanny to overwhelm the British forces, as she could allegedly catch bullets and redirect them back to the enemy. Another way Nanny used her magic was when her people were close to starvation. She found some pumpkin seeds in her pocket, so she planted them and they grew within weeks, saving her people.

Nanny can also use her powers from beyond the grave, as there is a legend stating that if any straight-haired, white man steps into the original Nanny Town in the Blue Mountains, he will immediately be struck dead. These Obeah powers also helped establish Nanny as a wise woman, who passed down legends and music from her people in Africa, instilling confidence and pride in the Maroons. But magical or not, Nanny was recognised as an incredible military leader, by both the Maroons who she led and the British who she fought.

As with the rest of her life, there is a mystery surrounding Nanny's death. Many believe that she never lived to see New Nanny Town, as she was thought to be killed by a Black Shot in the First Maroon War. But this is unlikely, as there is evidence that New Nanny Town was granted to Nanny as the leader of the Maroons in 1740. So it seems that Nanny lived to be an old woman who died of natural causes; however, it is difficult to know, as "Nanny" is an honorific title, with many high-ranking women sharing the name. It is thought that Queen Nanny is buried at Bump Grave in Moore Town. More recently, in 1975, Nanny was named as a National Hero by the government of Jamaica, and given the title of Right Excellent. She is also honoured by having her portrait on the Jamaican $500 note, which is now referred to as a "Nanny" in Jamaican slang.

Overall, Nanny was a determined and courageous woman, who escaped slavery, liberated people, and protected her community. It is a shame that Quao signed the treaty in 1740, which went against everything Nanny stood for. Instead of fighting for the liberation of slaves, they were bound to protect British interests, even capturing and returning their slaves, which must have been terrible for Nanny, even though it meant that they could live freely in New Nanny Town.

As a National Hero, Nanny must be remembered for her services to her people. She was a strong leader and an accomplished woman whose greatest desire was for the freedom of her people.

Empress Elizaveta Petrovna (1709–1762 CE)

The Bloodless Empress

Elizaveta ruled the Russian Empire as empress in her own right for 20 years; this was never expected of her growing up, making her rather remarkable. She became popular for promising to be an empress who refused to execute her people, yet history seems to have brushed over Elizaveta's successful and stable reign. She was successful in foreign policy and enabled Russia to thrive in an Age of Enlightenment, due to her accomplishments in many areas, including the education system and the development of culture.

Elizaveta's father was Peter the Great of Russia; however, her blood was tainted by that of her mother, Catherine, who was the daughter of a Latvian peasant, and Elizaveta's parents were not married at the time of her birth Elizaveta also had a sister named Anna, and both girls were legitimised and given the titles of tsarevna after Peter and Catherine's secret marriage. However, neither girl was expected to rule, as Peter had a son with a previous wife. This meant that Elizaveta lacked an education suitable for a ruler, as she was expected to become the wife of a European prince.

Elizaveta's mother was responsible for organising her children's education, which was a difficult task as she had not been educated herself. But Elizaveta was bright and had a French governess who taught her mathematics, arts, sports, architecture, Italian, German, French, riding, and dancing. The most important of these was Elizaveta's French lessons, as Peter was hoping to marry Elizaveta into the Bourbon dynasty of French royalty.

But despite Peter's seeming lack of interest in Elizaveta's education, she was his favourite child as she resembled him both physically and temperamentally. She was a very sociable girl, and so beautiful that she was regarded as the leading beauty of the Russian Empire, so she was doted on by her father and those around her.

However, despite her beauty, Peter struggled to marry Elizaveta to any princes due to her being illegitimate at birth. Russian tsars had previously avoided marrying their daughters into the royal houses of Europe, but Peter worked hard to arrange to have Elizaveta betrothed to Charles Augustus of Holstein-Gottorp. However, before the marriage took place, tragedy struck Elizaveta's life. Her loving father, Peter, died in 1725, leaving Catherine as the Empress of Russia, as his heir had already died in prison. But her reign was short and she died in 1727; just weeks later, Elizaveta's betrothed died not long before their intended marriage.

In her will, Catherine had arranged to leave Elizaveta and Anna equal divisions of her estate, and that they should be appointed as primary members of the council, which was the regency for her successor, Peter II, who was the grandchild of Peter the Great and his first wife. But this will was ignored. Soon after her mother's death, Elizaveta's sister died while giving birth to her son, the future Peter III.

So Elizaveta retreated to her rural estate, and spent her time hawking and hunting, which she loved. She also spent her time with the local peasants, dancing, and singing, and even becoming involved with pages and local young men. As she was not seen as a threat, Elizaveta was invited back to court, where she spent her time attending balls and hunting with her half-nephew, Tsar Peter II. But in 1730, Peter died.

According to Catherine I's will, Elizaveta should have been declared as the next empress; however, her cousin, Anna of Ivanovna, managed to take the throne. After her brief reign, in 1740 the throne passed to Ivan VI, who was still a baby, with Anna Leopoldovna as his regent. Anna and Elizaveta did not get on at all. So Anna prevented Elizavta from having any chance of marrying a Russian noble or a foreign prince, but Elizaveta did not want to marry a commoner, as this would remove her royal status.

Their rift was partially caused by Anna's jealousy and resentment of Elizaveta's famed beauty. Once, when Anna asked the Chinese minister in St Petersburg who he thought was the most beautiful woman at court, he pointed to Elizaveta.

Although Elizaveta could not marry, she did take lovers. One of these was Alexis Shubin, but when Anna found out about their affair, she cut off Alexis' tongue and banished him to Serbia. After this incident, Elizaveta was followed by Anna's spies, so she tried to remain politically discreet, but she did have many sexual relations with handsome coachmen and footmen, and eventually found a long-term lover in Alexis Razumovsky. He was a Ukrainian peasant serf who sang for the church choir.

Anna had required Elizaveta to take an oath of loyalty, so she no longer saw Elizaveta as a threat. This meant that Elizaveta and Alexis could be more open about their relationship and may have had a secret marriage, as the pair were devoted to each other. Eventually, Alexis would become a count of the Holy Roman Empire, and in 1756, he would become a prince and field marshal. However, Alexis never showed much interest in the affairs of state.

While Anna was keeping Elizaveta in the background, the latter was gathering support. Anna was unpopular due to her encouragement of German dominance of Russian politics and culture, making the people feel as though their national identity was being repressed. The Russian people longed for the times of Peter the Great. Also, Anna was becoming known for her high taxes and economic issues. As Elizaveta was the daughter of two monarchs, Peter the Great and Catherine I, she was the obvious choice for a replacement. So Elizaveta was able to gain support from the Russian guard regiments, and she encouraged this by becoming close with them by planning events with the officers and becoming a godmother to their children.

Eventually, the French ambassador in St Petersburg began to plan to depose Anna, because her foreign policy was opposed to the interests of France, so he bribed people to support Elizaveta. Then, in late 1741, Elizaveta staged a coup d'état. With the help of the Preobrazhensky Regiment, she seized power. She wore a warrior's metal breastplate over her dress and held a silver cross, then marched into the Winter Palace and arrested Anna, who was sleeping with her lover at the time of the coup, and the baby Ivan.

All of this was conducted without bloodshed, and Elizaveta vowed that she would not sign a death sentence during her reign, and she kept this promise. To gain her support and seize power, she said, "Whom do you want to serve: me, your natural sovereign, or those who have stolen my inheritance?" This reference to her father, Peter the Great, was enough to secure the throne.

Although Elizaveta did not use capital punishment, she did display strength and cruelty. Those who supported her were rewarded generously, with titles and lands, but Ivan and his mother were imprisoned for the rest of their lives. Elizaveta had planned to allow them to flee; however, she feared a coup supported by foreign powers, so instead she imprisoned them. To remove Ivan's authority, Elizaveta destroyed anything depicting him, including all coins, then issued an order that if any attempt was made for Ivan to escape as an adult, he would be eliminated.

Years later, this order was upheld by Catherine the Great. Finally, Elizaveta crowned herself as empress in the Dormition Cathedral. She had very little political experience but began by exiling the unpopular German advisors, replacing them with Russians in a senate. Like her father, Elizaveta had good diplomacy skills; however, was accused of procrastinating, as she occasionally took months to sign documents. Although, many thought she did this purposefully so that she could spend longer on important decisions.

Her procrastination did not limit her abilities as a stateswoman, and she still could act quickly when necessary. One example of this is early in her rule when she found out about a plot to replace her with Ivan. She rounded up the conspirators, had them stripped down in front of a crowd, then they were flogged. Plus, their tongues were torn out and they were exiled to Siberia, much like her previous lover.

Concerning foreign policy, Elizaveta was successful. Throughout her reign, Russia grew into a European power. As empress, Elizaveta had a pro-Austrian, anti-Prussian policy, due to her hatred of Frederick of Prussia, perhaps Europe's greatest warrior. In pursuit of this, Elizaveta annexed a portion of southern Finland after fighting a war with Sweden from 1741 until 1743. Russia's relations with Great Britain also improved, and Russia was successful in fighting against Prussia during the Seven Years' War, from 1756 until 1763. Elizaveta had sent an army of nearly 100,000 strong to fight Prussia in this war, which put Prussia on the defensive for two years before Frederick surrendered and agreed to sign a peace treaty with Russia.

Sadly, Elizaveta died just days before her victory, and her successor, Peter III, who admired Frederick of Prussia, returned all of the territories that Russia had conquered back to Prussia. This meant that Russia had lost more than 100,000 people in an unnecessary war and gained nothing from it. Peter's decision to do this may have been due to his resentment of Elizaveta and his adoration of Frederick.

Despite Elizaveta not receiving the education that she should have had herself, she did understand the value of education, so made education freely available for all social classes except for the serfs. She also encouraged the establishment of the first university in Russia in Moscow and funded the establishment of the Imperial Academy of Fine Arts. In addition to this achievement in domestic policy, Elizaveta financed many construction projects, including on the Winter Palace. Many celebrate Elizaveta for bringing about an Age of Enlightenment in Russia. She allowed nobles to gain dominance in local government, modernised Russia's roads, and financed baroque projects. Also, the arts became more important, with Shakespeare being introduced to Russia by Alexander Sumarokov, with his adaptation of *Hamlet*. So in terms of domestic policy and culture, Elizaveta was incredibly successful.

Elizaveta is also known for her splendid and glamorous court. It was full of gold and luxury, with expensive foods, rare drinks, and a huge number of servants. They ordered a thousand bottles of French champagnes and wines to be served at just one event and even served pineapple, which was difficult to get hold of. The language of nobility was exchanged from German to French, and it was so widely spoken that it was in use until the 1917 Bolshevik Revolution. Music was also highly important at court because Elizaveta's lover enjoyed music, so Elizaveta imported musicians from Germany, France, and Italy, to satisfy him and the court.

Elizaveta also adored clothes. She owned 15,000 dresses, thousands of pairs of shoes and seemingly unlimited stockings. This was perhaps necessary, as Elizaveta banned anyone from wearing the same dress twice, and she had her men stamp gowns with ink to enforce this. Due to her vanity, Elizaveta also banned anyone from wearing the same hairstyle, dress or accessories as herself. One woman accidentally did so and was lashed across the face for her crime. She also ensured that French fabric salesmen would sell first to the empress; if they did not, they would be arrested.

An example of Elizaveta's vanity is when she had to cut off a section of her hair because she got some powder caught in it, and she then made all of the court ladies do the same. As Elizaveta aged and her beauty dwindled, her outbursts of anger became directed towards women whose beauty rivalled her own.

Although jealous of other beautiful women, Elizaveta loved hosting two balls a week. The first would be a large event of roughly 800 guests, whereas the second was reserved for her closest friends. These smaller gatherings began as masked balls but evolved into Metamorphoses balls by 1744. This involved having the guests dress as the opposite sex, which the courtiers hated, as they felt they looked ridiculous. But Elizaveta loved wearing men's tight trousers because they showed off her beautiful legs, and her dominating figure suited being in men's clothing.

The empress also threw children's birthday parties and wedding receptions at court, even providing dowries for her ladies-in-waiting. Behind the glamour of court, Elizaveta was hiding the shameful fact that she was constantly on the brink of poverty. The ballrooms were covered in gold, but the living quarters were cramped and dirty. There was such little furniture that when travelling, they had to take it with them, so Elizaveta was not as glamorous as she made out to be.

As a childless empress, Elizaveta had to choose a legitimate heir to secure the Romanov dynasty. She eventually chose her nephew, Peter Holstein-Gottorp, and he was proclaimed heir in 1742, after having to convert into the Russian Orthodox Church. He was provided with the best Russian tutors and was forced to marry the future Catherine the Great, at the time known as Princess Sophie of Anhalt-Zerbst. When Catherine gave birth to Paul, it was uncertain whether the baby was fathered by Peter, but Elizaveta did not mind that.

At his birth, Elizaveta took Paul from Catherine and did not allow her to see the baby for six months. By that time, the child had become a ward of the state. Unfortunately, Elizaveta was not a good guardian to the baby Paul. Sometimes she smothered him with love, but other times she would neglect him; once, the baby fell out of his crib and spent the entire night unnoticed on the floor.

As Elizaveta aged, she became prone to depression, particularly as her looks faded. She began to gain weight as she never exercised, and she suffered from asthma, colic, dropsy and constipation, and doubted her accomplishments as empress. In the 1750s, Elizaveta suffered from dizzy spells and strokes that left her barely able to walk, but she refused medicine. Although she was so ill, Elizaveta forbade the word "death" in her presence until 1761, when it was clear she was dying.

Elizaveta took a fever and began to haemorrhage from her mouth, recovering just enough to sign decrees regarding taxation. But just days later, she relapsed. Quickly, the empress made her confession and prayed, before saying goodbye to a few people, including Peter and Catherine. Elizaveta then died on Christmas Day and was dressed in a shimmering silver dress before being buried in the Peter and Paul Cathedral in St Petersburg.

Despite being less well-remembered than Catherine the Great, Elizaveta was certainly great herself and set a lot of the groundwork for Catherine's accomplishments. Elizaveta should be remembered for her bloodless accession and upholding her vow of banning capital punishment, which she kept throughout her reign. Not only this, but with such a lack of appropriate education, Elizaveta gained diplomacy skills and successfully made Russia into a more peaceful country which prospered into an Age of Enlightenment, brought about by the stability and popularity of Elizaveta's reign.

Elizabeth Sugrue
(1740–1807 CE)

The Woman from Hell

Elizabeth, also known as Lady Betty, is not a good role model, like many of the other women in this book; however, she is an interesting character. Her life was more difficult than most and she lost everyone who she loved, which led her to become a cruel and callous woman. Eventually, she would escape her own death by volunteering to become Ireland's first female executioner, a job she completed with a terrifying lack of empathy.

Other than that she was born in County Kerry in Ireland, not much is known about Elizabeth's early life. Her story really started when she was widowed after the death of her farmer husband, with two young children. This left Elizabeth devastated and destitute, and she was evicted from her home and had no choice but to search for a better life with her children. This led Elizabeth to travel a massive 300 km to Roscommon. It is uncertain what drew her to Roscommon in particular, but the journey was arduous, and Elizabeth's youngest child died of starvation and exposure on the way.

It is probable that Elizabeth was forced to bury her deceased child in a shallow roadside grave before continuing the journey with her remaining son, Pádraig. When the pair arrived in Roscommon, with no money or any means to earn money, they moved into an empty roadside hovel, having to beg, scavenge, and rob for their food. Perhaps to give her son a better chance in the future, Elizabeth taught him how to read and write, as she was fortunate to be literate herself.

Elizabeth was described physically as being middle-aged, dark-eyed, with a swarthy complexion, but not forbidding-looking. The locals also described Elizabeth as an angry woman who had a "violent temper", and this temperament led Pádraig to threaten to leave her, but she begged him to stay, afraid of the loneliness she would face if her one remaining son left. But in 1775, after a particularly violent assault, Pádraig left home. Some claim that he enlisted in the British Army, but others state that he emigrated to British North America and joined the Continental Army. Although he left Elizabeth completely alone, he did write to her during his absence and sent her money; however, as time went on, Pádraig contacted his mother less often, making her more and more bitter with the world.

In 1789, a tall, dark, bearded stranger came to stay at Elizabeth's house. There had been no room in the inn, so he was looking for lodgings, and Elizabeth had been taking in lodgers for money. That night, he lay a gold piece on the table and told Elizabeth to buy food with it, so she did so, purchasing bread, meat, eggs, and spirits. But despite the young man's kindness, Elizabeth saw his fine clothes and became jealous that he was so rich and she so poor, so Elizabeth murdered him while he slept so that she could take his expensive belongings.

It is uncertain whether Elizabeth had killed before, some claim that she often butchered lodgers for their wealth, but this may have been the first time. When Elizabeth sought through the victim's belongings to see what was for the taking, she discovered from his documents that he was her long-lost son, Pádraig. He had hidden his identity when his mother had not recognised him as he wanted to see if she had mellowed in their years apart—unfortunately, it seems that she had not.

Elizabeth reacted by screaming and weeping in the streets that morning, announcing her crime to the locals when she had discovered what she had done.

Quickly, Elizabeth was arrested, convicted and sentenced to be hanged by the neck until death. About 25 others were due to be hanged on the same day as Elizabeth, but the crowds were there to watch her death, as filicide was a terrible offence. The others to be hanged were mostly cattle thieves and teenagers who had torn down fences and hedges surrounding what had once been common land.

But to the crowd's disappointment on the day of the hangings, the hangman had fallen ill, or perhaps he sympathised with the teenagers he was supposed to execute that day. Three men were asked to take the hangman's place, but all refused, as many sympathised with the young boys who were to be executed. After a short while of wondering what to do, a voice shouted out amongst the shackled prisoners. It was Elizabeth.

"Set me free and I'll hang them all!" she yelled. To the Sheriff, this was an acceptable offer, as no one else was willing to execute the prisoners, so Elizabeth hanged every prisoner without a shred of emotion. Her job was to open the trap door where the noosed prisoners stood so that they would fall to their deaths. It was a particularly long fall, as these gallows had the longest drop in Ireland, standing at three floors high.

After this, Elizabeth lived in the prison as the Provincial Executioner, carrying out executions and floggings, which she apparently completed with relish. She was known to execute some rebels from the 1798 rebellion, and she used to draw portraits of those she hanged on the walls of her room using a burnt stick. In 1802, Elizabeth's death sentence was lifted, due to her service to "the safety of the public", and five years later she died. Some say that she died of natural causes, but others insist that Elizabeth was murdered by a prisoner. Whatever the cause of death, Elizabeth was buried in an unmarked grave within Roscommon Jail, so although she got herself out of a death sentence, she still spends eternity behind bars.

Due to her callousness and desire to flog and kill others, Elizabeth became known as the "woman from Hell". Her life was incredibly difficult, as she was widowed, evicted, lost a child, then lived in poverty for years, and it seems it was the murder of her child which pushed her over the edge from being a destitute, angry woman, to becoming an unemotional murderess. Elizabeth's legacy lingers still, as a generation of naughty children would be threatened with a visit from Lady Betty to encourage good behaviour.

Sybil Ludington (1761–1839 CE)

Teenage Revolutionary

At just the age of 16, Sybil rode all night to rally soldiers against the British during the American Revolutionary War. This was an important mission, enabling the Patriots to push the British back, and inspiring others to join the Patriot cause. At the time, Sybil was highly praised for completing her dangerous and successful mission, but since then, she seems to have been forgotten by history. Even during her own lifetime, Sybil had to live in poverty, despite now being known as a heroine.

Sybil was born in Fredericksburg, New York, now known as Ludingtonville, to Henry and Abigail Ludington, and was the oldest of 12 siblings. With so many younger siblings, Sybil spent much of her time busy helping her mother with the cooking, cleaning, and taking care of the younger children. Henry was a farmer and a military man, who served for over 60 years and was loyal to the British until 1773. However, Henry joined the Patriots during the American Revolutionary War.

Due to his experience, Henry quickly became a militia Colonel of Westchester County, New York. His land was used as a route between Connecticut and the coast of Long Island Sound, which was vulnerable to British attack. This militia which he volunteered to join pre-dated the Revolutionary War, so it consisted of colonists who had volunteered to protect their communities whenever they were needed, and supplied the Continental Army, who served full-time during their conscription.

But Henry's experience as a military man meant he was in constant danger from the British, as they knew of his talent. So when he switched sides to the Patriots, they offered a bounty of 300 guineas to anyone who could capture him. Because of this threat, the loyal militia guarded the Ludington house; however, because they worked part-time, sometimes the family was unprotected. Therefore, the family arranged a plan for what they would do if they were attacked and practiced this. Also, when there was no one protecting them, Sybil and her sister, Rebecca, kept watch on the woods from the second floor of their house, watching for an attack.

One evening, the sisters heard a commotion on a night when there were no guards, so leapt into action. They discovered that roughly 50 Loyalists were trying to capture their father, but from their training, knew exactly what to do. Sybil woke up the next oldest siblings and gave them Patriot hats to wear and a musket each to shoulder. Then Sybil lit candles in their room which cast light through the window, and the siblings marched back and forth in front of the candle in military-style. This cast long shadows through the window, making it appear as though militia were standing guard, rather than a group of sleepy children.

The Loyalists saw these shadows and quickly fled, preventing Henry from being captured. This displays Sybil's quick thinking and organisation skills, and her loyalty to her father. As well as planning for instances like this, the children were told code words used by the Patriots, so if a traveller wanted hospitality at their home, the child would know who was to be trusted and permitted to be fed and sheltered.

In 1777, a messenger arrived at the Ludington house and announced that the nearby town of Danbury was going to be attacked by British troops. This was a huge disaster because the area was a stockpile for the Continental Army in that region, containing their munitions and stores for the militia. But Henry's regiment of 400 men was disbanded for planting season, so were scattered miles apart. The messenger could not gather the men because he and his horse were exhausted from the journey he had already made, and he did not know the area. Henry could not gather the men either, as he needed to focus on the preparation for the battle. The only people who knew the area well enough, from passing messages from their father to the other militiamen, were Sybil and Rebecca.

As Sybil was known to be very capable on a horse, it was her who agreed to round up the men; however, it is uncertain whether Sybil volunteered to do this or if she was asked to by her father. He reportedly instructed Sybil to "ride to the men, and tell them to be at this house by daybreak", and to not stop to dismount, but to take a stick and rap on their doors and windows to alert the men. While she was gone, the rest of the family would all be busy making cartridges to use in the muskets.

So the 16-year-old Sybil jumped on her horse named Star and rode from nine at night until dawn. It was a dark and rainy night and the roads were dangerous, as outlaws roamed the area. Along the way, a highwayman attacked Sybil, but she fought him off with her father's musket, although some claim that she had no musket and beat him away with her stick. Whenever Sybil came to a house, she banged on their shutters with her stick to wake them and shouted, "The British are burning Danbury."

All through the night, because of Sybil's actions, men were arriving at the Ludington house, ready to fight, while she rode 40 miles, rounding up 400 men. By the time she arrived home at dawn, Sybil was exhausted and soaked through but was met by her mother, who gave her young daughter a warm breakfast before putting her to bed.

Unfortunately, the Patriots could not save Danbury; however, did meet up with the Continental Army at the Battle of Ridgefield, where they drove the British back to their fleet at Long Island Sound, preventing them from attacking more American cities. This led to a surge in support for the Patriot cause, with 3,000 residents joining the Connecticut Army of Reserve after the British had sailed away. So even though the stores in Danbury were destroyed, the Patriots had been successful. Alexander Hamilton wrote to Sybil's father saying "I congratulate you on the Danbury expedition. The stores destroyed have been purchased at a pretty high price to the enemy." This success was partly due to

Sybil's bravery and success in her night ride mission, so she was congratulated not only by the locals but also George Washington.

A year after America gained its independence, Sybil married Edward Ogden, a farmer and an innkeeper. The pair had a son called Henry, named after Sybil's father, but in 1799, Edward died of yellow fever. So it was left to Sybil alone to run the inn and support her son in becoming a lawyer. Eventually, Sybil bought a tavern and sold it for three times the price, so that she could buy a home for herself and her son and his family, but in 1838, disaster struck, and Henry died.

After this, Sybil had no one supporting her and could not make an income, so she applied for a Revolutionary War pension because her husband had served in the military. But due to insufficient proof of marriage, the application was denied. For the rest of her life, Sybil lived in poverty, until she died at the age of 77 and was buried near her father. Although she died penniless, and as if everyone had forgotten her service to the Patriot cause, more recently, Sybil has been recognised for her bravery. In New York, there is a statue built depicting her as a young girl on her horse during her night mission. Also, in 1935, New York State erected a series of historic markers along Sybil's route, and since 1979, runners have challenged themselves with the Sybil Ludington 50K run, which is along Sybil's approximate route which she travelled in her famous night ride.

Not much else is known about Sybil's life, as until 1880, her story was mostly shared orally by her descendants, except for a brief mention in her father's memoirs. But it is clear that Sybil was incredibly strong, as, at the age of just 16, she displayed extreme strength, loyalty and authority. She managed to ride for 40 miles, all night long, brought together 400 men and avoided capture in the meantime. And it rained heavily for the entire journey.

Wang Zhenyi (1768–1797 CE)

Self-Taught Polymath

Zhenyi was a self-taught astronomer, mathematician, and poet. Despite having no formal education, she was extremely knowledgeable, and spent her tragically short life learning, discovering, and making education more accessible for others. Although she was in a male-dominated environment, Zhenyi was content in her life as she loved to study. But when she did become angry with the societal misogyny, she expressed it beautifully in poetry.

Born during the Qing Dynasty in China, Zhenyi was born in Jiangning (present-day Nanjing) and lived with her father, grandfather, and grandmother. Despite living in a time when women did not have legal rights or access to higher education, instead, they were educated in areas such as cooking and child-rearing, Zhenyi was strongly encouraged to read and learn by her family. This gave her a love of reading and she was naturally a very bright young girl, who thrived under the tutorage of her learned family. Zhenyi's grandfather was a previous governor of Fengchen County and Xuanhua District, and taught Zhenyi all about astronomy, whereas her grandmother taught her poetry.

Zhenyi's father had previously failed the imperial examination to become a bureaucrat, so instead studied medical science, enabling him to tutor his daughter in medicine, as well as geography and mathematics. He had also previously written a book entitled *Collection of Medical Prescriptions*, all about medical science.

In 1782, Zhenyi's grandfather died, so the family travelled to Jiling for the funeral and settled there for five years. During this time, Zhenyi attempted to read her grandfather's entire collection of books, which were so numerous that they took up 75 bookshelves. The wife of a Mongolian general named Aa also took the time to teach Zhenyi martial arts, horse riding, and archery, even having her practice martial arts while on horseback. So by the age of 16, Zhenyi had a huge range of knowledge, including astronomy, poetry, and martial arts.

Next, Zhenyi's father decided to educate her further by taking her travelling to places she had never been, including Shaanxi, Hubei and Guangdong. He strongly believed that creating new experiences was the best form of education, and he wanted to enrich her life before moving back to their home in Jiangning. When they returned, Zhenyi met other female scholars and they influenced her to focus her studies on astronomy and mathematics, which was all self-taught.

In the field of astronomy, Zhenyi was very successful. She wrote many articles, including "The Explanation of a Lunar Eclipse" and "Dispute of Longitude and Stars". Within these articles, Zhenyi discussed many topics, such as the number of stars, the revolving direction of the sun, and the relationship between lunar and solar eclipses. Not only did Zhenyi read and learn from other astronomers, but she also gave her own contributions through original research. As she did not have a laboratory of her own, Zhenyi set up scientific experiments in her own house.

This included an experiment demonstrating a solar eclipse, using a round table to depict the Earth, a crystal lamp demonstrating the sun, and a round mirror as the moon. She then moved the objects using astronomical principles to simulate a lunar eclipse, which had previously been thought to be caused by the gods. Zhenyi wrote about these observations in her article called "The Explanation of a Solar Eclipse", which gives a very accurate explanation of why a solar eclipse happens.

As a mathematician, Zhenyi was especially apt in trigonometry. As she had not had a formal education, but rather was taught by family and herself, Zhenyi found the texts on mathematics very difficult to understand. This frustrated Zhenyi, as she felt that everybody should have access to education. So after reading *Principles of Calculation* by Mei Wending, a mathematician who she admired, Zhenyi rewrote the book. She wrote it in a simpler language that others would be able to understand, even if they were beginners. She named this *The Musts of Calculation*, and the book simplifies multiplication and division. By the time Zhenyi was 24, she had written her own book on the subject named *The Simple Principles of Calculation*.

Throughout her career in trigonometry, Zhenyi did have many moments of difficulty in understanding the complexity of it, stating, "There were times that I had to put down my pen and sigh. But I love the subject, I do not give up." This is an inspiring statement from Zhenyi, who knew that to pursue her interests, especially without access to a formal teacher like a man would, she had to keep going and never quit doing what she loved, no matter how difficult it could be.

Because of her grandmother's tutorage, Zhenyi was proficient in poetry. This skill improved after travelling with her father, as she was inspired to write about the lives of the commoners and working women who she met on her journeys, as well as the contrast between the lives of the rich and the poor. Throughout her life, Zhenyi wrote 13 volumes of poetry, prose, prefaces, and postscripts for other works. Although she was taught by a woman, Zhenyi's work was described as masculine, due to the lack of flowery words, which were stereotypically used by women.

So many in the Qing Dynasty enjoyed Zhenyi's works, including a scholar called Yuan Mei, who said that Zhenyi's poems "had the flavour of a great pen, not of a female poet". Not only did she write about traditional topics, such as history and her experiences while travelling, but Zhenyi also wrote poems about equality between men and women, writing:

It's made to believe,
Women are the same as Men;
Are you not convinced,
Daughters can also be heroic?

It seems that Zhenyi just could not understand the misogyny of her society, as she complained about how people immediately thought of scientists as male, and women as just working in the home. She claimed that men and women are all people, and all have the same reason for studying. These modern views seem completely sensible now but were uncommon while she lived. When Zhenyi was 25, she married Zhan Mei, and it was around this time that she began focussing on poetry and her thoughts on gender. But she continued with her scientific endeavours too, even becoming a teacher to male students, which was completely unheard of.

But by the time Zhenyi was 29, she became fatally ill. Before her death, she gave her works to her best friend, Madam Kuai, who eventually passed them to her nephew, the scholar, Qian Yiji.

Had she lived longer, Zhenyi may have discovered so much more and may have written many more inspiring poems. But the fact that she only lived to 29 demonstrates how incredible she was, that she made such an impact on science in such a short time, especially because she had no formal education. Zhenyi was very lucky to have such a progressive family who encouraged her to learn, but it is still a sentiment to her motivation and skill that she could become so knowledgeable without an education. Zhenyi was aware of her privilege, so made it her mission to make education as accessible as possible to others by simplifying other texts, which is an admirable task. As a nod to her contributions, one of Venus' craters is named after Zhenyi.

Ching Shih
(1775–1844 CE)

The Terror of South China

When Shih was a teenage prostitute living in poverty, no one would have imagined that she would end up as a pirate lord. Many argue that she is the most successful pirate, because of her military successes and because she was never captured. Instead of making the reckless decision to continue her immoral life as a pirate, Shih retired to live a peaceful life after being pardoned by the Chinese government. With her strict rules and harsh punishments, Shih was not a woman to cross; however, this strength and firmness kept her massive Red Flag Fleet united to rule the South China Sea.

Shih was born into poverty in the Guangdong province of China during the Qing Dynasty. From the age of 13, like many other girls, she worked on a floating brothel, which was known as a flower boat, as a Cantonese prostitute to help support her family. During her time working as a prostitute, Shih became known for her beauty, and she was a talented conversationalist, making her very popular to clients, including politically powerful clients. But in 1801, Shih became the favourite prostitute of a notorious pirate, Zhèng Yi (also known as Cheng I). Some say that he was astounded by her beauty, others claim he was more attracted to her cunning and resourcefulness, which were skills he looked for in a business partner.

Very quickly, he proposed marriage to Shih, either by ordering a raid to plunder the brothel and bring her to him, or just by asking nicely, it is uncertain. Some even say that Shih proposed marriage to Zhèng Yi. But before they agreed to marry, Shih insisted on contributing to the piracy and having equal control and shares of the pirating business, which Zhèng Yi agreed to.

Marriage to Shih seemed to do well for Zhèng Yi and his pirating business. At the time of their wedding, he controlled a fleet of about 200 ships, but within months of marriage, this number had grown to over a thousand, and about 70,000 men were under Zhèng Yi and Shih's control. They did this by using Zhèng Yi's reputation to bind together rivalling Cantonese pirate fleets into a unified alliance. Their alliance consisted of six fleets who came together as the Red Flag Fleet. Soon, Zhèng Yi and Shih adopted a young man who was the illiterate son of a fisherman, who had been taken by the pirates as a child, his name was Chang Pao. As well as Zhèng Yi's adopted son, Chang Pao was allegedly his lover, and was expected to take over the Red Flag Fleet after Zhèng Yi's death.

But when Zhèng Yi died in 1807 while in Vietnam, the fleet began to scatter. Shih did not want to go back to being a prostitute and she knew she was capable of pulling the Red Flag Fleet together again. So Shih seduced Chang Pao, who was easy to manipulate due to his lack of education, and the pair eventually married. Then she used her connections with Zhèng Yi's family and his loyal followers to build up the fleet. To gain the loyalty of those who would not take orders from a woman, Shih used Chang Pao, as they would follow her orders if the orders came through her husband.

Quickly, Shih was back in a leadership position and earned the respect and loyalty of her pirates by sharing the power and having an organised system with any loot they collected. It was agreed that the original seizer of any loot would keep 20%, and the rest would be put in a public fund which was shared by all. After pulling back together the scattered fleet, Shih announced "Under the leadership of a man you have all chosen to flee. We shall see how you prove yourselves under the hand of a woman."

In addition to organising the public fund, Shih put in place many other strict rules and punishments, to keep her hold on power. Anyone who gave their own orders or disobeyed a superior would be beheaded on the spot; no one could steal from villagers who supplied the pirates; any deserters would have their ears cut off; and anyone who withheld booty would be whipped at their first offense and killed at their second. There were also special rules regarding female captives, as often pirates would want to take the most beautiful captives as their wives. Shih did allow this; however, decreed that if a pirate chose to marry a captive, he must remain loyal to her and take care of her.

Any captive deemed too ugly to marry would be released or ransomed, but would not be harmed. Shih also stated that if a pirate raped a female captive or was unfaithful to his wife, then he would be executed. However, if the captive consented to sexual contact with a pirate, then the pirate would be beheaded and the captive would be drowned. So although pirating is not a moral career choice, and looting villages is in no way excusable, at least Shih did put in place some rules enforcing the protection of innocent captives.

By 1809, Shih commanded far more than Zhèng Yi ever managed, with the Red Flag Fleet as formidable as ever. They built power by raiding government camps and ships, and sailing into Chinese river towns and coastal villages, taking their wealth and levying taxes. To support their piracy, the Red Flag Fleet took control over coastal villages from Macau to Canton, and the people in those villages knew Shih as "The Terror of South China". Some also claim that Shih smuggled opium; however, she probably just looted.

The Chinese government quickly had enough of pirates having this much control, so planned to destroy the Red Flag Fleet in a series of battles. But Shih was not defeated. Instead, she captured and commandeered several of the Chinese government's ships, so eventually, the government had to start using fishing vessels in battles. Not only did Shih face these threats from the government, but she was also attacked by other pirate fleets, including some who she had been allied with, who had started working with the Chinese government to bring the Red Flag Fleet down. Even European bounty hunters had been hired by the Chinese government to capture Shih. At one point, Shih even was able to capture merchantmen from the East India Company, but she released all eight captives, who went on to tell tales of the ferocious Red Flag Fleet pirate lord.

In late 1809, Shih began to suffer defeat during the Battle of the Tiger's Mouth, when she faced the Portuguese Navy. In their final battle at Chek Lap

Kok in 1810, Shih and the Red Flag Fleet were forced to surrender, as she knew they could not go on fighting forever. However, Shih had previously been offered an amnesty from the Chinese government on the condition that she surrendered to them. So Shih began to negotiate with them and eventually agreed to end her pirating career and disband her fleet. Fewer than 300 of the pirates from the fleet would be punished, all others could keep their loot, as long as they gave up their weapons. Shih also convinced the Chinese government to give her husband a job as a captain in the Guangdong Navy, as well as keep 120 of his ships to be used in the salt trade. Several other pirates were also given positions in the Chinese bureaucracy.

So, in her mid-30s, Shih retired from pirating, instead was involved in the salt trade, and had two children with Chang Pao. Sadly, he died at sea in 1822, so Shih relocated with her family to Macau, where she opened a gambling house and brothel where she spent her remaining life. At the age of 60, Shih worked as an advisor to a military leader to help fight the British in the First Opium War, due to her renowned skill in leadership. Finally, with her family around her, Shih died at home, after having lived to an unusually old age for a pirate.

Throughout her life, Shih worked as a prostitute, a pirate lord, a gambling house owner and finally as a military advisor. Although Shih and her pirates committed atrocities when with the Red Flag Fleet, Shih should be regarded as a strong leader. She was empowered in how she used her relationships to keep thousands of men loyal to her, and used her cunning and intelligence to control and organise an entire fleet.

She was such a successful pirate that rather than being captured and executed as a young pirate lord, she knew to stop while she was ahead. This enabled her to negotiate to end her career in a way that worked for her so that she could live peacefully to old age.

Mary Baker
(1792–1864 CE)

Princess Caraboo

Princess Caraboo is an interesting and exotic character, who thrived in the attention of the British press. Dressing in unusual clothes, speaking a mysterious language and having odd eating habits, Caraboo was unlike anything anyone had seen, and many curious members of society would come to visit her. However, as Caraboo's fame grew, it turned out that not all was what it seemed.

In April 1817, a cobbler from Gloucestershire in England met a disorientated, starving, and exhausted young woman. She was wearing unusual clothes, including a turban, and was carrying a small bundle containing necessities, such as soap, a few halfpennies, and a bad sixpence. The mysterious woman spoke to him in a language he could not understand, so he assumed her to be a foreign peasant, and he kindly took the young woman to his home. He could not understand her but knew that she was hungry, so gave her bread and milk, afterwards, she mimed that she wanted to sleep; however, the cobbler's wife was not happy to have a stranger in her home, so they took her to the overseer of the poor. He was an official who administered relief for the poor, and he placed the woman into the hands of a local county magistrate, who was also the Town Clerk of Bristol, Samuel Worrall.

Samuel and his wife, Elizabeth, also could not understand the young woman. But they tried hard to listen to her to see what they could work out. They did not get much but realised that she was identifying herself as Caraboo, and was interested in Chinese imagery, which confused the couple, as she appeared European. Due to her lack of documents and possession of a bad sixpence, Samuel could not let Caraboo stay in his house. This is because the possession of a counterfeit coin was a serious crime, and as a magistrate, he could not take in a criminal. But the Worralls still wanted to ensure Caraboo's safety, so they took her to a local inn to stay.

At this time, botanical prints were popular, and the inn had many of its own. One such was a drawing of a pineapple, and when Caraboo saw it, she pointed and said "nanas", which translated to "pineapple" in some Indonesian languages. This seemed further evidence to suggest that Caraboo was from somewhere that grew pineapples, such as Asia.

Probably getting fed up of dealing with this mysterious woman, Samuel declared that Caraboo must be a beggar, due to her lack of documents and bad sixpence, so he took her to Bristol where she was tried for vagrancy. After this, Caraboo was kept in a hospital that cared for vagrants, where she would only sleep on the floor and refused to eat certain foods. She caused so many problems that Caraboo was sent back to live with Samuel and Elizabeth. While living with her, the couple noticed more eccentricities of their visitor.

When Elizabeth offered Caraboo a cup of tea, before drinking it she would repeat a prayer while holding a hand over her eyes. Once she had finished her cup, Elizabeth offered her a refill, but Caraboo insisted on thoroughly cleaning her cup before it would be refilled with tea. At mealtimes, Caraboo would only eat vegetables, and at night, seemed to not understand the purpose of the bed. It was not until someone showed her how comfortable it was that she said her prayers and then lay down on the bed rather than the floor.

While Caraboo stayed with the Worrals, she attracted a lot of attention from curious members of society and they were all trying to find someone who could understand what she was saying. Eventually, a Portuguese sailor claimed to be able to understand Caraboo's language, so she told her story to him, then he recounted it to Samuel and Elizabeth. He claimed that she was Princess Caraboo from the island of Javasu in the Indian Ocean. She had been captured by pirates and after a long voyage, had jumped overboard in the Bristol Channel and swam ashore.

Now knowing that their visitor was royalty, Caraboo began to be treated by the locals as a visiting head of state. Many people flocked to visit the princess, and Elizabeth, pitying the lost girl who must be missing home, tried to make her feel welcome. To do this, she bought Caraboo exotic clothes and allowed her to do activities that she would do at home. This included using a homemade bow and arrow, fencing, swimming naked while alone and dancing exotically. Most importantly, Princess Caraboo prayed often to Allah-Talla. Sometimes she would even climb to the top of a tree to pray.

As Caraboo's fame grew, a doctor visited her and identified her language. Then he inspected her body and found strange marks at the back of her head, he determined that these were the work of oriental surgeons. However, there was disagreement over the identification of Caraboo's language, as she wrote down examples of her language to be sent to Oxford for analysis, but they returned this, calling her examples "humbug".

But Princess Caraboo did not mind. She continued to communicate to those around her by miming and she gave even more details of her story. Caraboo claimed that her mother had been killed in a fight amongst cannibals. That the day Caraboo was kidnapped, she had been walking in the gardens with servants. The pirates captured, bound, and gagged Caraboo, then carried her to their ship. But when they untied her, Caraboo killed one pirate and wounded another. After a few days, she was sold to the ship's captain, who set sail for Europe, where Caraboo made her escape and wandered around for six weeks before meeting the cobbler who found her.

The more Caraboo told of her story, and the more unusual activities she did, the more attention she gained. Eventually, Princess Caraboo was such a celebrity that she had a portrait painted of her, and in Bath, a ball was held in her honour. But this fame led to Caraboo's downfall. A landlady named Mrs Neale recognised Caraboo's portrait in the *Bristol Journal* to be a young woman who she had lodged six months prior.

Rather than an exotic princess, Caraboo was actually a servant named Mary Willocks from Devon who had been struggling to find somewhere to stay. She took on the persona of Princess Caraboo to make herself more interesting and to be provided for. Mrs Neale claimed that Mary invented her own language from imaginary and gypsy words, and used this to entertain children. The marks on her head were scars from a cupping operation, conducted to relieve pressure in an "overheated brain", in a poorhouse hospital in London.

When Mrs Neale confronted Mary and told the Worralls, Mary suddenly had no trouble speaking English and accepted that the ruse was over. Just as they had enjoyed the story of a lost exotic princess, the British press also took pleasure in the turn of events. Instead of portraying Mary as a fraudulent servant, they hailed her as a working-class heroine, who had deceived high society for 10 weeks. Despite the reveal, Elizabeth still pitied Mary, so she arranged for her to travel to Philadelphia, as she had previously expressed a wish to go to America. While there, Mary briefly continued her role as Princess Caraboo but struggled to find success, so returned to Britain in 1824.

Again, Mary tried to find fame and fortune as Princess Caraboo, by dressing and acting like a foreign princess and charging people to see her, but now the ruse was up, people were not interested. So eventually, Mary married a man named Richard Baker, and she gave birth to a daughter called Mary Anne the following year. After giving up on Princess Caraboo, Mary sold and imported leeches for a living. Eventually, Mary died on Christmas Eve 1864 and was buried in an unmarked grave. Her leech business was continued by her daughter, who lived in a house full of cats.

Despite not finding success as Princess Caraboo, Mary did manage to fool everyone for a long time. Her secret was to pretend to be foreign and not understand English, as this meant that people would speak about her in front of her, so she could grasp how to act convincingly and always be one step ahead. Also, Mary was successful in managing to be fed and sheltered for free for an entire 10 weeks, and this would have been a big relief for a servant who had nowhere to stay. Mary was especially lucky to find Samuel and Elizabeth, who tried to make her feel at home, and still helped her even when they found out she was lying to them.

Policarpa Salavarrieta (1795–1817 CE)

The Colombian Woman

As a young woman, Policarpa's life was full of change and political strife. This, and her Revolutionary family, led her to believe in revolution and the independence of her home. Policarpa gave her whole life to this cause, and used the skills she had, such as seamstressing, to help end the oppressive regime of the Spanish colonisers. In an attempt to make an example of Policarpa and other Revolutionaries, the Spanish instead turned her into a martyr for the cause, inspiring others to fight for independence.

The name "Policarpa" is not the name that this spy was born with; however, her real name is not known because her birth certificate was never found. In her father's will, Policarpa is referred to as "Apolonia"; her forged passport gives the name "Gregoria Apolinaria"; and some knew her as "La Pola". But history remembers this woman as Policarpa because this is the name she chose while armed forces began looking for her, after she became known as a Revolutionary.

Policarpa lived in the Viceroyalty of New Granada, a Spanish viceroyalty that was established in 1717. The region included present-day Columbia, Panama, Ecuador, and Venezuela, and its capital was Santa Fé (present-day Bogotá). In around 1810, the viceroyalty began to disintegrate when some regions began to reject the Spanish officials, even though the governments swore allegiance to the Spanish monarch. Eventually, a series of civil wars, between Revolutionaries (or Patriots) and Royalists, led to the reconquest of the United Provinces of New Granada by Spain between 1814 and 1816. After a few more years under Spanish rule, the area was liberated in 1823 and named the Republic of New Granada.

Policarpa was born in the late 18th century to a well-off, respectable family living in the city of Guaduas, New Granada; however, they moved to Santa Fé while Policarpa was a child, to a much smaller house. In 1802, life took a turn for the worse for Policarpa, as a smallpox epidemic broke out and killed her parents and two of her siblings, tearing the family apart. Policarpa's older sister, Catarina, took Policarpa and their younger brother, Bibiano, back to Guaduas, to live with their godmother and aunt. When Catarina eventually married, she ensured that her two younger siblings could continue to live with her and her new husband. During this time, it is uncertain how Policarpa lived, but she gained some education, as she may have been a teacher in a public school, and worked as a seamstress.

Guaduas was an important rest stop on the road through New Granada, so soldiers, farmers, Spaniards, and Grenadines often passed through, making it a centre of news and information. This access to information such as the political strife, and her Revolutionary family members influenced Policarpa into sharing these revolutionary views. Margarita, Policarpa's godmother, had family members who actively fought the Spaniards when they began colonising the area in 1781, and Catarina's husband had fought and died in patriotic battles against the colonisers.

In the same battle that he lost his life, Policarpa's brother, Bibiano, had fought, and on his return to Guaduas, he was badly injured after being imprisoned by the colonisers. So during this time, Policarpa's patriotic values and spirit grew. Eventually, Policarpa and Bibiano were noticed for their rebelliousness towards the colonisers, so fled to Santa Fé in 1817, this is when she started using the name "Policarpa".

Santa Fé was mostly made up of Spanish Royalists, so it was difficult to get in and out of the city; however, the two siblings managed this by forging documents, and had a letter of introduction written by Revolutionary leaders. These letters recommended that Policarpa and Bibiano should stay in the house of Andrea Ricaurtey Lozano working as servants. However, Andrea's house was actually a centre of intelligence gathering and resistance, so the siblings worked as spies against the Spaniards. As newcomers to the city, they were perfect for the role, as they were unrecognised, so could move freely and meet with other spies unsuspected.

Previously, Policarpa had learned to be a seamstress, so patriotic leaders encouraged their new recruit to become the official seamstress for the Spanish royals. Policarpa managed to do this with the help of Alejo Sabarian, her alleged lover. She would offer her services as a seamstress to the wives and daughters of Royalists and officers, altering and mending for them. At the same time, she listened to their conversations to obtain information, such as their plans; the number of soldiers and their weapons; who the major Royalists were; and who was suspected of being Revolutionaries. When she was not doing this, Policarpa and Bibiano recruited young men to the Revolutionary cause and helped those who wanted to switch sides to leave the Royalists.

One day, two Revolutionary spies were apprehended while carrying information that linked Policarpa to the Revolution. These documents implicated Policarpa in helping soldiers desert the Royal Army; transporting weapons to the Revolutionaries; and helping spies to escape from prison. However, the Royalists did not have enough solid evidence to arrest a seamstress for treason. But they did not have to wait long until they found further evidence. Another spy was arrested, and he was found with a list of Royalists and Patriots, which was given to him by Policarpa, so the Spaniards wasted no time and arrested both Policarpa and Bibiano. The siblings were then transported to a makeshift prison and sentenced to death by firing squad in four days.

The night before her execution, Policarpa viciously and relentlessly cursed the Spanish. When a guard offered her a glass of wine, she tossed it back at him, continuing to berate her captures and the Spanish regime.

The next day, Policarpa was escorted by two priests with her hands bound. They told her she must ask for forgiveness, but instead, Policarpa cursed the oppression of the Spanish regime, and predicted their defeat. She was led to the public square, where a crowd was watching, and was told she must take a bullet to the back because she had betrayed the Spanish. So Policarpa bared her back by dropping her dress slightly and knelt with six other prisoners, including Alejo.

As she knelt, Policarpa shouted out "Although I am a woman and young, I have more than enough courage to suffer this death and a thousand more!"; then the squad began shooting. After this, the six other prisoners had their bodies paraded and exhibited through the streets of Santa Fé, to scare off potential Revolutionaries. As a woman, Policarpa was spared this final humiliation. Instead of putting off potential Revolutionaries, Policarpa's execution inspired sympathy and many others joined the Revolution. Eventually, the Revolution had enough support to achieve its independence from Spain in 1823.

Many people now regard Policarpa as a martyr, and the anniversary of her death, the 14th of November, is celebrated as the Day of the Colombian Woman. In her short life of just 22 years, Policarpa inspired many by fighting for a cause that put her in immense danger. Not only was Policarpa extremely brave for participating in these activities, but she was also very skilled in her abilities, gaining useful information from her enemy whilst also remaining completely unsuspected, making her a very competent spy and a strong woman.

Sojourner Truth
(1797–1883 CE)

Preacher of Freedom

Sojourner was born into slavery and suffered working as a slave until she was almost 30. But when Sojourner gained her freedom, she did not remain quiet. She fought for the liberation of her son, then went on to speak out against slavery and for women's rights for the rest of her life. This was not an easy feat, but Sojourner was a natural public speaker, with a demanding presence and calm composure, to make herself heard.

Born with the name Isabella Baumfree as a slave in New York, Sojourner was the daughter of a slave who had been captured in modern-day Ghana. From an early age, Sojourner was very spiritual, as when she was a child, she saw visions and heard voices that she attributed to God. Although she was illiterate, Sojourner could recite sections of the Bible by heart; however, her faith would be tested throughout her life.

In 1806, when her master died, nine-year-old Sojourner was sold at an auction with a flock of sheep for $100; tragically, she was split up from her family. With this new master, Sojourner suffered greatly as she was beaten daily, once even with a bundle of rods. Then Sojourner was sold for $105 to a tavern keeper, and just 18 months later, in 1810, Sojourner was sold to John Dumont.

This was the last time Sojourner was sold, but it was not a nice place to be. John was a rapist, which was already bad enough, but his wife was jealous of the attention her husband was showing Sojourner, so she harassed Sojourner and made her life even more difficult. It was around this time when Sojourner learned how to speak English, as her first language was Dutch. After some years, in 1815, Sojourner met a slave called Robert, who worked on a nearby farm, and the pair fell in love. However, Robert's master forbade the relationship because if they had any children, then they would be the property of Sojourner's owner.

One day, Robert sneaked over to see Sojourner, but the pair were caught, and Robert was savagely beaten, so the pair never met again. From this meeting, Sojourner did have a daughter called Diana, although it has been argued that this child was the result of a rape by John. Years later, John encouraged Sojourner to marry Thomas, another of John's slaves. The couple had three children, Peter, Elizabeth and Sophia.

As Sojourner was a hard worker and had worked for John for many years, John had promised Sojourner that he would grant her freedom a year before the state emancipation. Unsurprisingly, when this time came, John changed his mind because he claimed that a hand injury was making Sojourner less productive. But Sojourner would not accept this change of heart, so in 1826, Sojourner took her youngest child and walked away to a nearby abolitionist family, called the Van Wageners. When John saw that Sojourner had left, he went to this house to demand that they return his property. The kind family offered to pay John $20 for her services for the remainder of the year until the state's emancipation took effect, so had bought Sojourner's freedom.

Soon, Sojourner found out that John had illegally sold her five-year-old son, Peter, into slavery in Alabama to abusive owners. So the Van Wageners helped Sojourner go to court against John so that she may recover her child. She won the case in 1828 and was reunited with Peter, making Sojourner the first black woman to win a case like this against a white man.

With her freedom, Sojourner moved to New York City to be a housekeeper, and eventually, in 1842, Peter was able to take a job on a whaling ship. He wrote a few letters to his mother, but when the ship returned to port, he was not on board, so Sojourner never saw her son again, who she had worked so hard to free. A year later, Sojourner declared that the Spirit had called her to preach the truth, so this is when she began to call herself "Sojourner Truth". This meant that she could no longer work as a housekeeper in the city, as she had been called to go to the countryside to give speeches preaching about the abolition of slavery. So gathering all her possessions into a pillowcase, Sojourner went on her way.

In 1844, Sojourner joined the Northampton Association of Education and Industry in Massachusetts, which was an organisation founded by abolitionists, but also supported women's rights, pacifism, and religious tolerance. The members of this organisation lived in a 500-acre community that was completely self-sufficient, and Sojourner's job was to oversee the laundry. It was here when Sojourner took part as a preacher in the Northampton Camp meeting. However, during this meeting, a band of young men turned up and refused to leave, threatening to burn down the tents.

Sojourner was the only black person present, so she was terrified that they would attack her first, so she hid. But then when Sojourner saw how scared others were, she resolved to do something to help. Sojourner walked onto a small hill and began to sing hymns with her powerful voice, and this gathered the rioters and quietened them. The band of men then encouraged Sojourner to continue singing, preaching and praying for their entertainment, so after an hour of this, Sojourner negotiated with them. She agreed to sing one more song if they promised to leave afterwards, and the mob agreed and did as she asked.

After this first successful preach, Sojourner met other abolitionists, including William Lloyd Garrison and Frederick Douglas, who encouraged Sojourner to speak to groups about the evils of slavery. In 1850, Sojourner began dictating her memoirs to William Lloyd Garrison, who published them in a book entitled *Sojourner Truth: a Northern Slave.* Sojourner was able to live on the sales of this book and it gave her national recognition. Around this time, Sojourner also met Elizabeth Cady Stanton and Susan B. Anthony, who were women's rights activists. They inspired Sojourner to talk not only about slavery but also about women's rights.

In pursuit of her new focus on women's rights, Sojourner conducted a lecture tour in 1851 in Ohio, in which she delivered her famous, improvised "Ain't I a Woman?" speech, where she challenged the notion of racial and gender inferiority and inequality. In this speech, Sojourner explained that women were no weaker than men and used herself as an example, due to her six-foot height and physical strength despite her being a female. Sojourner spoke with such authority and composure that some of the audience members did not even believe that Sojourner was a woman. Not long after this, Sojourner left her husband, because he believed that formally enslaved men should gain suffrage before women, whereas she could not see why both could not happen simultaneously.

In 1853, Sojourner was at another convention to speak; however, she was greeted by the male audience members groaning and hissing at her. But as always, Sojourner maintained her composure and responded saying "you may hiss as much as you please, but women will get their rights anyway. You can't stop us." Like many successful public speakers, Sojourner adapted her speeches based on the response of her audience. So in this particular speech about women's rights, Sojourner incorporated many religious references and went on to say that just as the women in scripture, women today are fighting for their rights. Sojourner also scolded the crowds for their rude behaviour previously, and reminded them that God says to "Honour thy father and thy mother."

During the 1850s, Sojourner lived in Michigan, near her three daughters, and often spoke nationally. When the Civil War began, Sojourner encouraged black men, including her grandson, to join the Union cause and organised supplies for the black troops. After the Civil War, she was invited to the White House and met President Abraham Lincoln, with whom she spoke about her beliefs and experiences as an escaped slave. Then, she became involved with the Freedmen's Bureau, helping freed slaves to find jobs and build new lives. She also rallied people to donate food, clothes, and other supplies to black refugees. In addition to this, Sojourner lobbied against segregation by riding in streetcars that were designated for white people.

One day, a streetcar conductor tried to block Sojourner from riding due to the colour of her skin, so Sojourner ensured that the man was arrested and convicted. Sojourner also worked on a petition, which had thousands of signatures, to provide former slaves with land; however, Congress never took action.

In 1867, Sojourner addressed a speech to the American Equal Rights Association. This time, rather than hissing and groaning, Sojourner was received with loud cheers, perhaps because she was more established. In the first section of her speech, Sojourner spoke about rights for black women, as it was unfair that black men were receiving more rights but not women, and she feared that the black women would get left behind in the civil rights movement. In the second section of Sojourner's speech, she used a story from the Bible to strengthen her argument for women's rights and accused men of being self-centred for keeping all the rights to themselves.

In the third and final section, Sojourner spoke about women's suffrage, explaining that because she owned her own house and paid taxes, she should also have the right to vote. She argued that black enslaved women were capable of much larger difficulties than voting, such as hard manual work, so why would they not be able to do something as simple as voting? In another speech, Sojourner argued that women's rights were not only essential to the wellbeing of women, but also for the benefit of the whole of creation, including men.

As well as speaking about the abolition of slavery, and women's rights, Sojourner gave speeches on other subjects, including prison reform, and she spoke against capital punishment. However, as Sojourner neared the end of her life, she moved back to Michigan and was cared for by two of her daughters. Eventually, Sojourner died at home, and her funeral was attended by nearly a thousand people.

Throughout her life, Sojourner spoke up for those who were treated unjustly. With no education, not even the ability to read or write, and having grown up abused and isolated, Sojourner became a brave and powerful woman, who had a strong grasp of public speaking. She made herself listened to, by speaking with authority and composure. Although Sojourner saw and aided the abolition of slavery, she never experienced desegregation or women's suffrage; however, she aided these causes significantly. In 2009, Sojourner became the first African American woman to have a memorial bust in the Capitol building, so to this day, she is remembered for her life of speaking out for others.

Mary Anning
(1799–1847 CE)

The Greatest Fossilist the World Ever Knew

Mary lived her life constantly on the brink of poverty, only sustaining herself and her family by selling the fossils she found in the cliffs near her home. But while collecting these fossils, Mary made many very significant scientific discoveries, despite not having any formal education. Because of her discoveries, Mary was friends with many geologists, but due to her sex and working-class status, some geologists would present her findings without crediting her for them. But now, Mary is remembered as an incredibly intelligent woman who changed people's view of our history, and she assisted in the development of palaeontology.

Born in Lyme Regis in Dorset to a carpenter, Mary's family was very poor. Due to the crowded living conditions of their town, infant deaths from smallpox and measles were high. Out of her nine siblings, only herself and Joseph made it to adulthood, and Mary had been a sickly baby. When she was just 15 months old, Mary was being held by a neighbour who was standing under a tree with two other women, when lightning suddenly struck the tree and all three women were killed. Mary was rushed home and revived in a bath of hot water, and a local doctor declared this a miracle. Despite the close encounter with death, from this point, Mary was no longer a sickly baby, and she thrived. Members of the community attributed her curiosity, intelligence, and liveliness to this incident.

Lyme Regis is located on the cliffs along the English Channel and is sometimes referred to as the Jurassic Coast because of the Jurassic marine fossil beds in the cliffs. The Anning family lived so close to the cliffs that the storms would sometimes flood their home, once forcing them to crawl out of an upstairs bedroom window to avoid drowning. During the winter months, landslides would expose new fossils which had to be collected quickly before they were lost to the sea. Mary's father would go out to collect these fossils and sold them to tourists to increase his income.

Even though it was not typically a feminine pastime, Mary would often accompany her father with his fossil collecting, from the age of about five. She was greatly encouraged in this, and he taught her how to find and clean fossils so that they could be sold in his shop. The lack of wealth in the family may be partly due to food shortages caused by the French Revolutionary Wars and the Napoleonic Wars. This created tension in the working class because the price of wheat had nearly tripled in just 20 years, but their wages had remained almost unchanged. So unsurprisingly, Mary's father and other members of the working class were involved in organising protests and riots against this.

Mary had little education. She could not attend school but was part of a Dissenter chapel so attended Sunday School which taught Mary to read and write, and taught her about the importance of educating the poor. Although being a Dissenter taught Mary valuable skills, such as reading, Dissenters were not allowed into universities or the army and were excluded by law from many professions.

Of course, as a child, this did not affect Mary, and she loved learning to read. Her prized possession was a book called the *Dissenters' Theological Magazine and Review,* in which the pastor had published two essays, one insisting that God had created the world in six days, the other ironically encouraging Dissenters to study the new science of geology. Mary was happy to oblige and spent her free time teaching herself about geology and anatomy.

In 1810, disaster struck the Anning family. Mary's father died from tuberculosis and other injuries caused by falling from a cliff. His death left the family with debts and no savings, forcing them to apply for parish relief; however, even with this support, the family had to burn furniture to keep warm. It was also apparent that Joseph and Mary had to start contributing money to the family for their survival so that they did not have to go to the workhouse. So Joseph took up a post as apprentice upholster, and their mother encouraged Mary to continue selling fossils from the beach.

At the time, Lyme Regis was full of tourists because the English were told to holiday at home rather than abroad because of the French Revolutionary Wars and Napoleonic Wars. Many travelled to Dorset to go fossil hunting, as it was a fashionable tradition, so fossil hunters like Mary had many customers. For a long time, the locals had sold fossils as "curios" to tourists, and they gave them made-up names, such as "snake-stones" (ammonites), "devil's fingers" (belemnites) and "verteberries" (vertebrae). Sometimes the locals would sell these by claiming that they had mystical and medicinal properties.

But in 1811, Mary and her brother made a huge discovery to make Lyme Regis even more of a significant holiday destination. Joseph found a huge fossilised skull, but could not find the rest of the animal. So after a few months of digging out an outline, Mary found the entire skeleton, which was over five metres long. It seemed as though Mary had uncovered a monster.

Eventually, the creature was completely dug up and this was covered by the local press, who identified the creature as a crocodile. A lord of a local manor purchased the mysterious skeleton for £23, it was then passed to a public display in London. This caused a lot of intrigue because, at the time, many scientists still believed that Earth was just a few thousand years old and that a species did not evolve or become extinct. Therefore, they believed the creature must be something alive, yet undiscovered. The father of palaeontology, George Cuvier, had recently introduced the theory of extinction, but most were sceptical; however, Mary's discovery provided some evidence for this theory, raising huge questions about the history of the planet.

At first, scientists thought the creature was some sort of fish, then considered it could have an affinity to the duck-billed platypus. But finally, in 1819, an assistant curator of the British Museum, Charles Konig, suggested the name Ichthyosaurus, meaning "fish lizard". The name stuck; however, now we know it is actually a marine reptile. The skull of this ichthyosaurus, the first ever correctly identified of its kind, is still in the possession of the Natural History Museum in London.

The discovery of the ichthyosaurus gained Mary more customers, including Lieutenant-Colonel Thomas James Birch, a collector from Lincolnshire; however, the Annings were still in a financial crisis. In 1820, a year after Mary's discovery, Thomas saw that the family was on the brink of selling their furniture to pay rent. Thomas was so disturbed by their poverty, that he auctioned all the fossils he had previously purchased from them. Although he was upset to lose his collection, he was satisfied to be helping out the Annings, as he liked the family, and he raised £400.

It is uncertain how much exactly he gave to the struggling family, but it certainly gave them some stability. Also, the auction made Mary more well-known within the geological community, as buyers came from Paris and Vienna for the three-day auction. So Mary was able to continue supporting her family by selling fossils, primarily invertebrate fossils, such as ammonites and belemnite shells, which were common in the area and sold for a few shillings.

Mary's luck improved in 1821 when she collected her second major specimen. This time it was a plesiosaurus, which translates to "near lizard". This creature was so strange in appearance, that it was even stronger evidence for the theory of extinction. However, in the scientific writings that followed about the discovery, Mary was not mentioned, even though she had discovered and prepared the skeleton. In 1823, Mary discovered another, much more complete, plesiosaur skeleton, and drew scientific sketches of it. But again, Mary was not mentioned in the presentation and analysis of the anatomy of the discovery, even though she had collected the skeleton and drew the sketch that was used in the presentation.

However, this finding proved controversial. As the neck of the creature had an unprecedented 35 vertebrae, many believed that this was a fraud, and Mary had combined fossil bones from different animals to fake a discovery. This controversy was discussed in a meeting, which Mary was not invited to, but fortunately, the skeleton was deemed to be legitimate. If it was concluded to be a fraud, Mary would have no longer been able to sell fossils to geologists, putting her finances in jeopardy. Instead, this ordeal established Mary as a competent fossil collector, giving her more respect in geologists' circles.

By 1826, Mary had saved enough money from her discoveries to buy a house with a glass store-front window for her shop. Mary's shop was so popular, that the moving of business was covered in the local paper. This shop served many important customers, including the geologist, George William Featherstonhaugh, who purchased fossils from Mary for the new New York Lyceum of Natural History in 1827. Years later, Mary even had a royal visit from King Frederick Augustus II of Saxony, who in 1844 bought an ichthyosaur skeleton for his natural history collection.

Some geologists did not visit Mary simply to purchase from her, but she was visited by those who wanted to collect fossils with Mary or have discussions about anatomy and classification. Henry De la Beche, one of Britain's leading geologists, was a close friend of Mary since childhood when the pair would go fossil hunting together. Mary was also visited by William Buckland, a lecturer in geology at the University of Oxford. At Christmas time they would go fossil hunting together. Sometimes Mary would lead other geologists on fossil collecting excursions around Lyme Regis, showing that she had positive interactions with the scientific community.

This large network of geologists was built up with the help of a lifelong friend of Mary's, named Charlotte. Her husband encouraged Charlotte to work with Mary for a few weeks and the pair became very close, then when Charlotte went travelling around Europe with her husband, she met many geologists and told them of Mary, creating new customers for her friend.

Mary's next major discovery was in 1828 when she found the partial skeleton of a pterosaur (the name pterodactyl would be coined later). This creature had large wings and a long tail, and was believed to be the largest ever flying animal. This time, perhaps due to her success in the plesiosaur controversy, Mary was credited with the discovery. This was an important discovery, as it was the first of its kind found outside Germany, and created a public sensation when it was displayed at the British Museum. This discovery, along with the ichthyosaur and plesiosaur, gave support to Cuvier's suggestion of an "age of reptiles". This suggested that there was a time when reptiles rather than mammals had been the dominant form of animal life.

To get a better understanding of the anatomy of the creatures she was uncovering, Mary would dissect modern animals, such as fish and cuttlefish. In addition to this, Mary continued to unearth and sell fossils, helping to increase public interest in geology and palaeontology. Another scientifically, yet unglamorous, discovery that Mary made, was that the strange conical objects known as bezoar stones, were actually the fossilised faeces of ichthyosaurs or plesiosaurs, and they were named coprolites by William Buckland. She dug up so many fossils that the museums struggled to keep up with the demand.

However, even with all of this business, Mary was still constantly on the brink of a financial crisis, forcing her to remain a commercial fossil collector, as she had to sell her discoveries to make ends meet. But selling the fossils was becoming more difficult due to difficult economic conditions in Britain reducing demand for the fossils.

This upset her friend, Henry De la Beche, and he was determined to help Mary. So he painted *Duria Antiquior – A More Ancient Dorset* in 1830. He then sold the prints to geologists and wealthy friends, then donated the profits to Mary. This piece of art is now known as the first form of palaeoart, which is a representation of prehistoric life based on the discoveries Mary was unearthing.

Although this helped Mary financially, in 1833, Mary came close to death, displaying to her how dangerous fossil hunting could be. The fossil hunters relied on landslides on the cliffs to uncover the fossils they could sell, however, in this incident, a landslide almost buried Mary. Fortunately, she got out of the way in time, but her black and white terrier, who accompanied her on the fossil hunts, was buried, devastating Mary.

Just a few years later in 1838, Mary suffered another disaster when her life savings of £300 were lost in a bad investment. She had invested in a conman who ran off with the money; however, others believe this man did not run away, but died, so Mary could not recover the investment. To help her out, an old friend, William Buckland, persuaded the British Association for the Advancement of Science and the British government to award Mary an annuity, known as a civil list pension, in return for her contributions to geology. This provided Mary with an annual pension of £25, giving her some financial security.

In her lifetime, Mary only published one scientific writing, which appeared in the *Magazine of Natural History* in 1839. This was an extract from a letter that Mary had written to the editor, in which she questioned their claim that the recently discovered fossil of the prehistoric shark, hybodus, represented a new genus. Mary claimed that this was a mistake since she made the same discovery years ago. Although Mary was recognised for her scientific contributions, the Geological Society of London refused to admit Mary, and would not admit women until 1904, or even allow women to attend meetings as guests.

This was not a good time to be a woman, especially a working-class Dissenter woman, as most of the scientific community were Anglican gentlemen, who refused to see past Mary's gender. Geologist men who bought her findings would publish scientific descriptions of these specimens without even mentioning Mary's name, even though she discovered the specimen, dug it up, cleaned it, and identified it. It seems as though fossils were credited to museums in the name of the rich man that paid for them, rather than the poor woman who found them.

Mary was aware of the discrimination she suffered and was resentful. Mary complained to friends, saying her brains were sucked by the men of learning and that the world had used her unkindly, making her suspicious of those around her.

In 1847, rumours spread that Mary had a drinking problem because she was taking increasing doses of laudanum. However, she used the laudanum as a painkiller because she had breast cancer. When the Geological Society heard of this diagnosis, they raised money to help Mary with expenses. After her death, they contributed to a stained glass window in Mary's honour, in the local parish church where she was buried. Since Mary's death, the National History Museum hailed her as the greatest fossil hunter the world has known.

Also, in 2010, the Royal Society included Mary in a list of the 10 British women who have most influenced the history of science, acknowledging her work in a way that it rarely was during her lifetime. In Mary's honour, a fossil that was identified as a new kind of ichthyosaur found in Lyme Bay has was named Ichthyosaurus Anningae. So although Mary was not respected enough during her time, now she is credited for her discoveries and scientific contributions, which changed views of the history of our planet.

Pine Leaf
(1806–1854 CE)

Woman Chief

Many have been entranced by Pine Leaf because of how different she seemed when comparing her to other women at the time. She has been compared to the mythological Amazon warriors because of her skills in warfare. But Pine Leaf was not just a skilled warrior, she was also a powerful leader, who worked her way up the ranks with her strength and intelligence. She became known as the "Woman Chief" in the patriarchal society in which she lived.

Pine Leaf was born to the Indigenous American Gros Ventres tribe in Montana; however, at the age of ten, she was kidnapped by the Crow tribe. A Crow warrior who had recently lost his son adopted Pine Leaf as his own and raised her as his daughter, encouraging her to enjoy typically masculine activities. The Crow tribe was patriarchal, as women were commonly the food preparers and child rearers, but they did influence leadership, and some even gave up their domestic roles to be career warriors. This would surprise their enemies, who feared that the female warriors possessed supernatural abilities.

So Pine Leaf was being raised to be a career warrior and she could rival any of the young men in their activities. Pine Leaf may also have had a twin brother who was also adopted by the Crow tribe, who was killed in an attack when the siblings were 12 years old. The young Pine Leaf vowed to avenge her brother and stated that she would never marry a man until she had killed a hundred of the enemy with her own hand. With this in mind, whenever there was a battle, Pine Leaf was the first to fearlessly volunteer to fight.

As she grew older, Pine Leaf was known to be a "Two-Spirit". This is a term used by indigenous North Americans, describing a gender-variant person. However, unlike typical Two-Spirits, Pine Leaf wore female clothing, but at the same time carried guns, lances, and bows. She also rode a warhorse and kept young women as wives. Two other women who were known to be warriors in the Crow tribe were Akkeekaahuush, meaning "Come Towards the Near Bank", and Biliíche Héeleelash, meaning "Among the Willows", the latter of the two was an important war leader. When Pine Leaf's father died, she took over the leadership of his lodge and quickly worked her way up the ranks.

Pine Leaf gained her reputation as a warrior during a raid by the Blackfoot. During this raid, Pine Leaf fought off multiple attackers at a time and helped to turn back the raid. She then raised her own warriors to raid the Blackfoot settlements as a response, claiming many horses and scalps from the enemy. After this, Pine Leaf was accepted to represent her lodge as "bacheeítche" (chief) in the Council of Chiefs, and was given the name "Bíawacheeitchish", translating to "Woman Chief". Pine Leaf continued to be remarkable, so she eventually became the rank of third among the council's 160 lodges.

In 1851 was the Treaty of Fort Laramie, which was an agreement of territories between the US treaty commissioners and representatives of many Indigenous American tribes, including the Crows. From this point, Pine Leaf would be involved in negotiations with the tribes of Upper Missouri, and even worked to bring peace between the Crow tribe and the Gros Ventres, the tribe of her birth. Unfortunately, after a few years of peace, Pine Leaf was ambushed by the Gros Ventres and killed.

Much of Pine Leaf's life was caught in the memoirs of James Beckwourth, a visitor to the Crows. He described Pine Leaf as brave, intelligent, and strong, and James fell in love with the Woman Chief. Eventually, he asked Pine Leaf to marry him, but it is uncertain what happened next. Some claim that he left the tribe until Pine Leaf had made up her mind and agreed to marry him, and the couple was married for five weeks until James left the Crow tribe forever.

The other story is that Pine Leaf refused to marry James, partly because she still had to kill a hundred men, and because she already had enough wives. But James persisted and lied to convince Pine Leaf to marry him. He claimed that a fortune-teller said he would be invincible in battle if he married Pine Leaf, so she laughed and said she would marry James "when the pine leaves turn yellow and fall from the tree". It took James a while to realise that pine leaves never turn yellow. But James stayed persistent and proposed marriage to Pine Leaf again. This time she said she would not marry him until he found a "red-headed Indian", which of course he never did. In this account, James finally left the Crow tribe without marrying Pine Leaf.

However, this account is unreliable. Due to James having a famously elevated sense of self-importance, it is likely his memoirs are exaggerated, or even fictional. Many others from outside the tribe who came across Pine Leaf were also fascinated by her, as she was so different from any woman they had met before, so they linked her to the mythological Amazon warriors.

Although the existence of Pine Leaf, and much of her life, can be questioned, there was certainly a Crow Woman Chief. She was a fearless leader who proved that women could be just as ruthless as men and as skilled in warfare. Rather than conform to gender stereotypes, Pine Leaf did what she wanted. She wore feminine clothes, but yielded weapons and rode horses as was typical of the men. This strong attitude enabled Pine Leaf to be successful and influential in her tribe so that she was able to work her way up the ranks through her brave and skilled actions on the battlefield.

Frances Dickens (1810–1848 CE)

Eclipsed Musician

Frances was always expected to become the famous name of the Dickens family, because of her talent and education as a singer and pianist. However, despite her parents choosing her education over her siblings', it would be Charles Dickens, rather than Frances, who became the household name. But Frances still found success in her own right, and perhaps if she had a longer life, she would have become better remembered by history.

Frances was born in Landport and was the oldest of eight siblings, one of whom would grow up to be the author, Charles Dickens. As a child, Frances always displayed a strong musical ability, which allowed her to gain a place at the Royal Academy of Music when she was 13, which had opened the year before. The fee for this school was 38 guineas a year, which was too much for the Dickens family, but they decided to spend all their money on Frances' education at the expense of the education of their sons. This was incredibly unusual at the time, to pay for their daughter rather than son to be educated.

John Dickens, Frances' father, was a clerk in the Navy Pay Office in Portsmouth; however, was later transferred to London, where he was paid £200 a year. But even with this income, John had trouble managing money, as he had expensive pastimes, such as dressing well, entertaining friends, and reading expensive books. Even in 1818, when his salary had increased to £350, John was struggling financially and had to ask for loans from other family members.

Perhaps his other children's educations did not all need to be sacrificed, as he could have spent less on himself. The births of more children into the Dickens family further worsened the family's financial situation. Eventually, in 1819, John borrowed £200 from his brother-in-law, but could not pay the money back, so his brother-in-law refused to allow him in his house again.

Meanwhile, Frances was studying singing and piano at school, with Ignaz Moscheles as her teacher, who was a former pupil of Ludwig van Beethoven. He was also a Jewish emigrant from Bohemia who had previously lived in Vienna. In her second year, Frances was awarded for her "good conduct and improvement in music", and she won a silver pencil case as the second prize on the piano. But Frances' education was being threatened by her father's financial struggles. At one point, John wrote to his daughter's school, suggesting a payment plan of £10 quarterly, but the school responded by saying that Frances would have to leave if he did not pay £15 quarterly.

Around this time, John was arrested for debt and taken to Marshalsea Prison. Charles then had to act as a messenger for his father, having to ask family and friends for money to help John, but he already owed these people money, so no one was willing to help. To make ends meet, Charles had to take their expensive books and furniture to a pawnbroker. Charles was also responsible for collecting his sister from school each Sunday to visit their father.

Eventually, in 1825, John's mother died, so he inherited £450, which could pay off his debts, enabling him to be discharged from prison, and he was able to get his job back. So it seemed Frances' place at the Academy was secure. But only for two years. By 1827, John was already back in debt, so Frances paid for her studies by taking on a part-time teaching job, as a sub-professor. She was paid seven shillings for two hours, three times per week. In this position, Frances showed herself to be an enthusiastic teacher, but she only had one pupil, so the school could not afford to pay her for more than two years.

After leaving the Academy, Frances became a professional musician and found success. There were excellent reviews of Frances singing in Academy concerts, and in 1834, Frances was awarded an associate honorary membership at the Royal Academy and took part in public concerts. Her brother was also finding success as an author, and Frances was the influence of many of his characters, including Little Fan, the sister of Ebenezer Scrooge in *A Christmas Carol,* and Florence Dombey, the sister of Paul in *Dombey and Son.* So not only in real life, but also in her brother's fiction would Frances be destined to be remembered as a man's sister, rather than her own accomplished woman.

In 1835, Frances was singing in a concert in a group containing Henry Burnett, who had also studied at the Academy. The pair would marry two years later and have two sons, Henry Augustus in 1839, and Charles Dickens Kneller in 1841. But Henry Augustus was a sickly child, shown by the fact that he was the influence for the character of Tiny Tim in *A Christmas Carol.* The family moved to Manchester and Frances spent much less time on her musical career, since becoming a mother and a wife. However, she and her husband did continue to sing together.

Unfortunately, Frances soon developed tuberculosis, so they returned to London for treatment, because Charles had told them he could provide the best doctors. But Frances' condition deteriorated. She was visited by her brother every day, and she confided in him that she was not scared to die, but was distressed to leave her children while they were so young. Sadly, Frances died of her illness at the age of just 38, and her son, Henry Augustus, died soon later. Both mother and son were buried at Highgate Cemetery with other members of the Dickens family.

Despite her parents' investment, Frances did not become as famous as her brother, but she was extremely successful and worked diligently for this success. It was uncommon for a woman to be so well educated, and especially for this education to be given to her over her brother. But Frances took all the opportunities that came her way and held onto them tightly because she never knew when her family's finances would deteriorate and her education would be taken away. As well as a talented singer and pianist, Frances was a loyal mother, wife and sister, as she would give up her career for her husband and children; she maintained a close bond with her brother, whose career would overshadow her own.

Rani Lakshmi Bai (1828–1858 CE)

The Most Dangerous of All Indian Leaders

In the 1700s, European powers were competing for control in India. In pursuit of this, the East India Company established its army in India, composed of British and native troops. As the East India Company grew in strength, British citizens built an Anglo-Indian society within India. So throughout Lakshmi's life, her country was being controlled by the British, but resentment was slowly building.

With all her wealth and education, Lakshmi could have lived a long, comfortable life in her palace after the death of her husband, as a rani who allowed the British to rule in her place. But she was a strong woman who refused to sit by while her home, Jhansi, was taken from her. Instead, Lakshmi was a leader in the Indian Rebellion of 1857 and became a symbol of resistance to Indian nationalists.

Lakshmi was born with the name Manikarnika Tambe, nicknamed Manu by her parents. Her father was a court advisor, but unfortunately, her mother, who was a learned woman, died when Lakshmi was just four years old. With just her father to raise her, Lakshmi was brought up more like a son than a daughter, with a good education. She was educated at home and was taught how to read and write, how to shoot, ride horses and elephants, and martial arts, alongside the boys in the Peshwa's household. Lakshmi was part of an important family, so she was well-known to the ruling Peshwa, who called her "Chhabili", meaning "playful". Two of Lakshmi's childhood friends were Tatya Tope and Nana Sahib, who would later become important in the Great Rebellion of 1858.

In 1842, at the age of just 14, Lakshmi married the Maharaja (the great ruler) of Jhansi, becoming his second wife. He was a recently widowed king, and this was when Lakshmi changed her name to honour the Hindu Goddess Lakshmi, as was tradition. As a rani (queen), Lakshmi refused to abide by the societal norms, she would not conceal herself from public view using a veil or curtain, as other women did at the time. She was also known to wear male attire, such as a turban, and she insisted on talking with advisers and British officials face to face.

Unfortunately, Lakshmi's husband would not allow her to continue learning martial arts with men, but Lakshmi would not accept this, so instead assembled a regiment of female soldiers from her maidservants to train with. Soon into their marriage, Lakshmi gave birth to her son, but the baby died just a few months later and the couple would have no more children. In 1853, Lakshmi's husband became very ill so he adopted a five-year-old distant cousin to be his heir, Damodar Rao. This adoption was completed in the presence of a British political officer, and adopting heirs was not unusual at the time, as the previous two rulers had been adopted themselves.

When Lakshmi's husband died, the British Governor-General of India, Lord Dalhousie, refused to recognise Damodar Rao as heir, using the Doctrine of Lapse. This stated that an area should lapse to the British if there was no appropriate heir. This angered Lakshmi and the people of Jhansi because Lakshmi's husband had instructed the British to treat his adopted child with respect, and to give the government of Jhansi to Lakshmi as a regent for Damodar Rao.

But instead, Jhansi was annexed, and an agent of the East India Company was sent to look after administrative matters. When Lakshmi was informed of this, she cried out "I shall not surrender my Jhansi", but she was given an annual pension and allowed to keep the town palace as a personal residence. While in this position, with her lack of control, Lakshmi spent her time writing letters asking to be given control of Jhansi. She was supported in this endeavour by two East India Company representatives who were sympathetic to Lakshmi's claims, describing her as a well-respected rani, and capable of being regent.

Meanwhile, discontent was building among the Indian soldiers within the British East India Company's army. This was because there was a rumour that the cartridges for the newly issued rifles were greased with cow or pig fat. This was regarded as an abomination by the Hindu and Muslim soldiers, who had been tearing the cartridges open with their teeth. They felt that the British were systematically trying to undermine their faith and convert them to Christianity. These feelings were exacerbated when 85 soldiers refused to use the cartridges and were put in irons in 1857.

The next day, three regiments stormed the jail, killing officers and their families, then marched on Delhi, 50 miles away, sparking the Indian Mutiny throughout the country. Others joined the rebellion because they had other grievances, so the violence spread quickly and became organised.

When news of the fighting reached Jhansi, Lakshmi asked the British for permission to raise an army for her protection, which she was granted. Then Lakshmi conducted a Haldi Kumkum ceremony, in which the married women would gather as a symbol of their married status to wish their husbands long lives. This reassured her people at a violent time, but Lakshmi was reluctant to rebel herself, even when the rebels seized the Star Fort of Jhansi. The rebels then persuaded the British to lay down their arms, promising that they would not come to any harm; however, they went back on this promise and massacred about 60 European officers, along with their wives and children. Four days later, the rebels left Jhansi with money they had received from Lakshmi after they had threatened to blow up her palace. As the only remaining source of authority in the city, Lakshmi assumed control.

But soon later, Jhansi was facing invasion from forces of the East India Company, to whom Lakshmi was still loyal. To protect her people, Lakshmi appealed for British aid; however, they believed she was responsible for the recent massacre, even though she had condemned the rebels, so they did not respond with help. The lack of British intervention gave more voice to Lakshmi's advisers who were advocating for independence. So when the British did arrive in 1858, Jhansi was defended with heavy guns, and the forces were assembled. The battle commenced, with both sides facing heavy fire.

When Lakshmi saw her troops beginning to falter, she appealed to her childhood friend, Tatya Tope, who led an army of over 20,000 to relieve Jhansi; however, this army was defeated. The British then scaled the walls and fighting took place in every street and within the rooms of the palace. Seeing that defeat was imminent, Lakshmi strapped her adopted son onto her back, put on a breastplate, yielded a sword and two revolvers then jumped onto her horse and escaped.

A few guards surrounded Lakshmi as she rode through the night until she made it to Kalpi, where she met Tatya Tope and other rebel forces. But Lakshmi was followed by the British army, and when they did attack Kalpi, it was Lakshmi who commanded the forces against the attackers; however, she was defeated.

Once more, Lakshmi escaped with other leaders, this time to Gwalior, where she joined Indian forces and quickly took control of the city with little opposition. They proclaimed Nana Sahib as Peshwa of a revived Maratha dominion, then it was Lakshmi who first began to prepare against the British forces who were coming to attack the city. She dressed in men's clothes and sat upon her horse, allegedly holding the reins between her teeth so she could fight with a sword in each hand. Lakshmi commanded the army of rebels made up of both men and women, and she fought viciously.

Despite her efforts, the British slaughtered 5,000 Indian soldiers and any Indian over the age of 16. Eventually, Lakshmi was unhorsed by a British soldier, and later, when she sat on a roadside and saw the soldier who had unhorsed her, Lakshmi shot him with a pistol, but not before he had also shot and killed Lakshmi with his firearm.

The British recorded Lakshmi's final battle and described her as "personal, clever and beautiful, and the most dangerous of all Indian leaders", so Lakshmi was loved by her people and acknowledged as brilliant by her enemies on the battlefield. She is remembered as a warrior rani who fought valiantly and died fighting for independence. Although Lakshmi lived for barely three decades, she did do her part for an important cause and established herself as a woman who would not follow the rules women were bound by: she would not cover her face, she demanded to speak with the men around her face to face and she not only fought in battles but also led troops and organised these battles herself.

The Indian Mutiny was far-reaching, and in late 1858, Queen Victoria issued a proclamation pleading for clemency to be shown to those who rose against British rule, but it was not until 1947 that India was fully independent.

Josephine Butler (1828–1906 CE)

The Constant Campaigner

Josephine took part in endless campaigning and fought to protect children from prostitution and for women's rights. While working with suffragists, Josephine did not just demand rights for women like herself, the wealthy and privileged, Josephine wanted to improve the lives of all women. Throughout her life, Josephine suffered terrible grief but dealt with this by throwing herself into charitable work, leading her to influence the laws of her country to make life better for all women.

Josephine was born in Northumberland, as the seventh child of the wealthy Hannah and John Grey, who was the cousin of the reformist British Prime Minister, Lord Grey, who led the country from 1830 to 1834. During Josephine's childhood, John acted as Lord Grey's political agent in Northumberland. In this role, John promoted political opinions, such as support for Catholic emancipation; the abolition of slavery; the repeal of the Corn Laws (tariffs and other trade restrictions on imported food and grain); and reform of the poor laws. Josephine completed her formal education at a boarding school in Newcastle upon Tyne, which she attended for two years, and at home she was exposed to politics and her father's political opinions.

Like all her siblings, Josephine was educated in politics and social issues and was often introduced to influential political visitors. She was also taught about religion by her mother, who particularly emphasised practical action, and this made Josephine extremely faithful. But at the age of 17, Josephine was out riding when she discovered the body of a suicide victim, and this led to a religious crisis. She attended church less frequently, and when she did attend, Josephine was not touched by the vicar's words. From then, Josephine did not identify with a single strand of Christianity and she was critical of the Anglican Church but continued to speak to God in her prayers.

Just two years later, Josephine was again moved by a display of others' suffering when she visited her brother in County Laois in Ireland during the Great Famine. During this visit, Josephine saw first-hand the huge, widespread suffering amongst the poor, which Josephine, from a privileged background, had not witnessed before.

In 1850, Josephine met a scholar named George Butler at a ball. George began sending Josephine love poems, and the pair were married just two years later. The couple lived in Oxford, and George shared Josephine's commitment to liberal reforms and her love of Italian culture. But Josephine suffered because of the misogynist community in Oxford, which she faced despite having a high level of education herself. Josephine also disliked being the only woman at social gatherings due to some of the men's opinions about women, but she felt that arguing with them would not help.

Instead, Josephine focussed on helping the "fallen women" of Oxford, by inviting them to live in her house. One such woman had been seduced and then abandoned, so murdered the baby who she had birthed as a result of the seduction and was serving a prison sentence at Newgate Prison. Josephine and her husband contacted the governor to arrange for this woman to stay in their house for the rest of her sentence.

Josephine's health began to fail in 1856 as a result of a lesion on her lung, which was exacerbated by the damp atmosphere of Oxford, so the couple immediately moved to Bristol. Around this time, Josephine gave birth to a third son, and she continued to support the liberal causes, including that of Giuseppe Garibaldi, who was unifying Italy. But the family were ostracised in Bristol because of their sympathy for the Union side in the American Civil War, and because they expressed support for the anti-slavery movement.

A few years later, Josephine gave birth to a daughter named Eva, but when she was just a young child, Eva fell from the top floor banister onto the stone floor and died three hours later. Josephine was distraught and suffered from disturbed sleep for years. Another of Josephine's children was suffering from diphtheria, so she decided to go to Naples with her son for the both of them to rest, as Josephine was suffering from depression. On the journey, Josephine had a breakdown in which she almost died when the ship faced rough weather.

In 1866, the family moved to Liverpool for George's work, where Josephine continued to mourn her daughter, but she began to focus her emotions on helping the less fortunate. This included visiting the workhouse at Brownlow Hill, which accommodated and employed 5,000 individuals who could not support themselves. Josephine would sit with the women in the cellars of the workhouse and pick oakum with them, whilst praying and talking of the Bible. Some of these women, many of whom were prostitutes dying of venereal disease, took shelter in Josephine's home, but eventually, there were too many women to provide for in the household.

So Josephine set up a hostel for these women which was funded by local men. In 1867, she had established another home providing work, such as sewing and making envelopes. She called it the Industrial Home and it was funded by the workhouse committee and local merchants. But Josephine saw that these hostels could not be a permanent means for employment, and the women would always struggle to find employment while they were not educated.

Josephine began campaigning for women's rights, such as the right to vote and to have a better education. She used the Liverpool hostels as a way for women to find employment while they were being educated in the hostels. With the suffragist, Anne Clough, Josephine established the North of England Council for Promoting the Higher Education of Women and was the president of this until 1873. This helped to raise the status of governesses and female teachers to that of a profession. Josephine then published *The Education and Employment of Women* in 1868, which was her first pamphlet arguing for women to have access to higher education, and a wider range of jobs. It was the first of 90 books and pamphlets she wrote.

To help women gain access to higher education, Josephine petitioned the senate of the University of Cambridge to provide examinations for women, and these were introduced the next year. This campaign to persuade the university to provide more opportunities led to the provision of lectures for women and the establishment of Newnham College, which was just for women. Another campaign Josephine took part in was related to married women, as at this time, women had no separate legal existence and could not own or control their own property, which was known as coverture. So Josephine and a suffragist, Elizabeth Wolstenholme, set up the Married Women's Property Committee. They pressured Parliament to pass the Married Women's Property Act 1882, which allowed married women to own and control property in their own right.

Josephine wrote *Women's Work and Women's Culture* in 1869, but her opinions upset other feminists, including Emily Davies. This is because the other feminists saw women as the same as men, whereas Josephine argued that men and women were different and had different roles in society. However, she argued that the women's role was just as important as men's and that women's suffrage was of vital importance to the morality and welfare of the nation.

Josephine became involved in yet another campaign in 1869 when she found out about the Contagious Diseases Acts, introduced in the 1860s. These acts authorised the police to detain women in specific areas who were thought to be prostitutes without evidence. After the arrest, these women could be given genital examinations, and then held in a lock hospital until they were cured, if they were found to be suffering from sexually transmitted diseases. If the woman refused to be examined, they could be imprisoned and made to do hard labour. Josephine objected to the fact that women, who had been forced into their prostitution by low earning and unemployment, were subjected to this humiliation, whereas their male clients were not.

To change this, Josephine met with Elizabeth Wolstenholme to discuss these acts. Together, they formed the Ladies National Association for the Repeal of the Contagious Diseases Acts, which published a *Ladies Manifesto,* explaining how the acts were discriminatory on the grounds of sex and class. Josephine then toured Britain in 1870, attending 99 meetings in a year, telling working-class family men of the examination these women underwent, which Josephine called "steel rape", and these men were outraged. There was some opposition to Josephine however, at one meeting, some pimps threw cow dung at her; at another, the windows in her hotel were smashed; and at a third meeting, some threatened to burn down the building where the meeting was held.

Everyone was shocked to hear a woman talking so openly about sexual matters and they criticised Josephine's husband for allowing her to do this, even saying it could harm his career, but he continued to support his wife. Eventually, Josephine was successful in her endeavours, as in 1883 the Contagious Diseases Acts were suspended, then repealed in 1886.

While investigating the Contagious Diseases Acts, Josephine found out that some prostitutes were as young as 12 years old, and there was a slave trade of young women and children from England to Europe for prostitution. In 1880, a campaign to combat trafficking led to the removal of the head of the Belgian Police from office, and the trial and imprisonment of his deputy and 12 brothel owners who were involved in the trade. Finally, 34 British girls were released from Belgian brothels.

Five years later, Josephine met Florence Soper Brooth of the Salvation Army. Together they exposed the problem of child prostitution, by persuading the campaigning editor of *The Pall Mall Gazette,* William Thomas Stead, to help. William thought the best way to prove that the purchase of young girls happened in Britain was to buy a girl himself. So William bought a 13-year-old girl from her mother for just £5 and took her to France. After this, he wrote some articles called "The Maiden Tribute of Modern Babylon", exposing the problem of child prostitution in London.

After this publication, Josephine spoke at a meeting in London, calling for more protection for young people, and for the age of consent to be raised. Just days later, the Criminal Law Amendment Act 1885 was passed, raising the age of consent from 13 to 16 years of age. Also, it was made a criminal offence to purchase girls for prostitution by giving them drugs, intimidating them, or using fraud. William was imprisoned for three months for purchasing the 13-year-old girl.

These new laws led to the formation of societies such as the White Cross Army, which aimed to force the closure of brothels and suppress indecent literature. But Josephine warned against this, as the "indecent literature" included information on birth control. Her warnings were unheeded by suffragists such as Millicent Fawcett, who was Josephine's biographer.

Although Josephine made changes in Britain, prostitutes were still allowed to be inspected forcefully in India. So Josephine began yet another campaign.

She could not visit India, as at 62, she felt too old to travel so far, but two American supporters visited on her behalf. Josephine compared the girls affected by this "steel rape" to slaves. This put pressure on MPs, as the British public was outraged by this, leading to the House of Commons in 1888 passing a unanimous resolution repealing the legislation allowing this.

After this feat, George's health began to fail, and Josephine spent her time caring for her husband. In Naples, George had contracted influenza during a pandemic, so the couple quickly returned to Britain, where he died in 1890. After her husband's death, Josephine stopped campaigning so much and moved to Wimbledon with her son and his wife. But she did not completely resign from her campaigning until 1901, then she spent her last few years with her family before she died at home.

Not many non-politicians have made such a profound difference to the laws of their country as Josephine. She influenced the decision to increase the age of consent, repeal the Contagious Diseases Acts in Britain and overseas, enabled women to own their own property, increased the standing of women's professions, and improved their ability to access higher education. Not only this, but even before campaigning, Josephine spent her time providing for, and sheltering, women who were less fortunate than herself in her own home, and enabled them to learn skills to further their chances in life. The death of her daughter pushed Josephine to help people who were looked down upon by society, as she threw herself into charitable work to cope with grief.

Isabella Bird
(1831–1904 CE)

The Adventuring Author

Isabella had a life that many people dream of. She was extremely well-travelled and supported herself by writing about her travels, giving those who could not travel the gift of her experiences. Isabella's travelling started because she sought a better climate for her health difficulties, but this led to a love for travelling, seeing new places, and meeting new people. At this time, it was very rare for a woman to travel, and unheard of to have a woman travelling by herself. So through her love of travel and her determination, Isabella broke down those boundaries.

Isabella was born in Yorkshire to an Anglican clergyman. As a child, Isabella moved around a lot with her upper-class family and eventually settled in Cheshire, where her younger sister, Henrietta, was born. When Isabella was just six, she displayed her critical mind and desire to express herself by confronting her local member of Parliament while he was campaigning. She asked him "did you tell my father my sister was so pretty because you wanted his vote?"

This strength of mind contrasted with Isabella's tiny, frail body, as she suffered from a problem with her spine as well as headaches and insomnia. Eventually, the family moved to Birmingham, because Isabella's father had lost a lot of his congregation due to his controversial views against Sunday labour, but he was still unpopular in their new home. So unpopular that people threw stones and mud at him and hurled insults. So in 1848, the family moved again to Wyton.

Because of her health difficulties, doctors recommended that Isabella should get a lot of fresh air and have an outdoorsy life. This meant that Isabella was able to ride a horse when she was very young and she rowed. The rest of Isabella's schooling was completed at home by her parents, learning botany from her father, and other lessons from her mother, who encouraged Isabella to be an avid reader. At the age of 16, Isabella published her first pamphlet about free trade and continued writing articles. But when she was only 19, Isabella had a fibrous tumour removed from her spine and she continued to suffer from many physical ailments, as well as depression. To help with this, the family spent many summers in Scotland, but later, doctors encouraged Isabella to go on a sea voyage for health purposes.

So in 1854, Isabella began her life of travel. Her father gave her £100, telling her to stay on her voyage until the money had run out, then she got on a boat to the USA, where she stayed with her second cousins. Isabella often wrote home, and these extravagant, detailed letters formed the basis of her first book, *An Englishwoman in America.* But in 1858, Isabella's father died, so she moved to Edinburgh with the remainder of her family. From there, Isabella took short trips to North America and the Mediterranean, and she continued to write so she could support herself after the death of her father.

In 1872, Isabella travelled to Australia but hated it, so instead went to Hawaii, which she loved. This inspired the book, *Six Months in the Sandwich Islands,* published in 1875. While in Hawaii, Isabella was very active, even climbing Mauna Kea and Mauna Loa, two of the volcanoes on the island. Next, Isabella travelled to Colorado, as the air there was said to be good for the sickly. While she was there, Isabella travelled 800 miles in the Rocky Mountains, riding a horse frontwards, rather than side-saddle, to reduce backache.

Throughout her travels in the Rockies, Isabella wrote to her sister, and these letters made up the content of her fourth book, *A Lady's Life in the Rocky Mountains*. As well as riding a horse in the "un-lady-like" manner, Isabella dressed practically, leading *The Times* to claim she was dressing like a man, for which Isabella threatened to sue. This practicality and independence meant that Isabella gained the attention of Jim Nugent, an outlaw with one eye, who was captivated by Isabella. She loved him too; however, he was violent and a drunk, so she refused his marriage proposals, describing him as "a man any woman might love but no sane woman would marry" to her sister.

So eventually, Isabella left Jim, never seeing him again, as he was shot and killed not long after. This love affair may have been Isabella's biggest adventure in the Rockies, but there were others too. At one point she had to ride alone through a blizzard with her eyes frozen shut, and another time, Isabella was forced to spend months snowed in a cabin with only two young men as company.

Isabella returned home after visiting the Rockies but did not stay for long. Soon Isabella was off to travel in Asia after being inspired by *My Circular Notes, 1876,* by John Frances Campbell. Isabella travelled to Japan, China, Korea, Vietnam, Singapore, and Malaya. However, it was around this time that Isabella's sister died of typhoid, so she returned to Britain. While home in 1881, Isabella married Dr John Bishop, who was a surgeon from Edinburgh, who had tended to Isabella's sister while she was sick.

But not long into their marriage, John's health began to deteriorate. In 1886, Isabella took him to southern Europe for a better climate, but John died, leaving Isabella with a large income. After her husband's death, Isabella decided to resume her adventuring, but first, she decided to study medicine and learn photography, so she could illustrate her later books with her own images. So, aged nearly 60, Isabella travelled to India as a missionary.

While there, Isabella was given a piece of land where she built a hospital with 60 beds and a dispensary for women. Isabella completed this while working with Fanny Jane Butler, and they named the hospital the John Bishop Memorial Hospital after her late husband, as he had left money in his will for this purpose. Isabella also co-founded the Henrietta Bird Hospital, in memory of her deceased younger sister.

When Isabella returned to Britain, she gave a speech in the House of Commons about the atrocities being committed against the Armenians in the Middle East by the Ottoman Empire, raising the issue with Prime Minister

William Gladstone. At this time, Isabella was well-known for her adventures and books detailing her travels, so she was the first woman to receive the Honorary Fellowship of the Royal Scottish Geographical Society in 1890, and later she became the first woman to join the Royal Geographical Society.

But as usual, Isabella did not stick around. Instead, she decided to travel in 1894 to Japan, then Korea, but had to leave suddenly because of the outbreak of the Sino-Japanese War, which led to the occupation of Korea by Japan. However, Isabella was not running from the conflict, instead, she went to photograph the Chinese soldiers who were headed to the front, then returned to Korea to view the devastation of the war. In 1897, Isabella returned to Asia, journeying up the Yangtze River in China; however, on this trip, Isabella was attacked by a mob who called her a "foreign devil", then trapped her on the top floor of a house which they set on fire.

Fortunately, Isabella was rescued by some soldiers at the last minute. This was not the only time Isabella had faced danger. Another time, Isabella had been stoned and knocked unconscious. When Isabella returned home after travelling in the mountains bordering Tibet, she wrote *The Yangtze Valley and Beyond,* which was published in 1900, one year before her final trip to Morocco.

When Isabella returned from Morocco, she soon became ill and died in Edinburgh while planning another trip to China. Her bag was even ready and packed for another adventure. Isabella was buried in Edinburgh with her family. Despite her constant ailments and health complaints, Isabella never stayed still to feel sorry for herself. Instead, she enabled herself to thrive, making the most of every day by seeing the world and telling others all about it through her writing.

Dr Mary Edwards Walker
(1832–1919 CE)

The Decorated Surgeon

From a young age, Mary was encouraged to do what she wanted with her life, despite her gender and the societal norms of the time. This led Mary to be determined and have a strong sense of identity, not caring what others thought of her career choice, the way she dressed, or her involvement in the suffrage movement. Mary was very successful in her career, and became the first female surgeon of the Union Army, leading her to become the only woman to ever earn a Medal of Honour for her services.

Mary was born in New York and was the youngest of seven children in her family, which consisted of five sisters and a brother. Their parents were determined to raise all of their children equally, and as "free thinkers", encouraging the children to question the restrictions of society. As well as these modern ideals, Mary's parents opposed slavery and believed that both genders were equal so should be granted the same rights and opportunities. This meant that Mary was not subjected to traditional gender roles, as Mary's mother would often do heavy labour on their farm, whereas her father often helped out with the household chores. All of the children were expected to help work on the farm and were encouraged to wear male clothing because it was more practical. They agreed that female clothes, such as corsets and tight lacing, were too restricting, to the point of being unhealthy.

As a young girl, Mary's parents wanted all their children to be well educated, so in the 1830s they founded the first free schoolhouse in Oswego, where their daughters could be educated alongside their son. After finishing elementary education, Mary attended the Falley Seminary in Fulton, New York, which emphasised social reform in gender roles, education, and hygiene. This encouraged Mary to defy the injustice of the traditional female role. It was around this time when Mary found her passion for medicine while spending her free time reading her father's medical texts on anatomy and physiology.

Once Mary's schooling had finished, she taught at a school in Minetto, New York to save enough money to go to medical college. In this endeavour, Mary was successful, as she graduated with honours as a medical doctor in 1855 from Syracuse Medical College in New York. She was the only woman in her class and graduated six years after the first female doctor in the USA, Elizabeth Blackwell. In the same year, Mary married Albert Miller, another medical school student.

On their wedding day, Mary refused to vow to obey her husband, she kept her last name and she walked down the aisle wearing a short skirt with trousers underneath. The couple then set up a joint practice in Rome, New York, but this did not flourish because patients did not trust a female physician. The marriage also did not flourish, as Albert had been unfaithful, so the pair eventually divorced. In 1860, Mary briefly attended Bowen Collegiate Institute in Iowa, but was suspended because she refused to leave the school's debating society, which had been all-male before her joining.

Mary was known for dressing in an unfeminine manner, as she hated long skirts with petticoats due to their discomfort and because they hindered her mobility. She also found these skirts unhygienic because they would collect dust and dirt from the ground. So Mary began experimenting with skirt length, always wearing men's trousers underneath, and by 1861 her normal attire was to wear a knee-length dress over trousers and suspenders. Mary's family encouraged this fashion choice; however, not everyone else was so supportive.

While a teacher, Mary was once assaulted by a farmer and group of boys, who chased her, then threw eggs at her because of the way she was dressed. Mary was also criticised by her female colleagues, and patients would tease Mary and stare. But Mary did not mind. She tried to reform women's dress so that women could wear clothes allowing for freedom of motion and circulation. With this in mind, Mary wrote to the women's journal, *The Sibyl: A Review of the Tastes, Errors, and Fashions of Society*, about campaigning against women's fashion due to its health issues, the expensive cost, and its contribution to the ending of marriages. This article made Mary popular with feminists and other female physicians.

When the American Civil War broke out in 1861, Mary volunteered to be a surgeon but was rejected due to her being a woman, despite having kept a private practice for years, and instead was offered the role of a nurse. Mary declined and volunteered to be a surgeon for the Union Army as a civilian, but at first, she was only able to practice as a nurse. She did this unpaid work at the Patent Office Hospital in Washington, DC. While there, she set up the Women's Relief Organisation which helped families of the wounded to travel to visit their loved ones. Mary also advocated for patient rights, so counselled soldiers about their rights to refuse an amputation, despite the risk to her job. She claimed that after examining soldiers herself, an amputation was almost always unnecessary.

In 1862, Mary moved to Virginia to treat the wounded soldiers near the frontline, where she saw women serving as soldiers. Delighted to see women doing "men's work", Mary told the press of Frances Hook, who served in the Union forces disguised as a man, to spread awareness of women's input in the Civil War. At one point, Mary wrote to the War Department, asking to work as a spy, but she was declined.

However, after petitioning for years, in 1863, Mary was finally employed as a "Contract Acting Assistant Surgeon (civilian)" by the Army of the Cumberland, becoming the first female surgeon in the army. She worked on the frontlines, often crossing battlefields to treat civilians, including at the Battle of Fredericksburg, and the Battle of Chickamauga. She continued to wear men's clothing to make her work easier; however, she wore her hair long and curled so everyone knew she was a woman, as she was proud to be a woman in this paid role, who was equivalent to lieutenant or captain.

In 1864, Mary was captured by Confederate troops and was arrested as a spy after she had finished helping a Confederate doctor perform an amputation. She was taken to Castle Thunder in Richmond, Virginia, and remained there for four months. While imprisoned, Mary refused to wear the clothes that had been provided for her, and her unusual attire intrigued the Confederate soldiers. Eventually, Mary was released in a prisoner exchange, and she was allegedly delighted to be part of a "man for man" swap.

After this, Mary, at her own request, became a surgeon for female prisoners of war, with the title "Acting Assistant Surgeon". But after only a few months, she became frustrated with the prison officials and prisoners who questioned her care, so transferred to the Refugee Home, where she returned to treating wounded soldiers. When the war ended, she returned home to New York and then was the head of an orphanage.

After the Civil War, Mary was awarded a Medal of Honour from President Andrew Johnson and is still the only woman to have received one. This was bestowed upon Mary for her efforts to treat the wounded during the Civil War. But in 1916, Mary was struck from the Army Medal of Honour Roll, because she had not engaged in actual combat with the enemy. When federal marshals arrived to take away the Medal of Honour from Mary, the 85-year-old met them at the door, wearing the Medal of Honour and holding a 12-gauge shotgun. They allowed her to keep it. For the rest of her life, Mary wore the Medal of Honour. In 1977, years after her death, due to the efforts of her family, her Medal of Honour was officially restored to her, due to Mary's gallantry in war.

Mary had suffered partial muscular atrophy while imprisoned in the Civil War, so was awarded a disability pension, permitting her to $8.50 a month, less than most war widows, but this was raised to $20 a month in 1899. As she was no longer a surgeon in the army, Mary decided to start campaigning for women's rights, starting with dress reform. In 1866, Mary was elected as President of the National Dress Reform Association, and wrote two books in the 1870s discussing women's rights and dress entitled *Hit: Essays on Women's Rights,* and *Unmasked, or the Science of Immorality: To Gentlemen by a Woman Physician and Surgeon.*

On multiple occasions, Mary was arrested for wearing men's clothing, but this did not stop her. In 1870, Mary was arrested in New Orleans because of the way she dressed, and the arresting officer twisted her arm and asked her if she had ever had sex with a man. She was released from custody after being recognised. Even this incident did not deter Mary. When people laughed at her for what she wore, Mary stated "I don't wear men's clothes, I wear my own clothes."

Mary also wrote and lectured, supporting movements related to health care, temperance, and women's rights. She was a member of the suffrage movement, with the view that women had always had the right to vote, Congress just needed to enact the enabling legislation. With this method of gaining suffrage, Mary attempted to register to vote in 1871; however, was turned away. It soon became clear that this method was not working, so the other women decided to adopt the method of a constitutional amendment, which undermined Mary's method. But Mary continued to attend suffrage meetings and distributed literature; however, the rest of the movement ignored her. She ended up receiving a better reception in England for her views on suffrage than in her home country.

Unfortunately, Mary's growing eccentricity isolated her from the other women. She had begun to wear full male attire, including a wing collar, bow tie and top hat. Others were afraid that this eccentricity would damage the suffrage cause as people would not take Mary seriously. Although Mary had become estranged from the suffrage movement, she still wanted to help others, so opened her home to those who were ostracised, harassed or arrested for not conforming to traditional ideas of how people should dress.

Mary died of a long illness at her home, after a fall on the steps of the Capitol Building in Washington DC left her infirm. She was buried in New York in a plain funeral; however, an American flag was draped over her casket, and she was dressed in a black suit rather than a dress. A year later, the Nineteenth Amendment to the United States Constitution guaranteed women the right to vote.

Mary has been remembered for her services, as in World War II a liberty ship, the SS *Mary Walker* was named after her. It is a shame that she never saw women achieve the right to vote, despite her efforts, and at the time of her death, Mary was not decorated for her role in the Civil War.

But Mary is an example of a woman who was not afraid to go against the societal norm, even though she was mocked throughout her life for the way she dressed. Mary seemed to care little about what people thought of her, instead, Mary wanted to save people and to make a change in the world. Perhaps her strength of character was because she was raised by such progressive parents and in a progressive, modern school, encouraging her to fight for every opportunity.

Yaa Asantewaa (1840–1921 CE)

Warrior Queen

Throughout her life, Yaa farmed, was chosen as queen mother, became the Gatekeeper of the Golden Stool, and was a warrior in a battle that she led until her capture. Yaa is an important historical figure who did what she could to prevent the colonisation of her land by the British. She inspired future generations to fight for their freedom and their home, so should be remembered as a strong and powerful female leader.

Yaa was born to the Asante people in Besease, in modern-day Ghana, and had a younger brother who became the Chief of Edweso, a nearby community. Despite being royal, Yaa worked by cultivating crops as a child. Eventually, she entered into a polygamous marriage with a man from Kumasi with whom she had a daughter. At this time, the Asante women had political obligations in legislative and judicial processes. The elderly women in the villages were responsible for looking after women's affairs and could serve as a member of the village council. So Yaa grew up seeing women make political decisions and act as matriarchs, giving her good female role models for her future.

A long time before Yaa was born, the Portuguese travelled to Africa, and they traded on the Gold Coast to other parts of Europe. Then, in the 16th century, the Dutch arrived in Africa. They traded in ivory and gold. But in the 19th century, a British expedition made it to the Gold Coast and developed trade relations with the Fante, another group of African people. It was custom for Europeans to provide for their African allies, so during the Asante-Fante War in 1806 and 1807, the British provided the Fante with military aid, solidifying the Asante antipathy towards the British Gold Coast government.

For the next few years, the British reduced the influence of the Asante, expanding British territory into their lands. In 1894, the British sent a resident minister to Kumasi, but an Asante ruler, King Prempeh I, rejected him, instead, he sent an Asante embassy to London to meet with Queen Victoria. While in London, the Asante embassy gained sympathy from the British media, and several members of Parliament, but many were angry at Prempeh, so decided to bring him to his knees.

Yaa witnessed the Asante being threatened by colonisers and saw the Asantes go through many other difficulties, including a civil war. During this time, Yaa's brother appointed Yaa as the queen mother of his region before he died in 1894. This was an important honour because the queen mother acts as the mother of the reigning king and helps to create public policy and serve as his main advisor and regent in the absence of the king. As the main advisor for the king, Yaa had the second highest position. As queen mother, Yaa had the right to nominate the next ruler, so she nominated her grandson.

But in 1896, the British colonial government was angry at the Asante for sending their embassy to London, so planned to crush them. They sent an official expedition to Kumasi to relay orders from Queen Victoria, and although he had not requested this expedition, Prempeh was ordered to cover the cost, but he refused, which the British expected. They used his refusal to argue that Prempeh was dishonouring Queen Victoria, so had him arrested, and Kumasi seized. Then, Prempeh, along with many other rulers in Asante, including Yaa's grandson, was exiled to Seychelles.

With so many of the Asante rulers exiled, Yaa became the regent of the Ejisu Juaben district, and she and the remaining leaders struggled to unite against the

British, as some even supported the colonisers. Eventually, some united in 1898 and formally requested the return of Prempeh, but they were refused. Then the British demanded to be given the Golden Stool which angered Yaa greatly.

In Asante culture, there are conventional stools occupied by chiefs or district rulers, and a Golden Stool (Asikadwa). This is an emblem of the Asante kingdom, and it was the queen mother's responsibility to be the Gatekeeper of the Golden Stool, as stools were usually connected with women. This was a highly important duty, as the Golden Stool is the most sacred object in Asante culture, as it harbours the souls of all Asante people, living or dead, and they believed it descended from heaven in a cloud of white dust. It is so important that the unity of the kingdom is believed to depend on the safety of the Golden Stool.

Yaa took her role as the Gatekeeper of the Golden Stool very seriously, so was furious when a representative of the British government sat on the Golden Stool, claiming that he had this right as Queen Victoria was the rightful ruler of Asante after the deposition of Prempeh.

After the British demanded the Golden Stool, the remaining members of the Asante government met secretly at Kumasi to decide what to do, but they disagreed, as they knew they would not win against the British. Many even suggested conceding to the British rule. Eventually, in this meeting, Yaa stood and spoke, saying that the Golden Stool meant nothing but money to the white people. She declared that if the Asante men would be cowardly and not fight, then they should exchange their loincloths for her undergarments. Yaa then called upon the women to rise and fight if the men would not, then she grabbed a gun and fired a shot to emphasise her point. This inspired the Asante leaders and they chose her to be the war leader of the Asante fighting force, making Yaa the first and only woman to have had this role in Asante history. This marked the beginning of the 1900 Asante-British War of the Golden Stool, sometimes referred to as the Yaa Asantewaa War.

Yaa led an army of 5,000, making it clear that the Asante were fighting because of the unlawful arrest and exile of Prempeh, and because of the British demanding the Golden Stool. The army besieged the Kumasi Fort for weeks so eventually the British ran out of supplies and disease was breaking out amongst them. Some fled to the Asante side. Their suffering led to the British suing for a ceasefire, so Yaa agreed, on the condition that the British must release Prempeh and guarantee that their southern allies would respect the rights of the Asante traders. Some of these demands were accepted, but the British refused to release Prempeh, so Yaa continued the siege.

Somehow, word got back to the British government, so they mobilised 1,400 troops from the other colonies in British West Africa. The Asante were outmanned and outgunned, soon Yaa and 15 of her advisers were captured and exiled to Seychelles, which marked the last battle in the Anglo-Asante wars. In 1902, the British seized the land that the Asante army had been protecting, making it a protectorate of the British Crown. However, despite the Asante's failure, the British never laid hands on the Golden Stool, as it had been hidden prior to the battle.

After years of exile, Yaa died in her sleep in Seychelles. Just three years later, other members of the exiled Asante court were allowed to return to Asante. Yaa's remains were also returned so that she could have a proper royal burial. In 1957, the Asante protectorate gained independence as part of Ghana, which was the first African nation in Sub-Saharan Africa to achieve this, and for her efforts, Yaa is immortalised in a song, translated as follows:

Yaa Asantewaa
The woman who fights before cannons
You have accomplished great things
You have done very well.

Although Yaa's army failed, she is remembered as a great leader, who did all she could to maintain the independence of her nation, when others were willing to give up. She inspired her people to rebel in the future and to fight for their freedom, and fought in a battle which she led. Yaa was an emphatic and inspirational speaker, a diplomatic and strong leader, and a fierce woman, who led her people to rebel.

Edmonia Lewis (1844–1907 CE)

Sculptor of Abolitionists

Despite a few setbacks, such as not being able to graduate from college, Edmonia constantly followed her passion, even travelling from Boston to Italy to pursue it. This determination led her to become the first professional African-American sculptor; however, her motivation was simply to excel at her profession. Although Edmonia faced racism throughout her life, she would do what she could to not let this be a detriment to her passion.

Edmonia was born in New York to a free African American father and a Native American mother, but by the age of nine, Edmonia was already orphaned. So Edmonia, at this time known as her Native American name, Wildfire, was adopted by her two maternal aunts, along with her half-brother, Samuel, known as Sunrise. With her aunts, Edmonia sold Ojibwe baskets and other items, such as embroidered blouses, to tourists who were visiting Niagara Falls. While living with her mother's family, Edmonia would spend her free time roaming the forests and fishing, but after a few years, Samuel left to mine gold in California.

In 1856, Samuel made a fortune in the Californian gold rush, so financed his 12-year-old sister's schooling. Edmonia enrolled in a pre-college programme in an abolitionist school. She claims that she was described as "wild" at school; however, her academic record states that her grades, conduct and attendance were all excellent. While there, Edmonia learned Latin, French, grammar, arithmetic, drawing, composition and public speaking.

When she was 15, Edmonia attended Oberlin Academy Preparatory School, then attended Oberlin College in Ohio, which was known for its acceptance of minorities and women, and it was one of the first colleges to accept these demographics. It was at this time when Edmonia changed her name to Mary Edmonia Lewis. At college, Edmonia was particularly interested in the fine arts. She boarded with the abolitionists Reverend John Keep and his wife, with a few other women. Unfortunately, Edmonia was still subject to daily discrimination and was rarely able to participate in the classes.

Edmonia's college life ended rather prematurely. One day, Edmonia served warm spiced wine to two of her friends who were boarding with her, and they both later became seriously ill with poison found in their system. Not much was done about this incident for a while, even though it was suspected that Edmonia had poisoned her friends. However, one night Edmonia was walking home alone when she was dragged into a field, beaten, then left for dead. Then the local authorities arrested Edmonia and charged her with poisoning her friends.

Edmonia's court hearing was delayed due to the seriousness of her injuries, but eventually, she went to court and was defended by John Mercer Langston, an Oberlin graduate who was also of racially mixed heritage. After a lengthy and publicised trial, Edmonia was found innocent; however, she was socially isolated for the remainder of her time at college. Later, Edmonia was accused of stealing art supplies, but was acquitted due to a lack of evidence.

Just months later, Edmonia was charged with aiding and abetting burglary. Either because she was forced or due to frustration with the constant accusations, Edmonia left college and was unable to graduate.

Despite her lack of qualifications, Edmonia was encouraged and financed by her brother to move to Boston to begin her artistic career. One day, Edmonia, encountered a statue of Benjamin Franklin in Boston and had never seen anything like it. She declared that she too could make a "stone man", and thus began her career as a sculptor. However, this tale may be exaggerated or false because after studying art for years in college she would probably have come across a sculpture before.

Now knowing she desired to sculpt, Edmonia just needed a teacher. However, this was more difficult than expected, as three sculptors refused to instruct Edmonia. Finally, she was introduced to Edward Augustus Brackett, who specialised in marble portrait busts. He lent Edmonia fragments of sculptures for her to copy in clay, and he helped her to craft her own sculpting tools. Eventually, Edmonia was ready to sell her first piece, a sculpture of a woman's hand, which she sold for $8.

After this, Edmonia spent her time sculpting medallion portraits of abolitionists. But soon, Edmonia decided to travel to Europe, declaring that "the land of liberty had no room for a coloured sculptor". She sold a portrait bust of Colonel Robert Gould Shaw, a white leader of the all African-American 54th Regiment of the Civil War, and used this money to move to Europe in 1865.

Edmonia travelled to London, Paris and Florence, but eventually settled in Rome, where she worked in the studio of an established sculptor, Hiram Powers. From there, Edmonia entered a circle of expatriate artists, receiving support from Charlotte Cushman, an actress from Boston, and Maria Weston Chapman, a worker for the anti-slavery cause. Edmonia loved Rome because there was less explicit racism and because she was a Catholic, so felt closer to her faith.

While in Rome, Edmonia quickly learned Italian and became close with many female American sculptors. Rome was popular with sculptors at the time because of the availability of fine white marble products, and at the time, they favoured the neoclassical style. Most sculptors employed Italian workmen and stone carvers, who could transfer a sculptor's plaster model into the finished marble products. But Edmonia did not do this, partly because she lacked the money, also because she did not want to give people the opportunity to claim that her work was not authentically her own.

As an artist, Edmonia was known for her portrait busts of abolitionists and subjects depicting her African American and Native American ancestry, as well as mythological and religious subjects. In 1867, Edmonia sculpted *Forever Free*, which depicts an African American man and woman emerging from the bonds of slavery. The sculpture demonstrates a positive, hopeful change for black people, as the man is holding his chained hand up high, and the woman is praying. A sculpture depicting Edmonia's Native American heritage is *The Old*

Arrow Maker, which shows a father teaching his daughter to make an arrow. This represents a portion of the story of Longfellow's *The Song of Hiawatha,* a poem inspiring several of Edmonia's works.

This piece is particularly important, as white people had previously portrayed Native Americans as violent and uncivilised; however, Edmonia portrayed them as peaceful, civilised people. What some believe to be Edmonia's masterpiece is her 3,015-pound marble sculpture called *The Death of Cleopatra,* which took Edmonia about four years to complete. It portrays the Egyptian queen while she is dying.

Unlike the Victorian custom of displaying death as refined and composed, Edmonia contrasts this by showing Cleopatra as dishevelled in her moment of death. This portrayal of inelegance was controversial, as some thought it too graphic; however, most were enthralled by this monumental sculpture.

In 1901, Edmonia moved to London and lived quietly, as the neoclassical style had gone out of fashion. She died of chronic Bright's disease, an inflammation of the kidney, and was buried in a Catholic cemetery in London. Although Edmonia faced discrimination and did not gain qualifications from her schooling, she was hugely successful in her career. Edmonia was fortunate to have the encouragement and support of her brother and enjoyed using tales of her Native American upbringing to support her business. It is unfair that Edmonia felt she had to leave her country to be successful due to the colour of her skin.

Edmonia was dedicated to her passion and refused to be praised simply because of her skin colour, she said, "some praise me because I am a coloured girl, and I don't want that kind of praise. I had rather you would point out my defects, for that will teach me something." This demonstrates Edmonia's commitment to sculpting and motivation to improve, as well as her desire to not let her skin colour influence the way people saw her art.

Emily Hobhouse
(1860–1926 CE)

The Noblest and Bravest of Women

Emily was a campaigner for many causes including female suffrage, peace, and improved treatment of Boer women and children in the Second Boer War. Whenever Emily saw an injustice happen in the world, she would do what she could to put a stop to it, even if it meant isolating herself from her own country. But this did not matter to Emily while innocent people were being treated poorly. Emily is well-known and loved in South Africa for her efforts in the Second Boer War, but should be a household name for her determination and sense of justice.

Born in St Ives, Cornwall, Emily was the daughter of the first Archdeacon of Bodmin. Although her family was well to do, Emily had a limited education at home, and she found life very boring because she itched to be out in the world helping people. However, her father would not allow this, instead, she was bound to help out at Sunday school and sing and play the organ at church. Sadly, when

Emily was just 20, she lost both her sister and her mother, so Emily's job was to take on parochial duties, which consisted of visiting parishioners and organising events for the church. But soon, Emily's father grew sick, so she spent the next 15 years nursing him.

When Emily's father died in 1895, she wasted no time in leaving the country to perform welfare work amongst Cornish mineworkers who had migrated to America and were struggling with poverty. While she was on this first adventure, Emily met John Carr Jackson, and the pair soon were engaged to marry. They bought a ranch in Mexico together; however, their relationship failed, and Emily lost most of her money on the land in Mexico, so she returned to England in 1898.

Despite losing her money, Emily was still determined to do welfare work and campaign, so she became the chair of the People's Suffrage Federation, supported by her aunt and uncle. This position enabled Emily to campaign for all men and women to achieve the vote, not just men or those with property. During this time, Emily was also elected as the executive of the Women's Industrial Council, where she investigated child labour.

Emily's most notable work took place during the Second Boer War (1899-1902). This war broke out between Britain and the Boer Republics in South Africa because Britain rejected the Transvaal ultimatum. This ultimatum demanded that all disputes between Britain and the Boer Republics must be settled by arbitration and that the British troops must stop building forces in the region and withdraw.

When the war broke out, Emily was quickly invited to become the secretary of the women's branch of the South African Conciliation Committee. In this position, she organised protests against the war, such as a mass meeting in London, where women protested the actions of the British Army in South Africa. Emily also set up the South African Women and Children Distress Fund, to raise funds for the relief of the women and children living in South Africa whose lives had been upturned by the war. However, very few people were willing to contribute to this fund except for members of the Society of Friends.

In 1900, Emily travelled to South Africa herself to supervise the distribution of the funds she had raised. She hoped to provide clothes and food to the women and children who were kept in a concentration camp by the British Army. But when Emily arrived in South Africa, she discovered that there was not just one concentration camp, but many more which were holding thousands of innocent

South African women and children in disgusting conditions. This was due to Lord Kitchener's "scorched earth" policy, which involved the killing of crops and livestock, poisoning of wells, and burning farms, so the women and children were forced into concentration camps.

Furious at her discovery, Emily persuaded the authorities to allow her to visit the concentration camps so that she could provide relief and report on the conditions at the camps. While in these camps, Emily discovered overcrowding and poor hygiene due to neglect and a lack of resources for the people. For example, they were not allowed soap because it was deemed a luxury. These dire conditions meant that diseases such as measles, bronchitis, pneumonia, dysentery, and typhoid were out of control, causing almost 28,000 deaths during the 18 months the camps were in operation. 24,000 of those people were children under the age of 16.

Emily met one young girl called Lizzie van Zyl while she was visiting, who was a seriously sick and malnourished seven-year-old girl. The child was placed on the lowest rations and went to hospital within a month because she was starving. As she was unable to speak English, the hospital staff labelled her as an "idiot". One day Lizzie cried out for her mother, so an Afrikaner woman comforted her, saying she would see her mother again soon, but this kind lady was interrupted and told not to interfere with Lizzie because she was a nuisance. The young girl died soon later.

Cases like Lizzie van Zyl and thousands of other children deeply upset and angered Emily. An unknown source described her as such: "None of the camp commandants were quite sure who this well-dressed, well-connected woman was, but they knew she was angry and they were not about to say no to her."

Emily worked hard to help these people while in South Africa, managing to list soap as a necessity, along with straw, more tents and more kettles to boil drinking water. She also gave out clothes and supplied pregnant women with mattresses after seeing that they had to sleep on the hard ground. In 1901, Emily reported back to the British, with disturbing descriptions of the suffering she had witnessed at the hands of the British. She also wrote several letters to newspapers about the treatment of those in the camps and included many testimonies from Boers describing the suffering they were facing. But no one would take her seriously, so Emily travelled back to England to speak to the government herself.

When she returned, Emily faced a lot of criticism from the British government and the media for fraternising with the enemy. However, she did gain support from the Liberal leader and gained more funding for the Boers, particularly after lecturing the Secretary of State for War for two hours. Also, Emily had bombarded the news with letters, so the concentration camps had become an international scandal. Eventually, a formal commission was set up to investigate Emily's claims, and this was headed by Millicent Fawcett. However, Emily was not permitted to be part of this commission due to her upsetting officialdom, and because she was unpopular with members of Parliament, with Lord Kitchener referring to her as "that bloody woman".

This did not stop her from trying though. Emily did return to Cape Town in 1901, but was not able to land and was deported with no reason given. When Emily refused to go back to England, she was tied up by the soldiers, and when she struggled against them, they called her a lunatic, leading Emily to respond with "Sir, the lunacy is on your side and those with whose commands you obey."

After the Fawcett Commission corroborated Emily's claims, Emily was able to return to South Africa after the war in 1903 to assist the rehabilitation of the people. She set up a home industries scheme, teaching young women spinning, weaving, and lace so they could have an occupation, and set up schools for the children, particularly encouraging the education of women and girls. Emily remained there for years until she returned to England in 1908 due to a heart condition.

In 1913, Emily returned to South Africa for the unveiling of a monument at Bloemfontein to the Boer women and children who had died. On this visit, she met Gandhi, who asked Emily for her help with the suffering Indian community, so Emily helped him to meet with Prime Minister Botha to discuss the situation. Gandhi greatly appreciated Emily's support, and when she died years later, he wrote in her obituary:

Miss Hobhouse was one of the noblest and bravest of women. She worked without thinking of any reward… She loved her country and because she loved it, she could not tolerate any injustice caused by it… She had a soul that could defy the might of Kings and Emperors with their armies.

When World War I broke out in 1914, Emily, a staunch pacifist, immediately tried to bring about peace, writing letters to Lloyd George and the newspapers arguing for peace. After this, Emily travelled around Europe, attending meetings where she spoke about peace. Emily even became the only known British civilian to visit Germany at this time, where she spoke very amicably to the German Foreign Minister to find a way to negotiate peace. From this meeting, Emily believed he wanted her to act as an intermediately between Germany and Britain, but when Emily returned home, no one would listen to her.

It seemed that no man would listen to Emily while she encouraged her leaders to negotiate peace. So as Christmas approached in 1914, Emily organised the writing, signing, and publishing of the Open Christmas Letter. It was a message of peace addressed to the women of Germany and Austria from 100 British women, saying "do not let us forget our very anguish unites us... We must all urge that peace be made. We are yours in the sisterhood of sorrow." By March, a similar letter was published from a group of German and Austrian women to the British. Although this letter may not have led to the end of the war, it is a heart-warming story of women from opposing sides coming together in peace, united by their grief.

When the war ended in 1918, Emily set up funds to help the children affected by the war. This included the fund to help "enemy" children, the fund to Aid Swiss Relief, and she chaired the Russian Babies Fund and represented the Save the Children Fund. These projects helped to feed thousands of women and children daily through central Europe, and South Africa contributed significantly towards this effort. For her work in helping the European children affected by the war, Emily was honoured by the City of Leipzig and the German Red Cross.

After she had become too ill to continue her work, Emily was made an honorary citizen of South Africa for her humanitarian work, and they collected £2,300 to give to Emily to thank her. She was delighted by this gift, and considered giving it back or using it for campaigning, but eventually decided to accept the gift and bought herself a house in Cornwall. When Emily died, her ashes were scattered at the Women's Monument in Bloemfontein in South Africa.

Emily was both greatly loved and loathed by her country. But she is an inspiration for continuing to work to support others, even though she knew it would turn her country and government against her. Although she is relatively unknown in her own country, in South Africa Emily is greatly loved. Her unworn wedding veil is hung in the head office of Oranje Vrouevereniging in South Africa, as a symbol of Emily uplifting the women there. She worked tirelessly throughout her life for others, despite constant health problems, and would never give up on the prospect of peace. Even during a war, Emily would do what she could to limit the suffering of the innocents involved on both sides.

Nellie Bly
(1864–1922 CE)

The Greatest Journalist of Her Time

Nellie was born with the name Elizabeth Jane Cochran, but she is known as her pen name, as it was as a journalist when Nellie changed the world. Although she came from humble beginnings, Nellie overcame adversity and misogyny to become a great journalist, reporting on events that mattered, such as life for Mexicans and those living in mental health asylums. This led Nellie to launch a new kind of investigative journalism, and later, she broke a world record by circumnavigating the globe in just 72 days.

Nellie was born in Pennsylvania and was one of 15 siblings and half-siblings, and experienced crisis at the age of just six years old when her father died suddenly. Because the death was so sudden, there was no will, so the family was left with no legal claim to his estate, causing a financial crisis. But as a young girl, Nellie seemed carefree and was known as "Pinky" because she wore a lot of pink as a child. However, as a teenager, Nellie reinvented herself as the sophisticated Elizabeth Cochrane while attending Indiana Normal School to become a teacher. But Nellie had to drop out of higher education after just one term because the family could not afford it, so Nellie moved to Pittsburgh in 1880 with her mother and helped her to run a boarding-house. Around this time, Nellie's mother remarried; however, divorced quickly because her husband was abusive.

Despite her lack of education, Nellie began her career in journalism in a particularly impressive way. She read an article in *The Pittsburgh Dispatch* entitled "What Girls Are Good For", which stated that women exist to give birth and run a house, and it labelled working women as a "monstrosity". Nellie would not endure this insult, so responded under the pseudonym "Lonely Orphan Girl". The editor was so impressed that he asked the writer to identify herself. When Nellie did so, he offered her the chance to write another piece for the newspaper under the same pseudonym.

So Nellie wrote a piece called "The Girl Puzzle", which discussed how divorce affected women and called for divorce reforms. The 21-year-old Nellie impressed the editor again, so he offered her a full-time job at *The Pittsburgh Dispatch*, and as it was customary for women newspaper writers to use pen names, they chose the name "Nellie Bly".

While working at *The Pittsburgh Dispatch*, Nellie focused on the lives of working women, particularly factory workers. However, when the factory owners began complaining about this, Nellie was only allowed to write the women's pages, covering fashion, society, and gardening. But Nellie soon grew bored of this, as she wanted to write about important topics which would appeal to both genders. So Nellie set off to Mexico to report about the lives of the Mexican people, exposing the oppression under Dictator Porfirio Díaz. Her findings were published in a book called *Six Months in Mexico,* which included her protests of the imprisonment of a journalist who had criticised the Mexican government. The Mexican authorities threatened Nellie with arrest, forcing her to flee home where she accused the Mexican dictator of being tyrannical and controlling the press.

In 1887, Nellie grew bored of working at *The Pittsburgh Dispatch,* so moved to New York City to pursue more exciting work. However, Nellie lacked money and struggled to find work, as she was rejected many times by different editors due to them not wanting to hire a woman. So Nellie realised it was time to stop asking, and instead, demanded work. She stormed into the office of the *New York World* and demanded to write a story about the immigrant experience in the United States. Although the editor was not interested in this idea, he did offer Nellie a job and assigned her to investigate a mental hospital in New York, called the Women's Lunatic Asylum on Blackwell's Island, which had been accused of neglect and brutality.

Nellie did not just investigate from the outside, instead, she faked insanity to gain admission to the asylum so she could expose the treatment of the patients first-hand. To feign insanity, Nellie stayed up all night so she appeared wide-eyed and disturbed, then claimed that the other women in the boarding house where she was residing were mad and refused to sleep. Eventually, Nellie disturbed the other women so much that the police were called and Nellie was taken away. After being examined by a police officer, a judge and a doctor, Nellie was committed to the asylum for 10 days before the *New York World* asked for her release.

Nellie wrote a six-piece exposé about her experiences called *Ten Days in a Mad-House.* In this, Nellie describes the terrible treatment that the patients faced, such as not being given water even when they cried out for it until their throats were parched. The food that the patients were given was spoiled and mouldy, and Nellie was even served a piece of bread with a spider baked inside. Although Nellie would not eat the disgusting food, other women were so hungry that they ate quickly and without complaint.

To make matters worse, the asylum was built to hold 1,000 patients, but there were 1,600 living there, making it overcrowded, and diseases were common. There were just 16 doctors to care for all of these patients, and their treatment was harsh. The patients had to take ice-cold baths and remain in wet clothes for hours, and had to sit in silence and completely still on benches for 12 hours at a time. They were also tethered together with ropes and forced to pull carts around and clean the building and their nurses' rooms and clothes. Those who complained or resisted were beaten, and some were even threatened with sexual violence.

Many of the patients were not even insane. Nellie stopped faking insanity as soon as she entered the asylum, but everything she did was perceived as the actions of an insane person. Others living in the asylum were immigrants who struggled to communicate and so were placed in the asylum. Nellie also met women who had been committed to the asylum simply for being poor and having no family to support them. Nellie pointed out that many arrived in the asylum with no mental illness, but while there had psychological damage inflicted upon them.

After the publication of Nellie's exposé, there was a grand jury investigation of the asylum, which corroborated with Nellie's findings, so brought about improvements in asylums across the country. This included giving more funds to the care of the mentally ill, additional physician appointments, stronger supervision of nurses and other healthcare workers, and regulations to prevent overcrowding and fire hazards.

In 1888, Nellie started a new assignment, which involved her taking a trip around the world to turn the fictional book, *Around the World in Eighty Days*, written by Jules Verne, into fact. For the 40,070 km journey, Nellie packed lightly, taking just the dress she was wearing, a coat, a few changes of underwear, a small bag of toiletries and some money in a bag around her neck. Another woman, Elizabeth Bisland, was sent by *Cosmopolitan* around the world in the opposite direction to attempt to beat Nellie. However, Nellie did not learn about this competition until reaching Hong Kong and claimed to not be bothered about racing.

Some reports suggest otherwise, as Nellie allegedly said, "I'd rather go back to New York dead than not a winner", while in Japan. To keep people interested in the journey, *New York World* organised a "Nellie Bly Guessing Match", in which readers estimated Nellie's arrival time to the second, and the winner was prized a free trip to Europe. On her journey, Nellie met Jules Verne, visited a leper colony in China and bought a fez-wearing monkey in Singapore.

Eventually, she completed her circumnavigation in 72 days, 6 hours, 11 minutes and 14 seconds, which was a world record, beating Elizabeth Bisland by four days. When Nellie arrived home, she was greeted by brass bands and fireworks; however, just months later, George Francis Train beat her world record by completing the journey in 67 days. After returning to New York, Nellie wrote *Around the World in 72 Days,* which was a bestseller.

In 1895, Nellie married a millionaire manufacturer named Robert Seaman, who was 40 years her senior. Because of his failing health, Nellie left journalism. When he died in 1904, she took over his company, Iron Clad Manufacturing Company, which made steel containers such as milk cans and boilers. While in charge, Nellie gave her employees several perks unheard of at the time, including fitness gyms, libraries and healthcare, but this grew expensive. Eventually,

Nellie returned to journalism, covering World War I, writing stories on Europe's Eastern Front. She became the first woman and one of the first foreigners to visit the war zone between Serbia and Austria, but she was arrested when she was mistaken for a British spy.

In 1913, Nellie covered the Woman Suffrage Procession for the *New York Evening Journal,* using the headline "Suffragists Are Men's Superiors". In this, she accurately predicted that it would be 1920 before women in the United States would be given the right to vote.

After a busy life of writing and adventure, Nellie died of pneumonia at the age of just 57. Although she died at a relatively young age, Nellie achieved more than most do in a lifetime. She was the head of a company and an incredibly successful journalist. In her journalism, Nellie put herself at risk to give voice to those who needed support, providing awareness for the Mexicans living under an oppressive dictator's rule, and women living in a mental health asylum. Coming from financial troubles and a lack of education, Nellie had to constantly work hard to achieve her goals in life, so that she could become the best female journalist of her time.

Edith Cavell (1865–1915 CE)

Nurse to All

As a nurse, Edith's purpose in life was to help people. She did this without any discrimination, as despite the war, she believed that everyone was entitled to be cared for. Not only did she treat injured soldiers on both sides of the war, but Edith also enabled hundreds of Allied soldiers to escape German-occupied Brussels. This braveness and kindness meant that Edith's death incited international fury, strengthening the Allied cause.

Edith was born near Norwich, England, and was the daughter of a reverend. She had three younger siblings, and the four of them had an idyllic childhood, drawing and painting flowers in the summer, and ice skating in the winter. As for her education, Edith was educated at Norwich High School for Girls, then in boarding schools. After her education was completed, Edith worked as a governess in Belgium; however, soon had to return home when her father became ill. Throughout her father's sickness, Edith nursed him until he eventually recovered. This is thought to be where Edith's interest in nursing began.

In 1896, Edith applied to become a nurse probationer at the London Hospital, then worked in many hospitals throughout England as a nurse. Edith also spent time as a private travelling nurse, treating patients suffering from cancer, gout, pneumonia, pleurisy, eye issues, and appendicitis in their homes. When there was a typhoid outbreak in 1897 in Maidstone, Edith was there to help and was awarded the Maidstone Medal for her skills and efforts.

At this point, nursing was relatively new as a profession, as it had previously been dominated by nuns who had little training. But in 1907, Edith was recruited as matron of a new nursing school in Brussels, the Berkendael Institute, which was Belgium's first training hospital and school for nurses. Within the year, Edith was training nurses for three hospitals, 24 schools, and 14 kindergartens in Belgium, helping to improve the standard of nursing.

However, in 1914, the First World War broke out. At the time, Edith was visiting her widowed mother in Norfolk but knew that she would be needed as a nurse. So Edith returned to Brussels when she heard of the threat of the advancing German troops, and the swift German occupation of Brussels. There was a huge demand for nurses at this time, so Edith felt it was her duty to return to her hospital, which had been taken over by the Red Cross, which treated civilians and casualties from both sides.

At the beginning of the war, Edith was asked to help two wounded British soldiers trapped behind German lines after the Battle of Mons. She treated these men in her hospital, then arranged to have them smuggled out of Belgium into the neutral Netherlands. From this point on, Edith became part of a network that sheltered Allied soldiers and Belgians eligible for military service and enabled their escape by providing them with false papers, money to reach the Dutch frontier, and guides to navigate the border. Over 11 months, Edith helped roughly 200 British, French, and Belgian soldiers to escape, and many of these had written to Edith to thank her after they managed to return to Britain. Also, Edith was happy to treat German and Austrian soldiers, which drew criticism; however, Edith was a nurse and believed it was her duty to treat anyone who was sick. She saw beyond the uniform and focused upon the person instead.

Despite her treatment of German and Austrian soldiers, the German authorities were becoming suspicious of Edith, partly because she was outspoken about her beliefs. In 1915, she was arrested for war treason, despite not being a German national, and charged with harbouring Allied soldiers. For 10 weeks, Edith was held in Saint-Gilles prison, the last two weeks were in solitary confinement. When questioned, Edith admitted to the German police that she had been instrumental in conveying about 60 British soldiers, 15 French soldiers, and 100 French and Belgian citizens of military age, to the frontier and sheltered them in her house. This meant that when court-marshalled, Edith was found guilty for aiding British and French soldiers to cross the Dutch border and eventually enter Britain. The penalty for this crime was death.

There was international outrage at this sentence. The First Geneva Convention normally guarantees the protection of medical personnel, but this protection is forfeit if it was used as a cover for belligerent action. So technically, the execution of Edith was legal. The British could do nothing to help Edith. But as the United States had not yet joined the war, they applied diplomatic pressure, claiming that executing Edith would further harm Germany's reputation. Spain also protested Edith's execution. Many stated that Edith should be pardoned because of her honesty and because she had saved so many lives on both sides, but the Military Governor of Brussels ordered the immediate implementation of the death penalty.

The night before Edith's execution, she claimed to have been thankful to have 10 weeks of quiet to get ready for death, and her final words are recorded to be: "Ask Father Gahan to tell my loved ones later on that my soul, as I believe, is safe, and that I am glad to die for my country." The next morning at the Brussels firing range, 16 men formed two firing squads who carried out the execution.

After the war, Edith's body was taken back to Britain on the same train that carried the Unknown Warrior, and she became the first female commoner to be given a state funeral at Westminster Abbey. She now shares this honour with Lady Diana Spencer and Prime Minister Margaret Thatcher. Throughout the remainder of the war, Edith's story became propaganda for military recruitment in Britain, as many saw her as a martyr. Her death had caused outrage in many neutral countries, so her image was used to demonstrate German barbarianism and moral depravity.

Before her death, Edith was quoted to have said "I must have no hatred or bitterness towards anyone." This quote summarises Edith's values as, despite the war, Edith saw no one as an "enemy", but instead saw people as simply people who needed her help and nursing skills, which she willingly provided, and she was executed for this display of humanity.

Edith Wilson
(1872–1961 CE)

The Secret President

Sometimes referred to as the "secret president", and the "first woman to run the government", Edith was a very powerful and controversial First Lady of the United States. When she married Woodrow Wilson, Edith knew nothing about politics and cared little, but she became incredibly involved in the running of government, particularly after her husband's disabling stroke, which made Edith the sole link between president and government.

Edith was born in Virginia and had 10 siblings. Although the family was impoverished, they were proud to be direct descendants of Matoaka, otherwise known as Pocahontas. After the American Civil War, Edith's father could no longer pay taxes on all his properties after the abolition of slavery, so the family moved to Wytheville and he supported his family by becoming a circuit court judge. Edith's household was full of people. In addition to her many siblings,

Edith lived with her grandparents, aunts, and cousins. Many women in Edith's family lost their husbands in the war, so chose to be supported by Edith's father.

Unfortunately, Edith's family were proud southerners who justified slave ownership. They claimed that their slaves were content and had little desire for freedom; however, Edith's views on the matter are uncertain.

Unlike her sisters, who were enrolled in local schools, Edith was taught how to read and write at home and had little education as a young girl. Edith's main teacher was her bedridden grandmother, who taught her to read, write, and speak French. She also learned to make dresses and inherited her grandmother's trait of making quick judgements and having strong opinions. In exchange for the tutoring, Edith washed her grandmother's clothing, put her to bed at night, and looked after her canaries. Edith's father also helped to educate his daughter by reading classic English literature to the family at night and allowed Edith to accompany him on travels. When she was not learning or doing chores, Edith attended church and became a lifelong Episcopalian.

At the age of 15, Edith was finally able to attend school at Martha Washington College, which was a finishing school known for its music programme. But Edith hated it. This is partly because she was undisciplined and unprepared as a student, but she also disliked the food and found the rooms too cold, and the curriculum too challenging and strict. So after one semester, Edith left, and years later enrolled in Powell's School for Girls, which Edith described as the happiest time of her life. But this school had to close because the headmaster suffered an accident costing him a leg, and Edith's father refused to spend any more money on his daughter's education, as he thought his sons' education was more important.

In 1896, Edith married Norman Galt, a jeweller who she met in Washington DC when visiting her sister. The couple had one baby, who was born in 1903, but the child died when he was just days old, leaving Edith unable to have more children. Then in 1908, Norman died unexpectedly, leaving Edith with a good inheritance. With this money, Edith paid off all of their debts, then toured Europe after hiring a manager to oversee her late husband's business. Edith became the first woman in town who drove her own car. She was so well-known for this that the police officers would often stop other traffic to let her pass.

Despite Edith's wealth, she was looked down upon by high society because her wealth was derived from a retail store. At this time, Edith had little interest in politics and did not even know who the 1912 election candidates were, which becomes less ignorant after considering that women were not yet given the right to vote.

One day in 1915, Edith was out on a muddy hike with her friends, including the White House physician, President Woodrow Wilson's cousin, and another friend. Afterwards, the cousin of the president suggested that the group had tea at the White House, which they did, and this is where Edith first met Woodrow Wilson. Woodrow was struck by this tall woman with striking blue eyes and black hair and soon fell in love with her, despite being recently widowed. Just weeks after meeting, Woodrow and Edith were engaged to marry. The couple went on romantic dinners and sent each other suggestive love notes, discussing political opinions.

This panicked political advisors as Woodrow was trusting an unknown woman with classified information. Also, he was up for re-election in 1916, and they feared that remarrying so soon after his wife's death would lead to lowered popularity with the American public. This was certainly worth worrying about as there were already scandalous rumours spreading. Some claimed that Edith and Woodrow's relationship began before the death of his wife. Others even believed that Edith and Woodrow murdered his wife.

These rumours had the potential to ruin both of their reputations, so Woodrow suggested that Edith back out of the engagement to protect herself. But Edith would not leave her betrothed and instead suggested that they marry after a year of mourning for Woodrow's wife. But many in government were still suspicious of Edith and tried to oust her by writing fake love letters as if written from Woodrow to a woman named Mary Peck, with whom he had previously had an affair. They hoped that when they released these letters to the press, Edith would be humiliated and leave the White House for good. But Edith and Woodrow's wedding went ahead in a small ceremony at Edith's home with about 40 guests. Woodrow was also successful in the 1916 election and remained the President of the United States for another term.

By 1917, Woodrow had involved his country in the First World War, so as the first lady, Edith's duty was to set a good example for the rationing effort. She observed gasless Sundays, meatless Mondays, and wheatless Wednesdays to encourage the American women to economise on food so that the soldiers could eat better. With her step-daughters, Edith volunteered at a Red Cross canteen and set up a Red Cross sewing group, which made pyjamas and woollen hats for the soldiers serving overseas. Edith then replaced the White House lawnmowers with sheep and when it was time for shearing, she auctioned the wool, giving the $50,000 it made in profits to the war effort.

In addition to these efforts at home, Edith also supported her husband throughout the war by accompanying him to Europe in 1918 and 1919, to visit troops and to sign the Treaty of Versailles at the end of the war. This made Edith the first American first lady to travel to Europe during her term. Edith enjoyed these visits, as she liked to socialise with the European female royalty, putting herself as an equal and keeping her country in its place as a world power.

Most first ladies spend their time acting as a hostess, focussing on the social aspects of the administration, which Edith would have done very well. However, this was not possible for Edith because she was the first lady during wartime, so instead, she focused on keeping her husband fit under the strain of being a war president. To the dissatisfaction of advisors, Edith had an active role in government, working with Woodrow in his private office, having access to classified documents and secret wartime codes, and his mail. At Woodrow's insistence, Edith sat in on meetings and afterwards would tell him what she thought of different political figures and foreign representatives.

Edith's role in government grew drastically in 1919 after the Paris Peace Conference. Woodrow returned to campaign for the senate's approval of the peace treaty and the League of Nations Covenant, a concept aiming for peace which he had created. This lengthy campaign involved a tour across America, which Edith disapproved of because she feared for his health due to the stress he was facing. During this tour, Woodrow did become sick, forcing him to return to the White House, and soon later, he had a stroke that was so severe that it paralyzed parts of his body.

Many believed that Woodrow should step down as president because he was too ill to govern; however, Edith thought this would be detrimental to his health, and the doctors agreed with her. So it was decided that Woodrow would continue as president, with Edith hiding how disabled her husband had become from the American public, saying that he badly needed rest so would work from his bedroom suite.

After this, Edith took over many routine duties, calling this task her "stewardship". Although she did not make decisions in public affairs, Edith decided which communications and matters were important enough to be brought to the president. This made Edith the single link between the cabinet and the president. Despite claiming to not have the power of a president, Edith did have the Secretary of State, Robert Lansing, removed after she found out he was conducting cabinet meetings without either the president or herself.

Edith also refused to be undermined or disrespected, for example, she refused to allow a foreign representative in the country until he had dismissed an aide who had made demeaning comments about her. Edith also helped Woodrow with his paperwork, including giving him suggestions in the margins of the classified documents she brought to him.

However, some in the White House did not trust Edith. She argued that she was acting on the recommendation of Woodrow's doctor, to preserve his mental health, but others did not believe her. Many still did not trust Edith due to her speedy marriage to the president, believing her to have had an affair with the president while his previous wife still lived. They also critiqued Edith for being too narrow-minded, preventing the president from being effective.

By 1921, after 17 months of Edith's stewardship, the president and first lady retired. For the next three years until Woodrow's death, Edith nursed him through his illness. After this, Edith went on to head the Woman's National Democratic Club's board of governors and published a memoir in 1939. For the rest of her life, Edith was present for presidential matters, including Roosevelt's address to congress encouraging the United States to join the Second World War in 1941, and she attended the inauguration of Kennedy in 1961. Just months later, on the anniversary of her husband's 105th birthday, Edith died of congestive heart failure. She was buried next to her second husband at the Washington National Cathedral.

Although a controversial figure, Edith was certainly a strong woman. She was not politically minded before her marriage to the president, but quickly went above and beyond to assist her husband with his duties, even more so after his stroke. With little formal education, Edith was able to understand politics fully, as she dedicated her life to her husband, nursing him through his sickness as well as taking on his duties. Although she may not have directly influenced public affairs, Edith certainly had power due to being the sole link between the president and the rest of America, before women even had the right to vote.

Constance Kopp
(1878–1931 CE)

Woman of the Law

"Kopp" is a very suitable surname for Constance, considering she became the first female undersheriff in the United States. She was a strong woman, with an imposing figure and personality, and believed that women should do whatever they wanted in life, whether that be run a household or work. Constance was determined to have a meaningful career in which she could help people, so persistently worked hard to achieve this.

Constance was born in Brooklyn, New York, but moved to a farm in New Jersey while she was a young girl. Her father was an alcoholic and absent; however, Constance was close to her two younger sisters, Norma and Fleurette. But calling them the Kopp sisters may be inaccurate, as although Fleurette was brought up to believe she was Norma and Constance's sister, she was actually Constance's daughter, born while Constance was unmarried, so raised to believe she was her sister. As the oldest of the three, Constance was the head of the household, and she was an imposing figure, standing at six foot tall, towering over many men.

As a young lady, Constance wanted to study to become a nurse or a lawyer, but her mother discouraged this, much to Constance's fury. But Constance was still able to receive some education, as she was able to speak French and two dialects of German. In addition to desiring a career, Constance had no interest in marriage, as this would confine her to the home. Despite her reluctance to marry and ambition for a career, Constance did not look down upon women who were satisfied to become housewives, as she believed that a woman should "have the right to do any sort of work she wants to, provided she can do it."

In 1914, Constance's family horse-driving buggy was hit by another vehicle while all three of the Kopp sisters were in the buggy. The buggy was damaged, so Constance asked the driver of the other vehicle, Henry Kaufman, a silk factory owner, to pay for the repair, as the crash had been his fault. But Henry would not cover these costs, so Constance decided to take legal action and sued. She was awarded a $50 judgement; however, Henry ignored this and still refused to pay, instead, he sent threatening letters to Constance. So one day, when Constance saw Henry's automobile in the street, she ran after it, demanding her money and calling on other pedestrians to help stop the car. Eventually, Constance had created enough of a scene that Henry stopped and paid the $50.

But Henry was angry and would not let the feud go. He wrote letters to Constance which were extremely threatening and signed "Friends of HK". Strange men would linger at Constance's family farm and fire upon it, sometimes even breaking into their home, damaging the house and threatening to burn it down. Once, Henry was driving drunk with some friends when he saw Constance on the street, so shouted at her until a patrolling officer arrested him and fined him $5 for harassment.

Although Constance went to the police about these threats, only one police officer took an interest in Constance's complaints. Sheriff Robert Heath took Constance's concerns seriously so provided the Kopp sisters each with a handgun and provided them with a guard at their home. One day, Constance received a letter instructing her to give $1,000 to a woman wearing black at a specific place and time. So Constance informed the police and waited at the meeting place with a concealed handgun and the police nearby. But the woman wearing black did not turn up.

Another incident occurred soon later, which was even more threatening. Constance received a letter from a friend of Henry, who wanted to meet because he had heard about a plot to kidnap the teenage Fleurette to sell her into white slavery. So Constance met up with this man, again with a concealed handgun. She was right to be wary, as Constance was attacked; however, she managed to get away and a nearby police officer captured and detained the attacker.

To collect evidence against Henry Kaufman, Constance went undercover twice to meet the writers of the threatening letters. Eventually, the police were able to obtain a handwriting sample from Henry, which matched the handwriting on the letters sent to Constance, so when on trial, Henry was found guilty of threatening and harassing Constance and fined $1,000. He was also told that he would face jail time if he did not stop harassing the Kopp sisters immediately. After this, Henry's wife divorced him, so he had to leave his home and family behind. The guilty verdict was possible because of Constance's help in the investigation, and her determination and bravery greatly impressed the sheriff, so he appointed Constance as his undersheriff. She was the first woman in the United States to have this position.

Constance took her new job very seriously. In one of her first cases, Constance tracked down and arrested an escaped prisoner. When she saw the target, she fearlessly put her arms tightly around him, pinning down his arms and keeping him still so that another officer could arrest the escaped prisoner. In another case, Constance and other officers were transporting a prisoner, but the prisoner escaped from the vehicle and jumped into a river, attempting to drown himself. So while the officers stood and watched, not knowing what to do, Constance undressed and followed the prisoner into the river, and brought him back into custody. She was then treated for shock and hypothermia due to the extreme cold.

Although Constance had proved herself on many occasions to be a competent and skilled undersheriff, in 1916 she was fired and replaced. This is because a less progressive, republican sheriff had been elected, and he claimed that he had nothing useful for Constance to do. She did challenge this decision, as there was a law protecting the jobs of civil servants that had been appointed by the previous political party; however, she was unsuccessful. Instead, Constance set up and managed her own private detective agency with her sister, Norma, but there is minimal information about this endeavour.

Constance was a well-accomplished woman and did something that no woman in the United States had done before, and did it very well. She did not keep her job as undersheriff for long, but this seems to be due to the prejudice of her superiors rather than any failings on Constance's part, as she proved herself to be a talented, quick-thinking and capable undersheriff. Constance's success over Henry Kaufman displays that she was a pragmatic and determined woman, who would persevere rather than put up with harassment; she worked hard to make life better for herself and her family, forcing Henry to face the consequences of his actions.

Raden Adjeng Kartini
(1879–1904 CE)

Advocate for Education

Despite only living a short life, Kartini accomplished something no one had before, the establishment of a school for native Javanese girls which did not discriminate based on social standing. Kartini was privileged to be born into a wealthy family, giving her more opportunities for education than other girls. However, she witnessed the poorer treatment of indigenous people in Java and of women and resented the fact that her culture meant that she was not entitled to education past the age of 12. So Kartini complained about these injustices to bring them to the attention of others and helped to improve the opportunities for Javanese women of future generations.

Kartini was born to an aristocratic Javanese family in the Dutch East Indies (modern-day Indonesia). Java was the largest island in the Dutch colony and was important for the production of spices, rubber, and tobacco. Polygamy was common amongst the Javanese nobility, so although Kartini was the daughter of her father's first wife, she was not the daughter of her father's chief wife. Kartini had about 11 siblings and half-siblings who she loved to play with as a child, and she was very active, so those around her gave her the nickname "little bird" because she was always flitting around.

As she was from a wealthy family, Kartini was able to attend a Dutch language primary school, in which she learned to speak Dutch, which was an unusual accomplishment for Javanese women. Here, Kartini was exposed to western ideals and saw how the indigenous Javanese people were treated differently to the Dutch. School gave Kartini a rare opportunity to be exposed to these new ideas, such as feminism, which was instilled in Kartini by her sewing teacher.

But at the age of 12, Kartini was removed from school due to a Javanese custom, which dictates that girls should be secluded at home and be prepared for marriage until their parents find them a husband. During this time, the young women are expected to learn homemaking skills and to be good, obedient, quiet Javanese wives. But Kartini also educated herself during her seclusion, by reading books, newspapers, and European magazines, teaching Kartini about European progressive thinking. This encouraged Kartini and two of her sisters to dream of having a meaningful career so that they may engage in the social and economic development of their country. While secluded, girls from rich families like Kartini could have whatever they wanted: rich foods, beautiful clothes and servants, but no freedom.

Fortunately for Kartini, her father was lenient, so allowed Kartini to leave the house in a closed carriage to attend embroidery lessons, and even allowed her in public for some special events. But Kartini's biggest joy in her seclusion was her pen pals. These included Mevrouw Ovink-Soer, a socialist and feminist, Stella Zeehandelaar, a Dutch feminist who Kartini found by placing an advert for a pen pal in a magazine, and Mr Abendanon, the Director of Education, Industry and Religion in Java. Kartini mostly wrote about how the Javanese traditions caused the oppression of women to her pen pals. She deeply wished for the emancipation of women, and the right to obtain freedom, autonomy and legal equality.

Kartini hated that men had educations and the opportunity to pursue a career in anything they wanted, whereas women had to be secluded for years. Then they were married off to a strange man, becoming their property and one of their many wives. Kartini called for Javanese education, the end of polygamy, women to autonomously be able to choose their career and their marriage, and the training of more Javanese teachers, midwives, and doctors. Although Kartini resented the Javanese traditions which suppressed her, she was also frustrated that the Javanese indigenous people were seen as lower in society than the Dutch colonisers, and wanted the end of colonial domination and exploitation.

Kartini deeply loved her father for allowing her to be educated until the age of 12, and for allowing a lenient seclusion, but he firmly prevented her from taking academia further in life. Kartini expressed a wish to study in the Netherlands, or enter a medical school in Batavia, but he would not allow this. Kartini's pen pals expressed disappointment when they found out that she would not be studying with them. However, eventually, Kartini was permitted to study in Tokyo, to become a teacher. But these plans were abandoned when Kartini's parents found her a husband, forcing Kartini to remain in Java to become a wife.

In 1903, Kartini was married to the Regency Chief of Rembang, Joyodinigrant, a man 26 years older than her, who already had three wives and many children. Although Kartini resented polygamy and being given to a stranger like property, she was excited to escape her isolation. Also, Kartini's new husband was happy to allow Kartini to follow her aspiration, so this enabled Kartini to develop a school for women. This school taught girls of all social standing a progressive, western-based curriculum, encouraging the lifelong pursuit of education. This was the first Indonesian primary school for native girls that did not discriminate based on social standing. After this impressive feat, Kartini decided to write a book, but never completed this because she died due to a complication in childbirth at the age of 25.

After her death, Kartini's sisters continued to advocate for the education of girls and women. Also, Kartini inspired other accomplishments, for example, the Van Deventer family established the R.A. Kartini Foundation, which builds schools for women which are known as "Kartini Schools". To further her progressive ideals, Kartini's pen pals published a book in 1911 entitled *Out of Darkness to Light,* a book full of Kartini's letters in which she discusses the idea of Javanese women having the freedom to learn and study so that they may be equal to European women. Her letters call for support overseas, which this book enables, as this publication changed the way the Dutch viewed native women in Java, making this book a symbol for the Indonesian independence movement and Indonesian feminists.

Although Kartini died so young, she achieved an impressive amount, even building a school so that young girls had more opportunities and a better life than she received. Although she never knew it, Kartini's letters inspired change in the way women and native people were perceived, beginning change in the world. In 1945, the Republic of Indonesia guaranteed women the same rights as men in the areas of education, voting rights, and economy, which is the change Kartini wanted to see in her society. Years later, since 1964, Kartini's date of birth, 21st of April, has been celebrated in Indonesia as "Kartini Day", so she is still an inspiration and guide to girls and women all over Indonesia.

Huda Sha'arawi (1879–1947 CE)

The Unvieled Woman

Huda fought for two causes: Egyptian independence and women's rights. While in seclusion from the outside world, Huda witnessed her brothers receiving better treatment and education, so decided that she would take matters into her own hands and be responsible for her own education. Huda saw that there was injustice in her society, so displayed this injustice to other women and fought to have her voice heard as an equal to the voices of men.

Huda was born to a wealthy Egyptian family and was raised in Cairo. Her father was the President of Egypt's Chamber of Deputies, so Huda had a relatively privileged childhood. Despite the official occupation of Egypt by the British in 1882, Huda's childhood seemed happy, with herself and her brothers receiving a good education in which they learned grammar, calligraphy, and multiple languages. At this time, it was common for men to have wives as well as concubines, who they called "second wives", and Huda was born from her father's concubine, but was very close to her father's wife. She would often discuss the injustice of being female born into a man's world, as even from a young age, Huda saw that her brothers were treated favourably compared to her.

Like many upper-class Egyptian women, Huda was sheltered for much of her early life in the harem system. This meant that the unmarried women were confined to secluded apartments within the home and wore face veils when outside. If they wanted to speak to a man inside the house, Huda would do so behind a screen, as was the custom. The only men that Huda had access to were the eunuchs, castrated men who were normally slaves from Sudan, who would serve as an intermediary between the women and the outside world. Huda was fortunate to be educated in her harem, as this was uncommon; however, she was constantly frustrated when she saw the superior education that her brothers received.

One day, as a young girl, Huda was inspired by a poetess named Sayyida Khadija, who spoke to the men comfortably as a peer, rather than being intimidated by them. After this incident, Huda realised that with learning, a woman was the equal of a man, if not more, so she focused on her own education.

At the age of 13, Huda was betrothed to marry her much older cousin who had a concubine and three daughters, all older than Huda. This man had also been Huda's guardian since her father had died years before, so Huda did not want to marry him because she saw him as a father figure. Knowing Huda's reluctance to marry, Huda's family tried to make the marriage easier by including in the marriage contract that their marriage must be monogamous, meaning the concubine would have to be abandoned. With this agreement, the marriage went ahead, but just a year later, the concubine gave birth to a child, fathered by Huda's new husband, so Huda immediately returned to live with her mother.

For the next seven years, the couple was separated, and Huda spent this time focused on advancing her education, such as learning to read the Quran and had tutoring in Quranic Arabic. In 1900, Huda was pressured by her family to reconcile with her husband. She did so, and three years later, gave birth to a daughter, Bathna, and then a son named Muhammad in 1905. Because Bathna was a sickly child, constantly on the brink of death, Huda lost contact with her female friends and devoted her life to her children, but once Bathna was strong again, Huda started to socialise.

Women in Egypt were usually confined to the home during this time, which Huda resented. So she began to make lectures for women about topics that she found interesting, bringing many women into the public for the first time to see these lectures in a safe space with other women. In 1909, Huda convinced these women to help her create a welfare society to raise money for the poor women in Egypt. This would be the first secular philanthropic organisation run by Egyptian women, and they offered social services for poor women and children. This not only helped the poor but also enabled the upper-class women who took part to demonstrate that women are not just delicate beings made for men's pleasure who need protecting. This organisation also ran a medical dispensary for underprivileged women and children.

A year later, Huda was able to open a school for girls, which taught academic subjects rather than practical skills, such as midwifery, which is all women were normally taught. By 1914, Huda had formed the Intellectual Association of Egyptian Women, to improve women's intellectual and social lives. As well as advocating for the education of the women around her, Huda was not afraid to ignore the societal rules restricting women, for example, Huda would go to a department store herself in Alexandria to buy clothes rather than have the clothes brought to her home.

With her husband, Huda was devoted to the idea of independence for Egypt and had many nationalistic views. In 1919, Huda organised a women-led protest which advocated for Egyptian independence from Britain and the release of nationalist leaders. This protest would be known as the "March of Veiled Women" and took place in the streets of Cairo, and never before had so many Egyptian women been involved in such activism. When the group of women came across British soldiers, she told her followers not to attack, as she did not want anyone to be harmed, so they stood firm. They all stood for three hours under the blazing sun until the British left the street.

Just a few years later, in 1922, Egypt was finally granted its independence; however, Britain did retain significant control. At the time of the protest, Huda's husband was the acting Vice President of the Wafd, a nationalist liberal party in Egypt. In 1920, Huda was elected as the first President of the Wafdist Women's Central Committee, due to her work leading the protests.

Before Egypt had achieved independence in 1922, Huda held a mass meeting of women at her house, where the women agreed to launch an economic boycott against the British. They refused to buy British goods and withdrew their money from British banks. This boycott was a useful weapon and a factor in achieving Egyptian independence that same year. However, when Egyptian independence was achieved, the Wafd government went back on their promise to give women the vote, and despite the women's contribution to the nationalistic cause, ignored their pleas for suffrage.

In the same year as gaining Egyptian independence, Huda's husband died and she turned her attention from nationalism, as Egyptian independence had been achieved, to women's rights. Therefore Huda attended many conferences about women's rights around Europe. At the International Women Suffrage Alliance Congress in Rome, Huda and her friends saw that they were the only delegates with veiled faces. However, wearing a veil hindered communication, so Huda and her friends agreed to remove them. On returning home, at a Cairo train station, Huda again removed her veil, then stamped it into the ground.

Initially, everyone in the station was shocked, but then many broke into applause and even removed their own veils, which Huda encouraged. Many people see this as a religious symbol; however, at this time, Egyptian women in poorer areas did not cover their faces, only their heads, so the face covering was a symbol of privilege rather than faith, so Huda was stripping off a divisive symbol. From this point, Huda decided to no longer wear her veil and headscarf, gradually encouraging other women to make this decision too. Slowly this convinced the stricter fathers and husbands to allow their wives and daughters to walk the streets unveiled.

In 1923, Huda founded and became the first President of the Egyptian Feminist Union (EFU), which sought to reform laws restricting personal freedoms, such as marriage, divorce, and child custody. She started this union partly due to her frustration at the Wafdist government's betrayal of refusing women the vote. Age of marriage was important to Huda, after her experience of being married without her consent when she was only 13. So after pressure from the EFU, the legislature increased the minimum age of marriage to 16 for girls, and 18 for boys. However, Huda was overruled on many other of her proposals on social reform due to opposition from the Muslim clergymen. But despite the opposition, Huda continuously publicised her ideas with a fortnightly journal entitled *L'Égyptienne*, with the first edition published in 1925.

Although Egyptian girls could attend primary school, there was just one Egyptian school for girls beyond this, which was a teachers' training college. So in 1924, the first secondary school for girls was opened. At the opening of

Parliament in 1924, Huda led Egyptian women once again, having submitted a list of nationalist demands, and demands relating to women's rights. However, these were ignored by the Wafdist government, so Huda protested this by resigning from the Wafdist Women's Central Committee. She did continue to lead the EFU until her death, including publishing the fortnightly journal. Huda fully committed to this, including representing Egypt at women's congresses in Graz, Paris, Amsterdam, Berlin, Marseilles, Istanbul, Brussels, Budapest, Copenhagen, Interlaken and Geneva. At these meetings, Huda advocated for peace and disarmament.

At the age of 68, Huda died of cholera. After her death, Huda's movement for women was banned by the Egyptian president. Sadly, the gains Huda made for gender equality and national liberation have been slowly reversed due to the autocratic rule in Egypt.

Huda had a good start in life compared to many of the other women who grew up in Egypt at this time. She used her status for the benefit of the other women around her. Despite the custom at the time, Huda would not allow herself to be hidden away or remain quiet, instead, she made her voice heard and her face seen. Understanding the harshness of some of the men in her society, Huda never forced other women to unveil themselves, but instead encouraged their learning and their unveiling by leading them. As well as fighting for women's rights, Huda fought for the independence of her nation, which she greatly contributed to along with many other women.

Anna Pavlova (1881–1931 CE)

Prima Ballerina

Physically, Anna was not suited to ballet, but she had such a passion for dance that she determinedly worked and practiced until she became the Prima Ballerina. In addition to being an impressive dancer, Anna choreographed many dances and became the first ballerina to tour around the world, where she learned new dances. As a performer, Anna was special to witness, and she danced as often as she could so that she could bring ballet to as many people as possible.

Anna was born in St Petersburg in Russia, to a peasant laundress mother who worked in the home of a Russian-Jewish banker, who may have been Anna's biological father. Unfortunately, Anna's step-father died when Anna was just two years old, leaving Anna's mother in poverty. As Anna was a premature child, she was sickly, so she was sent to live in the Ligovo village to be looked after by her grandmother. This was an upper-class suburb of the city, so Anna became acquainted with aristocratic society. Despite her family's lack of wealth, when Anna was a child, her mother took her to the theatre to see a performance of *The Sleeping Beauty,* and Anna was enthralled. It was from this moment when Anna knew she wanted to be a ballerina like those she saw on stage.

Happy to encourage her daughter's passion, in 1890, Anna's mother took the pair of them to the Imperial Ballet School so that Anna could audition. Unfortunately, Anna was rejected due to her young age and sickly appearance. But still determined, Anna practiced at home until a year later when she returned to the Imperial Ballet School. This time, Anna passed the entrance exam and was accepted into the school.

For a young child, the schooling was tough, as Anna had to practice her ballet routines for eight hours each day, then study music to give her perfect pitch. Along with the other students, Anna adopted a strict diet of mostly fish and vegetables, which she continued to eat for the rest of her life. Soon, Anna would have her first taste of performing on stage; the students of the school performed in *A Fairy Tale.*

Although she loved ballet, Anna did struggle through her schooling. This is because her body type was not typical of a ballerina. She had severely arched feet, thin ankles and long limbs, so her classmates taunted her, calling her names such as "the broom". However, Anna did not let this affect her, instead, she perfected her ballet by practicing each step many times, as she believed that "work transforms talent into genius". To improve, Anna took extra lessons from famous ballerinas of the time, including Christian Johansson, Pavel Gerdt, Nikolai Legat and Enrico Cecchetti. This extra work enabled Anna to enter the "classe de perfection" in 1898, then she graduated the next year, a rank higher than her classmates. This higher level allowed Anna to perform in smaller groups from earlier on.

In Anna's official début, she performed in a group of three at the same theatre where she fell in love with ballet as a young girl. Her performance in this collected brilliant reviews. Another of Anna's earliest roles with the Imperial Ballet was her role as the Fairy Candide in *The Sleeping Beauty.* But on the night, Anna was so nervous that she would not dance her part with the correct technique; she panicked in the wings, so two of the other fairies had to calm her down by coming up with new steps for her to use. When Anna used these newly choreographed steps, she was scolded and never cast as the Fairy Candide again.

During her first few years as a ballerina, Anna suffered nerves like these in many performances, but still always impressed the audience.

Anna was a surprise to the public due to her unorthodox style of dancing. At the time, the rules of dance were very strict; however, Anna broke these rules, by performing with bent knees, bad turnout, misplaced *port de bras,* and incorrectly placed *tours.* People thought that Anna's style was similar to the style of the romantic ballet of the 1840s. Anna was also known to lose balance while dancing due to her enthusiasm and unusual movements, sometimes she even fell on stage. This could also be caused by Anna's weak ankles, so she changed some of the movements slightly.

Anna was supported in this by her ballet master, who encouraged the young ballerina to do what she could to not damage her ankles and feet. She was encouraged to not attempt acrobatics, instead, remembered that daintiness was Anna's greatest asset, so she used this quality to her advantage. Despite Anna's unusual technique and stature, she rose through the ranks and became the Prima Ballerina in 1906, after her excellent performance in *Giselle.*

Arguably, Anna's breakthrough role was *The Dying Swan,* performed in 1905. This was a solo role choreographed specifically for Anna by Michel Fokine and is Anna's most famous role. In this performance, Anna's delicate movements and intense facial expressions convey a message about the fragility of life.

In 1907, Anna took part in a European ballet tour with a few other dancers to Riga, Stockholm, Copenhagen, Berlin, and Prague. She proved very popular in these and enjoyed travelling, so performed on another European tour the next year. Although Anna was showing herself to have great talent, she still found herself having to prove herself to others. One example is when the ballerina Mathilde Kschessinska was pregnant, so coached Anna to take her role in *La Bayadère.* Allegedly, Mathilde chose Anna to perform her role because she thought that Anna could not upstage her, as she believed Anna to be technically inferior due to her small ankles. But the audience loved Anna for this role, even preferring her to Mathilde, as they thought her frail look was perfect for the part.

After spending time working in the Ballets Russes, a ballet company based in Paris, Anna decided to leave in 1910 to form her own company and dance independently. She may have decided this because she did not like some of the music she had to dance to in the Ballets Russes, so wanted to have complete creative control over performances. This also gave Anna the chance to choreograph her own roles, such as *The Dragonfly,* in which she fixed dragonfly wings to her back, and these dances were performed all around the world. While on her travels to places such as Mexico, Japan, and East India, Anna learned from local teachers so that she may perform ethnic dances, which she compiled into *Oriental Impressions.* In 1916, Anna also produced a 50-minute adaptation of *The Sleeping Beauty,* which she performed in New York City with her company.

Although Anna travelled often with her company, in 1912 she moved to a house in London, which was her home where she returned between travelling. Her house had a lake with two swans, named Jack and Clara. Her other pets included a Siamese cat, various dogs, and many kinds of birds. While in London, Anna was influential in the development of British ballet and inspired many young British ballerinas. From her home, Anna established a dance school, which catered to those in her company. Initially, this consisted of eight Russian dancers but grew to 60 dancers and staff. These were all managed by Victor Dandré.

Victor was a French-Russian businessman who fell in love with Anna, and she loved him too. Early on in their relationship, Anna bailed Victor out of prison and paid off all of his debts and legal expenses, then a few years later, Anna and Victor were married in secret. From this point, Victor worked as Anna's manager and he supported her and her company throughout their travels. Years later, Victor would expose Anna's charity performances and efforts to support Russian orphans in post-World War I Paris. Anna also adopted 15 girls into her home near Paris, who she supported with the money from her performances and donations.

Throughout her life, Anna toured the world and made eight to nine performances per week. This continued into her 40s, leading Anna to be overworked and exhausted, but still, she continued. One day, Anna was travelling from Paris to The Hague when she became very ill. Later she was diagnosed with pneumonia and offered an operation; however, this would prevent her from ever dancing again. So Anna refused this operation as she claimed she would rather die than not be able to dance.

Just days before her 50th birthday, Anna died of pleurisy with her husband by her side. In her last utterance, Anna asked to have her *Swan* costume made ready for a performance. The next day Anna was supposed to be performing, and despite her death, the show went on. Instead of using an understudy, a single spotlight circled the empty stage where Anna would have been dancing.

Anna should be admired for her ability as a ballerina, but also her passion and enthusiasm for dance. Not only this, but throughout her life, Anna displayed such a strength of character, as she never gave up on ballet, even when she found out that her body type would hinder her. Instead of quitting, Anna worked harder and made the dancing work for her, so that although her performances were unusual, they were also unique and gave the audience something completely new.

Princess Alice of Battenberg (1885–1969 CE)

The Philantrophic Princess

As a member of a European royal family during the 1900s, Alice had an extremely turbulent life. She was exiled from her country twice, lived through two Balkan wars, two World Wars, and lost contact with her family after being sectioned. But despite the adversities that Alice suffered, she remained consistently kind and generous, giving up everything for the poor and hungry, even at great risk to herself.

Alice was born in Windsor Castle, in the presence of her great-grandmother, Queen Victoria. From birth, Alice was strongly connected to the royal families of Europe, with her father being Prince Louis of Battenberg, and Alice was christened Victoria Alice Elizabeth Julia Marie. As a child, Alice's parents noticed that she was slow in learning to talk and the words that she did speak were very indistinct, so after seeing an ear specialist, Alice was diagnosed with congenital deafness. But this did not hinder Alice, as her mother helped her to lip-read and speak in multiple languages, as Alice spent time all around Europe. As well as learning to speak multiple languages, Alice's education was excellent, and she was taught privately from a young age.

In 1902, Alice travelled to London to attend King Edward VII's coronation. Here she met Prince Andrew of Greece and Denmark. Very quickly, Andrew and Alice fell deeply in love and married in a civil ceremony in Darmstadt the next year. On the same day, they also had two religious marriage ceremonies, one Lutheran for Alice, and one Greek Orthodox for Andrew. This wedding was a huge event because together they were closely related to the ruling houses of the United Kingdom, Germany, Russia, Denmark, and Greece, so this event was one of the great gatherings of the descendants of Queen Victoria and Christian IX of Denmark held before the First World War, in which the houses would be in great conflict, and many fell from power.

After their wedding, Andrew continued to work in the military and Alice became involved in charity work, and by 1911 had three daughters, Margarita, Theodora, and Cecillie. However, as with many royal couples, Alice and Andrew wanted a son. Ten years after the birth of her youngest daughter, Alice gave birth to a son, Philip, who would grow up to be the consort of Queen Elizabeth II. From birth, Philip and his sisters were all Princesses and Prince of Greece and Denmark. In 1908, Alice was inspired by her aunt, the Grand Duchess Elizabeth Feodorovna of Russia, who was planning for the foundation of a religious order of nurses. Later this same aunt would give away all her possessions to undertake a completely spiritual life.

However, in 1912, Andrew and Alice faced adversity when the First Balkan War broke out. Andrew worked in the army, and Alice worked as a nurse, assisting in operations and setting up field hospitals, for which she received the Royal Red Cross from King George V in 1913, not long before the outbreak of the Second Balkan War. Unfortunately, conflict in Greece would not end soon, as just a year later, in 1914, the First World War broke out. The King of Greece at the time, Alice's brother-in-law, King Constantine I, followed a policy of neutrality, despite the democratic government supporting the Allies.

This unpopular policy led to the public rising against Constantine, so in 1917, he abdicated and went into exile in Switzerland with many other members of the Greek royal family, including Alice. With such strong anti-German sentiment in Britain during the First World War, Alice's father had to change his name at the request of King George V, from Battenberg to the more anglicised Mountbatten. A particular tragedy for Alice came in 1918, when two of her aunts who were part of the Russian royal family, Tsarina Alexandra Feodorovna and Grand Duchess Elizabeth Feodorovna, were murdered by the Bolsheviks after the Russian Revolution. By the end of the First World War in 1918, the Russian, German, and Austro-Hungarian Empires had fallen, and this revolutionary feeling around Europe put the other royal houses in a precarious situation.

Alice's luck seemed to rise again in 1920, during the Greco-Turkish War, when King Constantine I was restored as the King of Greece. However, this did not last long, as their army was defeated in the aforementioned war in 1922, so a Revolutionary Committee seized power and forced Constantine back into exile, and Andrew was arrested because he had commanded an army force in the war, so was blamed for Greece's defeat. Other former ministers and generals who had been arrested for similar reasons had been executed, so the British assumed that the same would happen to Andrew. To protect the Greek royals, the British gave them protection and enabled Andrew and Alice to escape Greece with their children, Philip was only a baby at the time and was placed in an orange box for the journey.

The family settled in the outskirts of Paris, where Alice worked in a charity shop for the aid of Greek refugees. For years, Alice had been through a lot, including fleeing her country twice, and this stress began to take its toll. In 1928, she converted to the Greek Orthodox Church and became incredibly religious, stating that she was receiving divine messages and had healing powers. This developed into Alice behaving in a disturbed manner, so in 1930, she was sectioned and forcibly removed from her family.

After being diagnosed with paranoid schizophrenia, Alice was placed in Ludwig Binswanger's sanatorium in Kreuzlingen, Switzerland. This institution was well-respected and had celebrity patients, so was not as bad as other asylums during this time in history, but it was still very unpleasant. Because of the nature of Alice's disorder, Sigmund Freud, the father of psychoanalysis, was consulted. He determined that Alice's delusions were the result of sexual frustration, so recommended that her ovaries should be X-rayed to encourage menopause and destroy her libido. In vain, Alice protested, claiming sanity, and tried to escape the asylum; however, she was held at the institution for two years.

During her time at the asylum, Alice drifted from her family. All of Alice's daughters were married to German princes, and Philip had been sent to boarding school in Scotland, cared for by his uncle. So when Alice was released, she lived quietly in Europe and remained in contact with just her mother for a few years. However, in 1937, Alice began to reach out to her family again, when her daughter, Cecillie, and her husband and young children, were killed in an aeroplane accident. So Alice and Andrew met for the first time in six years at their daughter's funeral, which was also attended by Philip. After this, in 1938, Alice returned to Athens to help the poor.

During the Second World War, which broke out in 1939, Alice was in the unfortunate position of having two sons-in-law fighting on the German side, and a son in the British Royal Navy. For the duration of the war, Alice lived in Athens, even after the occupation of Athens by the Axis forces in 1941. Alice spent her time working for the Red Cross, helping to organise soup kitchens for the hungry, and flew to Sweden to bring back medical supplies, under the pretence of visiting her sister. In addition to this, Alice organised two shelters for orphaned and lost children, and a nursing circuit for the poorer neighbourhoods.

Because her son-in-law was a member of the Nazi Party, it was assumed that Alice was pro-German. However, at one point after the German occupation of Athens in 1943 after the fall of Mussolini, a Nazi asked Alice what he could do to help, and she told him "You can take your troops out of my country." Alice saw the atrocities caused by the Nazis, particularly their treatment of the Jewish population, as 60,000 of the 750,000 Greek Jewish people who sought refuge in Athens were deported to concentration camps, and all but 2,000 of these died. Always wanting to help those in need, Alice took a Jewish widow, Rachel Cohen, and her two children into her home, despite the huge danger to her life.

At one point, the Gestapo became suspicious of Alice, they knocked on her door, desiring to enter her house to see if she was hiding Jewish people. Alice pretended not to hear the questions, preventing them from entering her property and discovering the Jewish family she was hiding.

Athens was finally liberated from Nazi control in 1944, and this was a huge relief to Alice, who had been giving all her rations to the poor. She wrote a letter to Philip, admitting that in the week before liberation, she had no food except bread and butter, and had no meat for several months. Unfortunately, even after the liberation, Athens was still an area of conflict, as communist guerrillas were fighting the British for control of the area. A curfew was put in place to protect the civilians from the fighting on the streets, but Alice would walk the streets to distribute rations to police officers and children. When she was warned that she could be shot by a stray bullet, Alice claimed that she was not worried. That same year, Alice received news that her estranged husband, Andrew, had died. Although Alice had not seen Andrew for many years, this was devastating as she had been hoping for a post-war reunion with her husband.

In 1947, Alice returned to London to attend the wedding of her son, Philip, and Princess Elizabeth, the presumptive heir of King George VI. Some of Alice's few remaining jewels, which were in a tiara gifted to her by Tsar Nicholas II and Tsarina Alexandra of Russia, were used in the engagement ring Philip used to propose with. In the wedding ceremony, Alice was sat at the head of her family in Westminster Abbey, but her daughters had not been invited due to the anti-German sentiment in British following the war, which had ended just two years previously.

After this, in 1948, Alice began wearing a grey habit and withdrew from the world to the island of Tinos. She never formally took vows or became a Greek Orthodox nun, but wore religious clothing for the rest of her life. In 1949, Alice founded a nursing order of Greek Orthodox nuns, the Christian Sisterhood of Martha and Mary, modelled after the convent that her aunt, the Grand Duchess of Russia, had founded in Russia four decades before. The order was dedicated to caring for the sick under Alice, who ran the institution as Mother Superior with the name Alice-Elizabeth. There were two houses set up for the order, one dedicated to caring for the sick, and one to train nuns, but funding this order was difficult.

Alice travelled to the United States in 1950 and 1952 to raise funds and sold almost all of her possessions to keep the order running; the order would eventually fail due to a lack of applicants. However, this did not stop Alice from giving everything she had, food and wealth included, to those who she felt needed it more.

In 1953, Alice again returned to London, this time to attend the coronation of her daughter-in-law, Queen Elizabeth II. She wore a two-tone grey dress and a wimple in the style of her nun's habit, which was incredibly subdued compared to the glamour of the British royalty at this event. Alice visited Philip and Elizabeth often and grew close to Elizabeth, even calling her "Lilibet" affectionately. In letters to Philip, Alice often expressed how proud she was of the pair of them. Years later, in 1967, Alice faced another conflict, which was the Colonels' Coup in Athens, in which King Constantine II was overthrown in a military coup.

Fearing the danger that Alice was in, especially considering her age, Philip and Elizabeth invited Alice to live with them at Buckingham Palace permanently. So after a lifetime of living isolated from her family, Alice spent her final two years reconnecting with her only son, and became close to her teenage granddaughter, Princess Anne, before she died in 1969, leaving almost no possessions, having given everything away.

Alice was buried near her aunt, the Grand Duchess Elizabeth, who she was inspired by, and she lies at the Church of St Mary Magdalene on the Mount of Olives in Jerusalem. Years after her death, in 1993, Alice was honoured as Righteous Among the Nations, for sheltering a Jewish family in her home during the Holocaust, despite the risks, and in 2010 was named a Hero of the Holocaust by the British government.

However, Philip has since said that his mother would never have seen aiding a Jewish family as heroic, but simply her duty as a human. Although Alice suffered so much in her life, being sectioned and diagnosed as schizophrenic, living with congenital deafness and losing her family, Alice always remained an incredibly kind person, who would always help those in need, without question.

Milunka Savić
(1888 –1973 CE)

Most Decorated Female Combatant

Despite her many acts of bravery and numerous medals for fighting in multiple wars, Milunka seems to have been forgotten in history. When she was discovered to be a woman, Milunka was allowed to continue fighting for her country because she was too good as a soldier to lose, and her skills and heroism on the battlefield would lead to Milunka becoming the most decorated known woman in the history of warfare.

Born in a village with fewer than 20 inhabitants, Milunka came from a humble background, near Novi Pazar in Serbia. Despite the lack of opportunities for a young girl, Milunka was educated and able to speak French and German. However, in 1912, the First Balkan War broke out, which was fought between the Balkan states (Bulgaria, Serbia, Greece, and Montenegro) and the Ottoman Empire. But when her brother received his conscription papers, Milunka went to war in his place, after chopping off her hair and donning male clothing. She successfully joined the Serbian army using the name Milun.

Milunka was a very successful soldier and received her first medal at the Battle of Bregalnica, where she was also promoted to the rank of corporal. However, during her 10th mission, Milunka was injured by a piece of shrapnel buried in her chest. As a result of this and her time recovering in hospital, a bemused doctor discovered Milunka's true sex when treating her chest injury, so she was immediately taken to a superior. This was very frustrating for Milunka's commander, because he did not want her punished as she was one of the best soldiers, and there were not enough so competent.

So instead, he decided to have Milunka transferred to the nurse's division. But Milunka refused this transfer, stating that she just wanted to serve her country in combat, so she waited for an hour while her commander decided her future. Eventually, Milunka was sent back to camp and told to keep fighting the enemy as a soldier.

Milunka continued to fight throughout the First Balkan War and then fought in the Second Balkan War of 1913, fought between Serbia and Bulgaria. After this, Milunka was able to fight in World War I using her real name. During this conflict, Milunka became known for her outstanding gut feeling and excellent timing, as she always launched attacks at the right time. Just months into World War I, Milunka was awarded a Karađorđe Star with Swords after the Battle of Kolubara, then her second after the Battle of the Cma Bend in 1916. In the latter battle, she captured 23 Bulgarian soldiers by herself; however, would not execute them as she claimed to be fighting for her life, not simply to kill enemies.

Her excellence as a soldier is displayed by the fact that Milunka was assigned to the "Iron Squadron", the most elite Second Squadron of the Serbian army. One of Milunka's comrades in this squadron was an Englishwoman, Flora Sanders, another female soldier. In 1915, Milunka suffered head injuries in battle, but after treatment in Corfu, returned to the frontlines to participate in battles without any complaint or fear.

In addition to the Karađorđe Star with Swords awards, Milunka received many medals from all around the world. Serbia presented Milunka with the Serbian Miloš Obilić medal, France bestowed upon her the Croix de Guerre and the Legion d'Honneur twice. Russia honoured Milunka with the Cross of St George, and Great Britain awarded her with the Medal of the Most Distinguished Order of St Michael. And this is just naming a few. The hordes of awards that

Milunka received made her the most decorated woman in the history of warfare. At the end of the war, France even offered Milunka a comfortable retirement; however, she decided to remain in her homeland in Serbia.

When she was demobilised in 1919, Milunka had a series of jobs, including working as a cook, a nurse, then a factory worker for military uniform control, then she settled as a cleaner. Eventually, in 1923, Milunka married Veljko Gligorijević and had a daughter, Milena; however, the couple divorced soon after their child's birth. After this, Milunka adopted three more daughters who had been orphaned during the war and, despite her lack of wealth, she paid for about 30 other children to attend school.

In 1939, World War II broke out; however, Milunka was not allowed to fight. So instead, during the German occupation of Serbia, Milunka organised an infirmary to provide aid to the Yugoslav Partisans and Chetniks, both groups working against Nazi Germany. At one point, Milunka refused to attend a banquet organised by Milan Nedić, a Nazi collaborator, because it would be attended by German generals and officers. For this, Milunka was beaten severely, in front of her children, then taken to the Banjica concentration camp, where she was supposed to have been shot to death. Fortunately, Milunka was not executed, and instead survived her imprisonment for 10 months before she was returned to Serbia after the war, where she was given a state pension for her services to her country.

With little money, Milunka returned to Belgrade, but by the late 1950s, her daughter was hospitalised and she was living in a crumbling house. Despite her services, Milunka seemed to have been forgotten by her country and was unknown. This began to change when Milunka attended jubilee celebrations wearing her military medals, as other military officers would speak to her and learn of her heroic story. Shocked at the conditions Milunka was living in, a newspaper article exposed Milunka's living and financial situations in 1972, so after some public pressure, Milunka was given a small apartment. Although the apartment was in a better condition, it was still not ideal because it was on the fourth floor and there was no lift, and Milunka was an elderly lady by this point. Just a year later, Milunka suffered a stroke while knitting, which led to her death.

Milunka was an incredibly skilled soldier, who did her job to a high standard without complaining or making a fuss. With so many medals, Milunka has demonstrated that a woman can fight and be a warrior. As well as her prowess on the battlefield, Milunka was a kind woman who did her part for her country after she could no longer fight by working against the Nazis, then later adopting children who suffered due to the war, and paid for other children to go to school, despite having no money for herself. So not only was Milunka a strong warrior, but she was also a selfless philanthropist who was forgotten by the nation she fought for.

Bessie Coleman
(1892–1926 CE)

The World's Greatest Woman Flier

Bessie was a woman with a lot of firsts, including but not limited to being the first woman of African American descent to have a pilot license and the first Native American to have a pilot license. Although no one in her country would teach a black woman to fly, this did not stop Bessie from pursuing her dream. Once she gained popularity as an aviatrix, Bessie used her platform to fight against discrimination and segregation in America, refusing to perform where black people could not attend, and she spoke out against racism throughout her life.

Bessie was born in Atlanta, Texas to a family of sharecroppers, which included 12 siblings, though only nine survived childhood. The family were African American with some Native American lineage. Every day from the age of six, Bessie walked four miles to attend school, which was tiny and segregated, yet Bessie loved to read and do mathematics, which she excelled at. As well as conducting her studies and attending church, Bessie was busy with chores, including washing the laundry and working on the cotton fields; however, she felt she wanted to do more in life.

In 1901, life was made difficult for Bessie's family when her father moved to Oklahoma to find better opportunities, but the rest of the family was left behind. This meant that Bessie and her siblings had to contribute to the family as much as possible to help their mother. This life was difficult, but Bessie was able to achieve an education, as from the age of 12, Bessie attended the Missionary Baptist Church School on a scholarship. When Bessie turned 18, she used all of her savings to enrol into the Oklahoma Coloured Agricultural and Normal University in Langston; however, after just one semester she returned home as her money had run out.

A few years later, Bessie moved to Chicago to live with her brothers, where she worked as a manicurist after attending the Burnham School of Beauty Culture. It was here where Bessie heard stories of pilots who were serving in the First World War from her brothers who had served in the military in France. These stories led Bessie to dream of becoming a pilot. But one day, Bessie's brother, John, came home drunk and teased Bessie that women in France were far more accomplished than American women. He stated that this was because French women had more opportunities and were so liberated that they could fly a plane if they wanted.

Spurred on by this daunting, Bessie took another job so that she could save money to train to be a pilot. But Bessie was rejected by everywhere she applied because American flight schools did not allow women or black people to train. Instead, Bessie was encouraged to study abroad, so after taking a French language class and receiving a financial sponsorship, Bessie travelled to Paris in 1920 to earn her pilot's license.

Bessie had been accepted to the Caudron Brother's School of Aviation and was taught to fly in a Nieuport 564 biplane, specialising in stunt flying and parachuting. Bessie soon found this work to be dangerous, she had to inspect the plane every time she flew, and at one point witnessed an accident that killed another student. But seven months after beginning training, as the only non-Caucasian in her class, Bessie became the first black woman and the first Native American to earn an aviation pilot's license. Bessie also became the first black person and the first Native American to earn an international aviation license from the Fédération Aéronautique Internationale, granting Bessie the right to fly anywhere in the world. After this, Bessie spent two months taking lessons from a French ace pilot in Paris to improve her skills. By late 1921, Bessie returned to the United States and became a media sensation.

To make a living as a civilian aviator, Bessie had to become a barnstorming stunt flier. This involved performing dangerous tricks for audiences; however, it was highly competitive, so Bessie decided to take more advanced lessons to improve her repertoire of tricks. But again, no one in Chicago would teach a black woman, so Bessie returned to Europe. First, she completed an advanced course in aviation in France for two months, then she travelled to the Netherlands to meet an aircraft designer and received training from a chief pilot. Finally, Bessie returned to the United States for a career in exhibition flying. Although no one had been willing to teach Bessie, she did prove popular and was known as "Queen Bess", "Brave Bessie" and "The Only Race Aviatrix in the World".

Bessie took part in important events and was often interviewed as she was admired by everyone, despite the segregation and discrimination she faced. The plane she flew was a Curtiss JN-4 "Jenny" biplane, and she also flew aircraft left over from the war. In 1922, Bessie made her first appearance in an airshow that honoured veterans of the all-black 369th Infantry Regiment of World War I. In this event, Bessie gave an aerial display with eight other American ace pilots and a parachutist. She performed figure of eights, loops, near-ground dips, walked on the wings of the plane while in the air and parachuted from her plane.

Soon, Bessie would become known as "the world's greatest woman flier". However, Bessie was criticised by the media for her opportunistic nature and flamboyant style, even though her career was in performance. In 1923, Bessie experienced the risks of her daring career. While flying to an airshow, Bessie's plane stalled and crashed. She broke three ribs and her leg in the crash; however, begged the doctor to patch her up in time for the show that day. Instead, Bessie was taken to hospital for several months to recover, but she sent a telegram to her fans on the day of the accident, writing "tell them all that as soon as I can walk, I'm going to fly!" So even after being seriously injured, Bessie was determined to continue flying and impressing her audiences.

Other than flying, Bessie's greatest passion was to fight racism. Throughout her career, Bessie spoke to audiences about her goals for African Americans, trying to encourage them to take up flying. She would also refuse to take part in aviation events that did not allow African Americans to attend and would not perform where there would be segregation. While on a speaking tour in Orlando, Bessie met Reverend Hezakiah Hill and his wife, Viola. They were activists and after hearing Bessie speak, they invited her to stay with them. They treated Bessie like a daughter, so Bessie lived with them for a long time. Around this time, Bessie opened a beauty shop so that she could earn enough money to buy her own plane, and eventually start a flying school for African Americans.

With her ambitious plans to buy a plane and start a flight school, Bessie was delighted when she was offered a role in a film entitled *Shadow and Sunshine*. This would earn her lots of money towards these enterprises, so she quickly accepted the offer. But during the first scene, Bessie was required to dress in tattered clothes with a walking stick and a pack on her back. She was directed to act in a manner that she felt was derogatory to black people, so Bessie refused and would not be part of the film. This meant that Bessie could never establish a school for young black aviators, but did inspire many with her values. Although she could not set up a school, Bessie did give some flight lessons between performing in flight shows, but most importantly, she taught people to stand against racial segregation.

In 1926, Bessie bought herself a Curtiss JN-4 biplane; however, it was very poorly maintained. When her mechanic and publicity agent, William Wills, flew it, he had to make three forced landings due to its poor condition. When Bessie's family learned of this, they tried to convince Bessie to not fly the plane, as they feared for her safety; however, she did not listen. While on a practice flight for a show the next day, William was flying while Bessie sat in the passenger seat with no seatbelt because she was planning a parachute jump so wanted to examine the land.

But soon after take-off, the plane went into a spinning dive 3,000 feet above the ground, throwing Bessie from the plane. She died instantly as she hit the ground, and William also died when the plane crashed as he failed to regain control. Tragically, Bessie was only 34 years old and William was just 23. At her funeral, 10,000 mourners attended and Ida B. Wells, the activist, led the funeral. Since 1931, the Challenger Pilot's Association of Chicago has flown over Bessie's grave annually, and in 1977, African American women pilots formed the Bessie Coleman Aviators Club.

Bessie's life was short, but she lived it to the full and never let her race or sex hold her back from fulfilling her dreams, even if that meant travelling to Europe. With her fame and popularity as a talented aviator, Bessie inspired many people and used her platform to fight against segregation in the United States, which she did publicly and consistently, even if it held back her career. In 1992, Dr Mae Jemison became the first black woman to travel into space, and she took with her a photo of Bessie, who had inspired her to be an astronaut.

Dorothy Lawrence
(1896 – 1964 CE)

An Ordinary English Girl

Dorothy was an incredibly strong-willed woman, as when she was just a teenager, she cycled herself to the World War I frontlines in pursuit of her dream to be a war correspondent. Dorothy was considered a spy and a prostitute before she was believed to be a war correspondent, and was never properly able to tell the world of her experiences as a woman on the battlefield. Eventually, due to her lack of family and the government forcing her silence, Dorothy lost her sanity and freedom.

Dorothy did not have the best start in life. She was orphaned as a teenager, so was adopted by a wealthy woman called Mrs Josephine Fitzgerald, who sent Dorothy to be educated at a private school in Salisbury. After finishing her education, Dorothy decided that she wanted to be a journalist. Although the suffragette movement was taking off in England, Dorothy struggled to find a job, as no one wanted to hire a young woman.

Eventually, Dorothy had a few articles published in *The Times,* but when the First World War broke out in 1914, she saw an opportunity. Dorothy spoke to many publications asking to be hired as a war correspondent; however, they refused to send a woman to the frontlines. After persisting, *The Times* did give a vague promise about publishing her work, then gave Dorothy a passport so she could travel to Paris in 1915, armed with her bicycle and notepad.

Once in France, Dorothy attempted to volunteer as a civilian employee of the Voluntary Aid Detachment, who provided nursing care for the British military, but she was rejected. Instead, she decided to enter the warzone as a freelance war correspondent, but two miles from the frontline, French police arrested Dorothy and ordered her to leave. That night, Dorothy slept in a forest and thought of another plan. She decided that the only way she could get to the frontline was while disguised as a soldier. With this in mind, Dorothy travelled back to the town and spent her time in cafés where she met British Army soldiers. After befriending these soldiers, Dorothy persuaded them to smuggle her a khaki uniform within their washing. The group of men who helped with this were called the "Khaki Accomplices" in Dorothy's book.

With her outfit ready, Dorothy just needed to turn herself into a man. So she flattened her chest using a corset, widened her shoulders using sacking and cotton wool, cut her hair short, darkened her complexion using a shoe polish and razored her cheeks to give herself shaving rash. Next, Dorothy learned how to act like a man by practicing drills and marching like a soldier. Finally, Dorothy obtained forged papers, taking on the identity of Private Denis Smith of the 1st Bn, Leicestershire Regiment, then she was off to the frontlines.

Dorothy cycled to the Somme, but on the way, her male attire failed somewhat, it was falling off and her tan was dripping down her face. To avoid unwanted male attention when she reached the frontline, Dorothy tried to make herself look less attractive; however, the soldiers had been starved of female company for months. Fortunately, a British Expeditionary Force (BEF) tunnel-digging sapper, named Tom Dunn, took pity on Dorothy and found her an abandoned cottage to sleep in, which was infested with bugs and she had to sleep on a soggy mattress and live off rations that Tom could spare. With her disguise reapplied, Dorothy worked as a sapper, a soldier who performed military engineering duties, including laying mines, operating just 400 yards from the front line. This work involved Dorothy laying mines in no man's land, while constantly under fire from shrapnel, rifles and shells. This work was exhausting and Dorothy worked hard; however, she refused to set off the fuse of explosives which may lead to someone's death.

With the disguise taking its toll, the strenuous and dangerous labour and living off little food, Dorothy's health began to suffer. She suffered from chills, rheumatism and fainting fits. Therefore, after 10 days, Dorothy handed herself in to the commanding sergeant. She feared that if she became so ill that she required treatment, she may be discovered as a woman, leading to the punishment of herself and her new sapper friends. Dorothy was immediately placed under military arrest.

Suspected to be a spy, Dorothy was interrogated at the BEF headquarters, then declared as a prisoner of war. After Dorothy convinced her interrogators that she was not a spy, she was taken to the Third Army headquarters in Calais, this time interrogated by six generals and 20 officers, accusing her of being a prostitute. Next, Dorothy was taken to Saint-Omer and interrogated again, where they believed that Dorothy was a war correspondent. However, the army was embarrassed that a woman had breached security, and they feared that Dorothy would go home and release details about a coming battle, which may compromise their position. They also feared that Dorothy would inspire other women to endanger themselves by travelling to the frontlines, so they kept Dorothy in a convent until the battle was over.

After witnessing the destruction of war, Dorothy wanted to help with the war effort by relaying urgent messages; however, they would not allow this. Instead, Dorothy was made to sign an affidavit, which meant that she could not write about her time on the frontline without being arrested. This was frustrating for Dorothy, as the reason she had travelled to the frontline was to write about her experience. Finally, Dorothy was sent back to London, journeying on the same ship across the Channel that the suffragette, Emmeline Pankhurst, was on.

As soon as she returned to London, Dorothy attempted to write about her experiences on the frontline in *The Wide World Magazine* but was silenced by the War Office. In 1919, a year after the war had ended, Dorothy moved to Islington and published her experiences in a book entitled *Sapper Dorothy Lawrence: The Only English Woman Soldier.* As the war had ended, Dorothy did not think she was still bound to the affidavit. But her book was heavily censored by the War Office, so it was not as successful as she had hoped. After this failure,

Dorothy's mental health began to decline, she suffered from a nervous complaint that caused her to shake so much that she could barely hold a pen. By 1925, Dorothy realised that she could no longer be a journalist, and she had no income.

To make matters worse, authorities began to notice Dorothy's erratic behaviour. Eventually, Dorothy went to a doctor about her mental health and confided in him that she had been raped as a teenager by a guardian. But she was not taken seriously because it was her word against that of a respected male member of the church. So with no family to care for her, as even Josephine Fitzgerald ignored Dorothy's pleas for help, Dorothy was taken into care and deemed as insane. For the next 40 years, Dorothy would be institutionalised at the Colne Hatch Lunatic Asylum, where she died, then was buried in a pauper's grave.

A quote in Dorothy's book reads: "I'll see what an ordinary English girl, without credentials or money, can accomplish. I'll see what I can manage as a war correspondent!" But Dorothy was not an ordinary English girl, she was one with extraordinary determination, independence and resilience. She managed to get herself to the frontlines, slept rough and coped with a copious amount of unwanted male attention. It is a pity that Dorothy was constantly silenced whenever she attempted to tell her story, and it could be this frustration that led to the breakdown of Dorothy's mental health.

Aloha Wanderwell
(1906 – 1996 CE)

The World's Most Widely Travelled Girl

At a young age, Aloha followed her dream to become an adventurer. This led Aloha to become the face of her first expedition and ended up being remembered as the world's most travelled girl. This was not an exaggeration either, considering Aloha circumnavigated the globe, travelled to previously unchartered areas of the world, and documented the lives of tribes that had never been documented before.

Aloha was born in Winnipeg, named Idris; however, her family gave her the nickname "Aloha" because she loved Hawaiian dancing. From a very young age, Aloha was inspired by the idea of travel and used to read her father's collection of childhood books about travel and adventure. At the age of three, Aloha's mother remarried, but when the First World War broke out in 1914, Aloha's stepfather joined the Canadian Expeditionary Force but was transferred to the British Army once he arrived in England.

The family followed him to Europe, and Aloha, with her mother and sister, travelled around England, Belgium, and France, being educated in boarding schools. But in 1917, Aloha's stepfather died in combat at Ypres. At this point, Aloha became a difficult student at her convent school, with her teachers complaining that the tall tomboy could not be changed into a proper young lady.

In 1922, Aloha was just 16 when she saw a job advert declaring "Brains, Beauty & Breeches – World Tour Offer For Lucky Young Woman… Wanted to join an expedition!" So, with a desire for adventure, Aloha applied to the job as a mechanic and filmmaker for a team racing Ford Model Ts around the world in an expedition created by Walter Wanderwell, also known as "Cap".

Cap was a controversial figure who had been jailed during the First World War, suspected to be a German spy; however, he was released at the end of the war. After his release, Cap started the expedition to promote world peace and disarmament. When Aloha met Cap, he gave her a job on the expedition, and she had many chores including translating, driving and helping to produce films of their travels. When she joined the team, Cap encouraged Aloha to take the stage name "Aloha Wanderwell", even though Cap was still married to his first wife. Quickly, Aloha became the face of the expedition, as the film of their adventures, *With Car & Camera Around the World*, mostly followed Aloha.

On this expedition starting in 1922 and ending in 1927, Aloha became the first woman to drive around the world in a Ford vehicle. The journey consisted of 380,000 miles, and they travelled across 80 countries. Within this expedition, Aloha travelled through war-torn France; Italy during Mussolini's rise to power; Germany during their riots and post-war suffering; to the Sphinx in Egypt; Palestine while it was being rebuilt as a new nation; through India, where Aloha almost died of thirst; and Mecca, where Aloha pretended to be a man so that she could pray with the rest of the team.

The expedition had been sponsored by the Ford Motor Company but was also financed by the team themselves, by filming and performing lectures during their travels. There were many times when the team would run into trouble, such as not being able to buy necessities for their cars. They resorted to using kerosene instead of gasoline, crushed bananas for grease, and elephant fat as engine oil. At one point while in China, civil warfare made it impossible to find fuel, so they had to pull the car for 80 miles. At the end of their expedition, one of the cars was donated to Henry Ford; however, this was crushed down to scrap metal to help with the war effort.

While on the Wanderwell Expedition in 1925, Aloha married Cap during the American leg of the expedition. This was because Cap was at risk of being arrested by the FBI under the Mann Act, which prohibits transporting women across the state lines for "immoral purposes". In the same year, Aloha gave birth to their first child, Valri, then two years later the couple had another child, Nile. The couple continued to travel the world together, and Aloha gave travel lectures against a backdrop of silent movies they had produced.

In 1930, Aloha learned to fly a German seaplane, which she landed in an uncharted area of the Amazon River. Aloha and Cap were searching for a lost explorer called Colonel Percival Harrison Fawcett, who had been searching for the Lost City of Z. But after landing the plane in Brazil, they ran out of fuel. So for six weeks, while Cap made his way back to civilisation to secure replacement parts, Aloha stayed with an indigenous tribe called the Bororo tribe.

She became friends with these people and was able to film a documentary, capturing a ceremonial dance, a first contact scenario with the villagers and the Bororo men experiencing sympathetic labour pains. Aloha compiled these scenes into two films, *The Last of the Bororos* and *Flight to the Stone Age Bororos*, which was the first filmed documentation of the Bororo people.

After years of exploring and adventuring together, in 1932, Cap was shot and killed while on his yacht in California, and the murderer was never discovered. Soon later, Aloha was remarried to Walter Baker, a cameraman she had previously worked with. The death of her first husband did not stop Aloha from her passion, as throughout the 1930s, Aloha and her new husband travelled to New Zealand, Australia, Hawaii, India, and Cambodia, just to name a few. At one point on their adventures, the team was surrounded by five herds of elephants and had to shoot their way out to avoid being trampled to death.

To pay for these expeditions, Aloha continued to make films and give lectures. She produced the travelogue *The River of Death* and *To See the World by Car*, in which she revisited some of the sites she saw with her late first husband, Cap. When the Second World War broke out in 1939, Aloha continued to travel but focused on making her films, such as *India Now* and *Australia Now,* less informative, and more about trying to rally troops for the war effort.

Still performing lectures, Aloha decided to also write her autobiography, *Call to Adventure!* This detailed her life as the world's most travelled girl, then eventually, Aloha settled with her husband in Ohio, where she worked in radio broadcasting and journalism. In 1982, Aloha gave a final travel lecture for 150 family members and guests, performed in the Natural History Museum in Los Angeles, before she died years later.

Since she was a teenager, Aloha was an accomplished woman for being the most travelled girl and for being the first woman to circumnavigate the globe in a Ford car. But she was also notable for her bravery as she left the safety of her school and family at the age of 16 to travel the world and to fulfil her passion. Aloha seemed to live a life that gave her a lot of happiness and a thrill of adventure, which was particularly special considering that at that time women were not often given these opportunities.

Irena Sendler
(1910 – 2008 CE)

Rescuer of Children

Irena was a completely selfless person, who put herself in immense danger to save as many Jewish children from the Warsaw Ghetto as possible. With a network of conspirators, Irena smuggled children away from danger and did all she could to reunite these rescued children with their parents after the war had ended. Since her activities during the Holocaust, Irena kept her heroism a secret, and only in the last decade of her life did Irena get the recognition that she deserves.

Born near Warsaw to a doctor, Irena was just seven years old when her father died of typhus. He had contracted this from a patient, who his colleagues had refused to treat as they feared contracting the disease themselves. But Irena's father was a kind man, one of the first Polish Socialists, who would treat the poor free of charge, even if they were Jewish, despite the anti-semitic feelings of the period. After his death, the Jewish community offered Irena and her mother financial support for Irena's education, but they refused this generous gift.

From 1927, Irena studied law and Polish studies at Warsaw University; however, was suspended for several years because she opposed the ghetto-bench system. This was a form of systematic segregation discriminating against Jewish people, and Irena defaced her grade card because it stated "non-Jewish". In the early 1930s, Irena married a man who would eventually spend over five years in a German prisoner of war camp. At this time, Irena began her work as a social worker with the Warsaw Department of Social Welfare and Public Health.

In this role, Irena took care of the poor in the city, paying special attention to young women and homeless single mothers, supporting and educating them about how to avoid venereal diseases and unwanted pregnancy. She also provided meals, financial aid, and other services for orphans, the elderly, the poor, and the destitute.

But when Germany invaded Warsaw at the beginning of World War II in 1939, Irena and her colleagues were barred from assisting the poor Jewish individuals. But this was not acceptable to Irena, so she continued to help the Jewish people of Warsaw by donating clothing, medicine, and money to them, but registering them under Christian names. To protect these people from being discovered, Irena reported these families as having highly infectious diseases, such as typhus and tuberculosis, so that the Nazis would not inspect their homes. Irena also offered food and shelter to the Jewish families; however, supporting the Jewish population became more difficult in 1940 when the Warsaw Ghetto was erected and sealed, with the Jewish community held within.

The Warsaw Ghetto was the size of New York's Central Park, with 450,000 Jewish people crammed inside. The overcrowding created poor hygiene conditions, and the lack of food and medical supplies resulted in epidemic and high death rates. Irena was still determined to help these people. She used her papers as a Polish social worker and papers from a worker of the Contagious Diseases Department, to enter the Ghetto daily, wearing a Star of David as a sign of solidarity to the Jewish population.

The Nazis allowed Irena to enter the Ghetto as they wanted her to check for signs of typhoid and inspect the sanitary conditions, as they feared diseases may spread to those outside of the Ghetto. While inside, Irena would help the Jewish people by providing them with food, clothes, and medical care. But Irena discovered that 5,000 Jewish people were dying a month from starvation and disease, so she decided to rescue Jewish children from the ghetto.

Irena joined the Children's Division of Żegota, an underground network aiming to help the Jewish community after 280,000 Jewish people had been deported to an extermination camp. Now with a codename, Irena and her colleagues made over 3,000 false documents to help smuggle Jewish children away from the ghetto. She also made contacts with orphanages and religious establishments, in addition to foster families who were willing to take in the escaped Jewish children. Finding people willing to shelter Jewish children at massive risk to themselves was difficult, as most Poles were caught up in their own struggles during the war and were passive in the face of the Holocaust.

However, asking Jewish parents to part with their children was more difficult, as these parents knew that although their child had a better chance of survival outside the ghetto, they feared never seeing their child again. Countless times, Jewish parents asked Irena if she could guarantee their children would live if she took them away, but all she could guarantee was that they would die if they remained.

Although escaping the ghetto and assisting Jewish people to escape was punishable by death from 1941, it became an urgent necessity in 1942, because of the Great Liquidation Action. This was the mass deportation of the ghetto residents to extermination camps. The Żegota had five techniques to smuggle away the children: using an ambulance a child could be hidden under a stretcher and driven out of the ghetto; they could escape through a courthouse on the edge of the ghetto; a child could be taken away using sewer pipes or other secret underground passages; the children could be carried out in a trolley while hiding in a trunk or suitcase; and if a child pretended to be sick, or really was sick, they could be legally moved away. Others carried the children out in body bags or coffins, and one mechanic took a baby from the ghetto in his toolbox.

Overall, Irena and the Żegota are thought to have rescued 2,500 Jewish children, both from the Warsaw Ghetto the streets of Warsaw. For each child, Irena documented their name, the address where they were hidden, the Christian name they were given after escaping, and their parents' names. These documents were coded and kept in a jar buried beneath an apple tree, and the hope was that after the war had ended, the jar could be dug up and the children could be reunited with their families.

In 1943, Irena was arrested but managed to stash away the incriminating evidence, including the list of rescued children and the large sums of money used to pay those sheltering the Jewish children. The Nazis took Irena to Piawiak prison where she was questioned and tortured. They demanded the names of the Żegota leaders and others involved in their scheme. During the torture, Irena's legs and feet were fractured, but she still refused to betray the Żegota and the rescued Jewish children.

However, Irena was sentenced to death by shooting as she had been informed upon for helping those within the Warsaw Ghetto. Fortunately, on the day of her execution, the Żegota had bribed the executioner so he helped her to escape. But Irena knew the Gestapo would pursue her, so she remained hidden with her second husband, a Jew who she had helped in the Warsaw Ghetto.

After the war was over, Irena dug up her jars hoping to reunite the rescued children with their families, but tragically, most of the parents had died in the Treblinka death camp. For the rest of her life, Irena continued to provide help for the needy, including organising orphanages for children and co-founding nursing homes and social welfare facilities. Despite the heroic actions of the members of the Żegota, they were harassed, interrogated, imprisoned, and executed after the war, due to Poland's communist government vilifying them. So for most of her life, Irena kept her heroism secret and lived in poverty, until a group of students uncovered her story in the early 2000s. This publicity enabled many people who had been rescued from the Warsaw Ghetto by Irena to call their rescuer to give thanks for their lives.

Most people would consider Irena a heroine who rescued children even though it very nearly cost her life to do so. But Irena disagreed, she stated, "I could have done more, this regret will follow me to my death." Despite her modesty, Irena has been presented with many honours and awards for her efforts in the war, including from the State of Israel, who recognised Irena as Righteous Among the Nations in 1965, a title given to non-Jewish people who helped them during the Holocaust. In 1991 she was made an honorary citizen of Israel. Irena was also awarded Poland's highest distinction, the Order of White Eagle, in 2003, but her favourite award was given to her in 2007 and was the Order of the Smile, an international prize awarded by children.

Irena believed that it is always important to offer help to someone when they need it, no matter what. With this value in mind, Irena risked her life to save 2,500 children and did all she could to reunite them with their families.

Noor Inayat Khan (1914 – 1944 CE)

Highly Dangerous Pacifist

Although a pacifist, Noor was determined to defeat the Nazis during World War II, putting herself in incredible danger to do so. Noor went beyond all expectations anyone had of her, surviving far longer than other radio operators who worked in Nazi-occupied France. Not only did Noor work exceptionally hard throughout her time working in France to get messages to London, but she also remained strong when facing interrogation and torture at the hands of the Nazis.

Noor was born in Moscow to an Indian Muslim father and an American mother but moved to London when she was very young, attending nursery at Notting Hill. Soon later, the family moved again, this time to an idyllic home near Paris. Here, Noor had a happy childhood, with a house full of music and meditation. She would play in the garden with her three younger siblings, and they would sit on the steps outside their house to look at the lights of Paris. But tragedy struck in 1927 when Noor's father died while on a visit to India. Because her mother was grief-stricken, it was up to Noor to become the head of the household, caring for her younger siblings and mother.

In addition to taking on this responsibility, Noor studied child psychology at the Sorbonne, and music at the Paris Conservatory, where she composed for the harp and piano. It was here when Noor fell in love with a Jewish musician and the couple became informally engaged. But Noor's family disapproved of this union, leaving Noor divided between her family and fiancé. Eventually, she broke off the engagement. After completing her education, Noor became a writer of children's stories.

When the Second World War broke out in 1939, France was soon invaded by German troops, so Noor and her family fled to England in 1940. The family were all pacifists; however, Noor and her brother decided that just opposing the fascist regime was not enough, so Noor joined the Women's Auxiliary Air Force (WAAF) that same year. While in the WAAF, Noor trained as a wireless operator; however, found this work dull. Soon, Noor was invited to a mysterious interview, without knowing what she was interviewing for. When she arrived, she spoke in fluent French to the interviewer, then was invited to join the Special Operations Executive (SOE), which was set up by Churchill to aid the Resistance movements in occupied countries.

Their job was to sabotage and provide arms to the Resistance, and they had decided that Noor would work well in this area because she was fluent in French, knew Paris well from living there, and was already trained as a wireless operator. Noor was told that if she accepted, she would be sent as an agent to occupied France with no protection, as she would have no uniform, so if she were captured, she would be shot. Immediately, Noor accepted the job offer.

During training, Noor had to undergo a mock Gestapo interrogation, which terrified Noor and she struggled, leaving her superiors uncertain of her ability to work in the field. She was also doubted because of her lack of athleticism, and they believed she was not incredibly intelligent. Others saw Noor's enthusiasm and determination and decided that she would be a brilliant agent and that the need for agents in France was so high that it did not matter too much anyway. In training, Noor was taught how to handle a gun, use explosives, kill silently, write in code and use Morse code. She was also taught how to identify the enemy based on their uniforms, and how to live with a false identity. Eventually, armed with a false passport, a few French francs, a pistol and a set of pills including a lethal cyanide pill, Noor was sent to France in 1943, wearing a pin on her lapel depicting a silver bird, given to her by a superior for luck.

Noor was the first female radio operator sent into Nazi-occupied France by the SOE and was aware that the work was incredibly dangerous. At the time, an operator's life expectancy was six weeks, because operators were highly vulnerable to detection. This is because if Noor stayed on air transmitting for more than 20 minutes at a time, then the signal would be detected by the enemy, and the source of transmission would be traced, leading to her capture. Noor was to be part of a mission called "Prosper", and her job was to maintain a link between the Resistance and London, to receive and send messages about planned sabotages.

Shortly after Noor arrived in France, many of the members of their network were arrested, eventually leaving Noor as the only operator in the field. It was suggested that she should return to London due to the danger of her arrest, but Noor declined and instead hid in different locations to send her messages to London. This increased Noor's chance of capture because she was forced to carry the bulky transmitter hidden in a suitcase or bundle of firewood. Noor also changed her appearance often by dying her hair.

As she was the only British operator remaining in Paris, Noor did the work of six radio operators and impressed her superiors by surviving for three months and always transmitting flawless messages.

But Noor did have a few incidents when she came close to capture. One example was when Noor moved to a new location and was setting up by hanging her aerial on a branch outside her room when a German officer suddenly appeared without Noor noticing. He took her by surprise by asking if she needed any help, but Noor thought quickly and told him she wanted to listen to the wireless, which was banned at the time. Using her charm, she convinced the German officer to help her set up a transmitter that would soon be transmitting to London. Soon, the work began to exhaust Noor and she worked so hard that she could barely sit up. To make matters more difficult, the Gestapo was searching for Noor, as they knew she was transmitting, but they could not find her and did not know what she looked like.

But after three months of transmitting, Noor was betrayed to the Germans by the sister of the head agent, who had been paid 100,000 francs for Noor's address. Noor was arrested and taken to the SD Headquarters in Paris. As soon as she arrived, Noor demanded a bath, and while the door was locked, she tried to escape out of the window but was caught. After this, Noor was interrogated but refused to give up any information. Later, Noor attempted to escape for the second time, but again was captured, and this time the Germans tried to have Noor sign a declaration renouncing future escape attempts, but she refused.

Noor was imprisoned at Pforzheim prison in Germany, and kept in solitary confinement because she was classified as "highly dangerous". They shackled Noor's hands and feet, so she could not feed or clean herself, and she was kept like this for 10 months, yet remained uncooperative. However, her stoicism was an act, as she was heard crying during the nights. Throughout her torture, Noor constantly refused to betray the SOE. Unfortunately, Noor's notebook, in which she kept details about the messages she sent as an SOE operative, was found by the Germans.

This meant that the Germans were able to send false messages imitating Noor, leading to the capturing and execution of other SOE operatives. Throughout these 10 months, Noor communicated with another inmate by scratching messages on her mess cup, and Noor told this prisoner her name and the address of her mother's house.

One day, Noor was handcuffed and driven to another prison, where she met some of her colleagues who were kept there. They were then put on a train to Munich together and told they were being sent to work as agricultural labourers. This was a lie, Noor and her colleagues were being taken to Dachau concentration camp. On the night of their arrival, Noor was singled out and beaten all night. The next morning, she was asked to kneel before she was shot in the back of the head and killed. Her last word was "Liberté."

Since her death, Noor has been awarded with George Cross in 1949, and the French Croix de Guerre in 1946. More recently, in 2012, a bronze bust depicting Noor has been unveiled by Princess Anne, and in 2020, in a virtual ceremony broadcast, Noor was honoured with a blue plaque at her London home. Noor was strong-willed and extremely hardworking, as she was determined to work for the SOE. At such a young age, Noor demonstrated incredible strength, far beyond what anyone expected of her, refusing to betray her country in the face of torture and execution.

Hedy Lamarr
(1914 – 2000 CE)

The Mother of Wi-Fi

Despite finding plenty of success as an actress, Hedy did not find much happiness. Because of her beauty, Hedy was typecast as the glamorous seductress in films, but was given few lines due to the expectation of leading actresses being beautiful objects to look at, but nothing more. Instead, Hedy's true passion was inventing and innovating, which she was also incredibly successful at; however, she was not appreciated for her contributions during her lifetime.

Hedy was born with the name Hedwig Eva Kiesler in Austria-Hungary, her father was a bank manager from a Galician-Jewish family, and her mother a pianist from a Hungarian-Jewish family. The family was affluent, so from the age of four years old, Hedy had private tutorage, and she was proficient in playing the piano, dancing, and speaking in four languages by the time she was

10 years old. As a child, Hedy was interested in performing and was already very beautiful, as she won a beauty contest in Vienna at the age of just 12.

However, Hedy was more interested in invention, a passion inspired by her father, who would explain how different technologies work while on walks together. Hedy used to take apart her music box and reassemble it to discover the inner workings, demonstrating her early passion for technology and invention.

From the age of 16, Hedy took acting classes in Vienna and worked as a script girl. After just a year, she achieved her first role in a film as an extra in *Money on the Street*. This led to a few other small roles until she landed her breakthrough in 1932 in a Czech film entitled *Ecstasy*, in which she starred as the main character, the neglected wife of an older man. The film was shocking, as Hedy simulated orgasm on screen, which was achieved through a colleague pricking her with a pin.

Also, Hedy was, briefly and tastefully, in nude scenes, which led to the film being banned in the United States for being too sexual; however, it was still a huge success. Later, *Ecstasy* was eventually banned in Germany due to Hedy's Jewish heritage. But despite the controversy, this film made Hedy well-known in the film industry.

Just a few years after the release of *Ecstasy*, at the age of 18, Hedy married Friedrich Mandl, a much older man who had been a fan of Hedy and was quite obsessed with her. He was also a very rich manufacturer and although he was of Jewish and Catholic descent, he forced Hedy to convert to Catholicism before they married, much to the dismay of Hedy's parents. This is just one example of Friedrich being a controlling husband, he also refused to allow Hedy from performing on stage or screen, and even spent $300,000 on copies of *Ecstasy* to destroy, as he did not want others to see his wife having an orgasm on screen.

Eventually, Hedy grew incredibly miserable, as she was not allowed to leave the house, and hated acting as the hostess to Friedrich's business partners, many of whom were associated with the Nazi party. Friedrich even had links to the Italian fascist leader, Mussolini, and was known to sell arms to the Nazis. The only benefit Hedy gained from this marriage was learning about military technology at business meetings with scientists, introducing Hedy to the idea of innovating in the field of weaponry. Eventually, Hedy had enough and disguised herself as a maid before fleeing the house on a bicycle. She divorced Friedrich in 1937.

In the same year, Hedy met Louis B. Mayer, who she agreed to work with as part of his company, MGM Studios. He took Hedy to Hollywood, advertising her as the "world's most beautiful woman". This is when she became "Hedy Lamarr", choosing the name Lamarr out of respect for a silent film star, Barbara La Marr. They chose to change Hedy's name partly to distance her from being the "*Ecstasy* lady", even though that was the film she was famous for.

In 1938, soon after moving to Hollywood, Hedy was cast as the lead in *Algiers*. In this same year, disaster struck Hedy's family and many other Austrian Jewish people, as Austria was annexed by Germany in the incident known as Anschluss. As the family had Jewish ancestry, they immediately fled to America, where Hedy was finding huge success as a beautiful, exotic actress.

But due to her beauty, Hedy found herself typecast as the glamorous seductress, which bored Hedy because she wanted more of a challenge. In this typical role, Hedy normally had very few lines, despite being the lead. To curb her boredom, Hedy took to conducting experiments in her trailer between takes. Once, she visited an aeroplane factory, so she could witness their building, and she was inspired to innovate. After seeing these planes and how they were built, Hedy bought a book of birds and a book of fish, then looked at the fastest of each kind. She combined the fins of the fastest fish and the wings of the fastest birds to sketch a new wing design for military aeroplanes. She was deemed a genius for these designs, demonstrating her natural ability in innovation and design.

However, Hedy was not just bored and unfulfilled, she was also homesick, and shy of the fame she was building. Hedy would not go to beaches because she hated the stares, and she did not enjoy giving autographs, as she could not understand why anyone would want one. Throughout her life, Hedy was married and divorced six times, the last of whom was her divorce lawyer! So Hedy was not getting satisfaction from her personal life or her career.

In 1940, Hedy allegedly claimed that she was not comfortable sitting in Hollywood making money when things in the world were in such a state since World War II broke out just the year before. Hedy believed that the knowledge she had gained from her first husband about munitions and various weaponry could be beneficial. So Hedy started working on an idea that would become the "Secret Communication System". This was a new communication system that could be used to guide torpedoes to their targets in war. She created the idea of "frequency hopping" amongst radio waves, which would prevent the interception of the radio waves by the enemy, meaning that the torpedo could find the intended target by blocking the enemy ships from jamming the torpedo guidance signals.

Hedy was awarded a patent for this in 1942; however, the navy would not use the system during the Second World War because it came from outside the military. However, in the Cuban Missile Crisis of 1962, the American ships were all armed with torpedoes guided by a frequency hopping system. Also, Hedy's idea of frequency hopping is used today as a precursor to secure Wi-Fi, GPS and Bluetooth, which are all used by billions of people around the world. However, Hedy never received any money from her creation.

Although Hedy was not able to help in the war effort with her skills of invention, she was able to use her celebrity status to sell war bonds, which help to finance the military. She travelled to 16 cities in 10 days to perform and encourage the public to buy war bonds, managing to raise $25 million ($350 million now, considering inflation).

During the 1940s, Hedy also formed her own production company and produced two films in which she starred, *The Strange Woman*, and *Dishonoured Lady*. Although these films both made profits, they were not massive successes, partly because many people in Hollywood did not approve of actors producing their own independent films, particularly when they were women. So Hedy continued to act in other films; however, became addicted to "pep pills" which were supplied by the studio, causing erratic behaviour. This was demonstrated in the late 1950s during the initial hearing of her and her fifth husband's divorce, when Hedy sent her movie stand-in in her place.

From 1966, Hedy had mostly finished with acting but did continue to invent. She created a tablet that would dissolve into water to make a fizzy drink, but this was unsuccessful, even Hedy admitted that the drink did not taste nice. Towards the end of her life, Hedy created a fluorescent dog collar, modifications for the supersonic Concorde airliner, and a new kind of stoplight.

Hedy's autobiography was released in 1966 entitled *Ecstasy and Me;* however, in 1969, Hedy claimed that she did not write this book and that much of it was untrue. It turned out that it was written by a ghostwriter named Leo Guild, so Hedy tried to sue the publisher to halt production, but she failed. Instead, Hedy found herself sued by Gene Ringgold because the book plagiarised material from an article he had written, even though Hedy had not written the book. Also in the late 1960s, Hedy was arrested for shoplifting but the charges were dropped. Hedy seemed to be suffering mentally at this point, as she lived in seclusion, not leaving her house because her eyesight was failing. However, Hedy was not completely isolated, as she spoke to her children on the phone for seven hours each day but never left the house to see them. In 1969, Hedy was distraught when her son, a Nebraskan police officer, shot and killed the 14-year-old African-American Vivian Strong, and was acquitted for her murder. After this, Hedy never spoke to him again. Eventually, Hedy died in her Florida home from heart disease, and her ashes were scattered in Vienna Woods in Austria.

Hedy was very successful as an actress, but this was not her true passion. This lack of satisfaction in Hedy's life is demonstrated by the fact that she was married and divorced so many times, and eventually lived secluded from society. Hedy often claimed that her beauty was her biggest curse. She believed that perhaps if she was not so striking, she would have never become an actress, and could have spent her whole life pursuing her true passion of invention and innovation. Although she did not find any reward for her ground-breaking creation of the frequency hopping technology during her lifetime, in 2014 Hedy was inducted into the National Inventors Hall of Fame, and has since been dubbed as "the mother of Wi-Fi".

Édith Piaf
(1915 – 1963 CE)

The Little Sparrow

After a difficult start in life, Édith worked hard to become a renowned singer. Named after Edith Cavell, a British World War I nurse, Édith demonstrated similar determination and passion as her namesake, but in a different line of work. In addition to becoming a hugely successful performer, Édith worked with the French Résistance to enable the escape of Jewish people from Nazi-occupied Paris. Despite many threats to her career, Édith always worked through them and became one of the greatest Parisian singers.

Édith was born with the surname "Gassion", and was allegedly born on the streets of Paris on a policeman's cloak; however, it is more likely that she was born in a local hospital. Her early life was tragic, as Édith's mother, a singer, abandoned her as a baby, giving Édith to her alcoholic parents. Édith's father left to fight in World War I in the French army very soon after her birth. When he returned, he found his two-year-old daughter to be neglected and malnourished, so took her to be cared for by his mother. Although Édith was no longer starving, she was now living in a Normandy brothel, where her grandmother worked as a cook.

The few prostitutes who worked in the brothel helped to care for Édith, and when the child was blinded by keratitis, the prostitutes spent all of their earnings to take Édith on a pilgrimage for St Thérèse of Lisieux. This miraculously healed Édith's sight. But Édith received little formal education while living in the brothel, and Édith's childhood environment may have led to her self-acclaimed weakness for men, as she claimed to have never seen a woman refuse a man.

When Édith grew older, she was taken by her father, a performing acrobat, to sing during his street performances. Then, when she was 14, Édith met Simone Berteaut, likely to be her half-sister, who became her life-long friend. The two girls sang together on the streets, and with the money they earned together, they rented a small room. But in 1932, this room grew crowded when Édith fell in love with Louis Dupont, who soon moved in with the girls, despite his dislike of Simone.

Louis also disliked the fact that his girlfriend earned her money by singing on the streets, so he tried to find jobs for her, which Édith resisted until she became pregnant at the age of 17. After the birth of Édith and Louis' baby girl, Marcelle, in 1933, Édith worked in a factory but quickly returned to singing. This angered Louis, so after a heated argument, Édith took Simone and Marcelle, then left Louis. However, Édith did not know how to care for her baby, so Marcelle was often left alone in the room while Édith and Simone went out to sing together on the streets or in clubs.

Eventually, Louis saw that his baby was being neglected, so took Marcelle away, saying that if Édith wanted to be with their daughter then she would have to return to live with him. But Édith declined this, however did help to pay for the care of Marcelle until she died of meningitis when she was two. To pay for her daughter's funeral, Édith allegedly resorted to prostitution.

In 1935, Édith was heard singing by a nightclub owner, Louis Leplée, who owned Le Gerny's. He immediately offered Édith a job singing in his club, which was visited by the upper and lower classes alike. This would change Édith's life; however, she was extremely nervous to sing in this club. This, along with her tiny height, led to Louis giving Édith the nickname "la Môme Piaf", translating to "The Little Sparrow", which is where Édith's stage name of "Édith Piaf" originated. Louis had Édith wear black dresses, then taught her about stage presence before her opening night, which was attended by celebrities, such as Maurice Chevalier, the French actor. Despite Édith's anxiety, the audience was impressed with the performance. From that night, Édith's career grew, and with Louis' help, she soon released two records in that same year.

However, in 1936, Louis was murdered by two mobsters who were associated with Édith, so she was questioned by the police, suspected of being an accessory to Louis' murder. Although Édith was acquitted, she knew this threatened her career, so quickly made efforts to improve her image. This included recruiting her future lover, Raymond Asso, to work with her, preventing unsavoury acquaintances from meeting with her, and hiring a songwriter who would allude to, and romanticise, Édith's previous life on the streets. These tactics were successful, by 1939, Édith was singing in sell-out performances. Perhaps because of her new found fame, Édith's parents both came back into her life. She was delighted to see her father, who visited weekly, but was frustrated to be called to the police station due to her mother's frequent drunken behaviour.

After the outbreak of World War II, Édith was determined to take the opportunity to improve her career. Before the German occupation of France in 1940, Édith joined a performance with Maurice Chevalier and Johnny Hess for the Red Cross, to support the war effort on the Allied side. Then, when the Nazis approached Paris, Édith fled, undertaking a tour of Toulouse to avoid the invaders, only returning to Paris once the German occupation was fully established. After registering with the German propaganda department and agreeing to have her song lyrics vetted, Édith found herself popular with the Nazis, allowing her to take some liberties. These included recording the song *Ou sont'ils mes petits copains?*, which was about friends who had gone to war, and during one performance, Édith draped herself in a French flag.

But due to her popularity with the Nazis, Édith became a controversial figure. This is because she often performed in Paris brothels and nightclubs for German officers and collaborating Frenchmen. She was even invited to be in a concert tour to Berlin sponsored by the German officials. This popularity enabled Édith's career to flourish, and she was able to live in a luxury flat close to the Paris Gestapo headquarters. But because of this fraternisation with the enemy, after the war there were plans to ban Édith's music from the radio, so she was forced to testify before a purge panel when she was accused of being a traitor and collaborator.

But Andrée Bigard, an important member of the Résistance, spoke in Édith's favour. He claimed that she had allowed him to act as her security, giving him a chance to do important work for the Résistance, such as forging documents and writing letters. She was also responsible for rescuing some Jewish people from Nazi-occupied France, including her colleague, who she paid to be hidden in unoccupied France until the liberation. Édith also performed at prisoner of war camps in Germany, where she would take photos with prisoners which could be used to make forged documents to help the prisoners escape. With this defence, Édith's career continued to thrive.

After the war, Édith remained popular, not only in France but internationally. Édith toured Europe, the United States, and South America. At first, Édith was unsuccessful in America, because her performance was simple, rather than a huge spectacle, but her popularity grew after a good review in the *New York Herald.* In 1946, Édith wrote and performed *La Vie en Rose,* which became her signature song. The song expresses joy at finding true love, which was appealing to the world so soon after the Second World War. Édith released many other of her most popular songs in the post-war period, including *Hymne à l'amour* in 1949, *La Foule* in 1957, and *Padam, padam...* in 1951, just to name a few.

Édith's songs were primarily autobiographical, all about love, loss and sorrow, as she thought that you could not have one without the other two. This idea became particularly true for Édith in the 1940s when she began her affair with the married boxer, Marcel Cerdan, famous for being the former middleweight world champion. Although Édith had many love affairs, she considered Marcel the love of her life, and the affair made headlines. But tragically in 1949, Marcel's plane which he had caught to visit Édith, crashed, killing everyone on board. The heartbreak that followed is likely to have inspired much of Édith's music. On the night of Marcel's death, Édith insisted on continuing with her performance, dedicating it to Marcel. Due to the sadness and shock, Édith fainted on stage but continued the performance after recovering.

In 1951, Édith was injured in a car crash, leading to morphine and alcohol addictions, which were exacerbated by two more near-fatal car crashes. To fight this addiction, Édith's first husband, Jacques Pills, took her to rehabilitation multiple times, but to no avail, and the pair divorced in 1957. These addiction problems continued throughout Édith's life, and she shared her addiction to alcohol with her second husband who she married in 1962. He was a performer called Théo Sarapo, and was 20 years younger than Édith and thought to be homosexual.

Near the end of her life, Édith had to undergo surgeries for a stomach ulcer due to her alcoholism and the medication that she took for arthritis and insomnia. In addition to this, Édith required a blood transfusion, and her liver was deteriorating. Due to these health issues, Édith died at the age of just 47 and was buried next to her daughter. Although she was denied a funeral Mass, Édith's funeral procession drew 10,000s of mourners to the streets of Paris.

Édith's last words were "Every damn thing you do in life, you have to pay for", which is a fitting quote for Édith, who had to work diligently to go from singing on the streets of Paris to becoming one the greatest singers of her time. However, Édith paid for the price of success with her health. Years later, in 1998, Édith's signature song, *La Vie en rose*, was voted a Grammy Hall of Fame Award, demonstrating that Édith's legacy has continued despite her early demise.

Andrée Borrel
(1919 – 1944 CE)

The Best of Us All

As the first female Special Operations Executive (SOE) agent to be parachuted into Nazi-occupied France, it is clear that Andrée was an incredibly brave woman. Before working for SOE, Andrée worked with the French Resistance on the Pat O'Leary Line, which involved her sheltering British airmen and aiding their escape out of Nazi-occupied France. While working as a SOE agent, Andrée quickly rose through the ranks because of her skills in the field, demonstrating her competence as an agent for the Resistance. Tragically, Andrée's time as a SOE agent was cut short when a double agent betrayed her and other members of the Resistance.

Andrée was born near Paris to a working-class family, and as a young child, she was described as a tomboy by her older sister, Léone, because she loved to climb and hike. At the age of 11, Andrée's father died, so she had to start supporting her family. This meant that when she was just 14, Andrée had to leave school, so she could work for a dress designer. Later, Andrée worked as a shop assistant in a Parisian bakery, then moved to a new job so she could have Sundays off to pursue her passion of cycling.

However, due to her mother's ill health requiring a warmer climate, Andrée and her family travelled to Toulon to live with family friends. From a young age, Andrée had socialist sympathies, so when the Spanish Civil War broke out, Andrée was determined to support the republican government in their fight against the fascists, who were supported by the Nazis. But by the time Andrée arrived in Spain, the war was lost, so she returned to France.

When the Second World War broke out in 1939, Andrée had another chance to fight against fascism. She trained in nursing with the Red Cross to join the Association des Dames Françaises, so that she could treat wounded soldiers. However, when France surrendered to Germany soon later, Andrée and her colleague, Maurice Dufour, decided to join the French Resistance. In 1941, they established the Villa Rene-Therese near the Spanish border, which was a safe house along the Pat O'Leary Line. This was a network of safe houses established by Albert Guérisse to enable injured British airmen, SOE agents, Jewish people, and others to escape Nazi-controlled France over the Pyrenees.

Andrée is thought to have aided and sheltered at least 65 Allied evaders, mostly British Royal Air Force airmen who were shot down over France. But within months, the escape network had been compromised by a double agent, so Andrée and Maurice abandoned their base and hid in Toulouse until they could escape to Portugal. While there, Andrée worked at the Free French Propaganda office at the British Embassy in Lisbon but travelled to London in 1942 to help in the war effort in a different way.

Once she arrived in England, Andrée was taken to the Royal Patriotic School, the MI5 security clearance centre, where she was interrogated as a double agent. They decided that Andrée was not a spy, but an "excellent type of country girl, who has the intelligence and seems a keen patriot". Understanding that Andrée wanted to help push the Nazis from her homeland, the British recommended Andrée to the Free French Forces. However, they were not interested in recruiting her because she had worked with the British on the Pat O'Leary Line and refused to divulge certain information. Instead, Andrée was approached by the Special Operations Executive (SOE), who wanted Andrée to work for them in France, supporting the French Resistance.

Andrée accepted this job offer and soon started training, in which she learned skills such as hand-to-hand combat and Morse code. When Andrée was asked how she would kill a Nazi with just what she had on her, Andrée responded with "I would jam a pencil through his brain. And he'd deserve it."

Soon, Andrée was cleared as a field agent, then promoted to lieutenant. Then, with the support of her commander, Andrée, now with the codename "Denise", and another agent, Lise de Baissac, became the first female SOE agents to be parachuted into Nazi-occupied France as part of the operation "Whitebeam". Andrée had been chosen to work as a courier, due to her intimate knowledge of Paris, for the new Prosper circuit in Paris. Her job was to raise bands of Resistance members in France to carry out guerrilla attacks against Nazi troops, coordinate aerial supply drops, and recruit, arm, and train Resistance members.

Francis Suttill ran the Prosper circuit and found Andrée so competent that she was made the second in command of the Paris circuit, with Francis describing her as "the best of us all". But in June 1943, Andrée and several other key members of Prosper had been betrayed by a double agent and were arrested by the Gestapo. Andrée was first taken to the Gestapo headquarters in Paris where she was interrogated; however, Andrée remained silent, so she was held at Fresnes Prison. During her time in Fresnes Prison, Andrée wrote many letters to her mother on cigarette paper, which she hid in her lingerie that was sent to her sister for washing. These notes were messages of love, reassuring her mother, and sending many kisses. But Andrée also wrote that she was betrayed by a man called Norman, who told the Germans everything.

In addition to writing these letters to her mother, Andrée also wrote coded messages to her sister, giving details about her captors. Then, Andrée was handcuffed to a guard and put on a train to Germany, where she was imprisoned in the civilian women's prison at Karlsruhe. She spent her time in the prison hard at work, peeling potatoes, sewing and completing other manual work, which helped pass the time. While at the prison, Andrée could hear the war coming closer, so hoped that she would soon be liberated.

However, just two months later, Andrée and three other SOE agents were given their belongings and escorted to the Natzweiler-Struthof concentration camp, located in Alsace in France. The four women were placed in isolated cells, before being taken one by one to the crematorium building. Once there, Andrée was asked to undress for a medical check, then given an injection, which the prisoners were told was to prevent them from contracting typhus. The injection was actually a strong dose of phenol, which the camp doctor believed to be fatal.

When the women fell unconscious due to the effects of the phenol, they were each placed into the crematorium oven and burned. Andrée was the last to be forced into the oven and when she was halfway inside, she woke up, and during the struggle, she left a severe scratch down the camp executioner's face before being burned to death.

Andrée lived for just 25 years but demonstrated such bravery by her willingness to fight the fascists in the Spanish Civil War, nursing for the Red Cross, working on the underground Pat O'Leary Line to rescue Allied forces, and working as an agent for SOE. When she was interrogated by the Gestapo, Andrée was said to have such a determined, disdainful silence that even the Nazis knew they could not break her, so Andrée went to her death refusing to betray her country, which she was so desperately trying to save from the clutches of the Nazis. After her death, Andrée was honoured with the Croix de Guerre by the French government, and the King's Commendation for Brave Conduct from Britain for her sacrifice.

Françoise Gilot
(1921–2023 CE)

The Astonishingly Good Artist

Since she was a young child, Françoise displayed huge passion and talent for art. Although she faced adversity, such as the Nazi's occupation of France and her turbulent relationship with Picasso, Françoise continued to focus on her art. As a painter, Françoise was magnificent and unique, using bright colours and was inspired by the cubism style; however, developed her own style, which is softer and more organic.

Françoise was born in France with two very different parents: her mother was a watercolour artist, and her father was a strict businessman. From a young age, Françoise was treated like a boy, which she enjoyed because it meant she was entitled to more opportunities. As he was a well-educated man, Françoise's father ensured that she received a good education at home from an early age, and Françoise could read and write by the age of three. Françoise also became ambidextrous, as she was naturally left-handed, but her father demanded that she write with her right hand. Françoise's father oversaw her learning of Greek mythology and hoped that his daughter would become a scientist or a lawyer.

From the age of five, Françoise began to learn about art from her mother, who tutored Françoise in using watercolours and India ink. But she never drew in pencil, because Françoise's mother thought artists rely too heavily on rubbers, and wanted her daughter to learn to incorporate her mistakes into her art. Françoise was also taught by her mother's teacher in art for six years, which helped to develop her passion. This early and vigorous tutorage gave Françoise a good eye for art. But this skill came naturally too, as when she was just five years old at a party, Françoise showed particular interest in a man who turned out to be the painter, Emile Mairet. After this event, Françoise was able to frequently visit his art studio, which helped to inspire her own art.

To her father's dismay, Françoise achieved a degree in philosophy, rather than science or law, at the British Institute in Paris in 1938. Soon after, Françoise then received a degree in English literature from the University of Cambridge, before her father sent her to Rennes in 1939, where she finally began law school. This was also when the Second World War broke out, and Françoise thought that Rennes would be safer than Paris from German bombing. Much of Françoise's very early work was destroyed during the war when her parents attempted to move it to safety out of Paris, but the truck carrying Françoise's valuable drawings and watercolours was destroyed. Françoise made up for this by painting constantly in her free time, even skipping morning classes to practice art.

Eventually, Françoise's lack of interest in law led to her dropping out at the age of 19 so that she could devote herself completely to art. Around this time, Françoise was back in Paris after the German occupation. Françoise found herself detained by the police for the act of laying flowers on the Tomb of the Unknown Soldier and was put on a list of agitators.

By 1943, Françoise had made a name for herself at art school and was already selling a lot of her art, partly due to her aptitude for business. One day, she was having lunch with some friends at a restaurant, when she was noticed by the 61-year-old Pablo Picasso. He was dining with his mistress at the time, Dora Maar, but at the end of the meal, he walked over to Françoise, offered her a bowl of cherries, and invited her to his studio. Françoise introduced herself to Picasso as a painter, and he laughed, saying "girls who look like you could never be painters." Françoise began a relationship with Picasso, despite expecting a catastrophe from this relationship, replacing Dora Maar as the painter's mistress. At first, the relationship was an intellectual friendship, but it soon blossomed into a romance. By 1946, Françoise abandoned her disapproving family and moved in with Picasso, as his mistress and his muse.

Soon after moving in together, Picasso took Françoise to meet another great artist, Matisse. This was an incredible moment for Françoise, who felt more akin to Matisse's work than Picasso's and had loved his art since she was a young teenager. But Matisse made Picasso jealous, by stating that he wanted to paint a portrait of Françoise with green hair and a light blue complexion. So that year, Picasso painted the La Femme-fleur series, in which Françoise was painted as a semi-abstract, pale green and blue flower.

During their 10-year relationship, Françoise and Picasso never married, as he was still married to Olga Khokhlova, who harassed Françoise on the streets. In the late 1940s, Françoise had two children, Claude and Paloma. Françoise did not really want children as she hated being pregnant, but Picasso insisted on it. Françoise believed this was because he preferred her being pregnant because she was weaker. Throughout their relationship, Picasso became increasingly controlling and cruel to Françoise, provoking her with his misogynistic views, such as stating that there were just two types of women: goddesses and doormats. Picasso even physically abused Françoise during their relationship by burning her cheek with a cigarette when he felt she was not paying him enough attention. However, despite Picasso describing himself as a man that no woman would leave, Françoise felt like a prisoner in their relationship and eventually left Picasso in 1953.

But Picasso did not take his rejection well and tried to sabotage Françoise's art career, which had flourished during their relationship. He told art dealers not to buy her art, or else he would not allow them to have his. So in 1961, Françoise moved to America, where 80% of her collectors were from, to escape Picasso's orbit. Fortunately, this decision proved successful, and Françoise's art kept selling. Years later, Françoise wrote *Life with Picasso*, which was an extremely successful book, despite Picasso attempting to legally stop its publication. After its release, Picasso refused to see Claude and Paloma again.

During her time with Picasso, Françoise was inspired by his art and cubist style. Although their art styles were similar, Françoise tended to avoid the sharp edges which Picasso is known for. This led to Françoise developing her own softer style, and she used organic figures in her art. Françoise's use of colour was magnificent and bright, and her layers of paint gave a less deliberate effect. Sometimes Françoise referenced stories in her art. Later in life, Françoise painted on a flat surface and then pressed the image onto paper, creating a beautiful effect.

In 1955, just a few years after leaving Picasso, Françoise married another artist, Luc Simon, and had another daughter named Aurélia in 1956. However, the couple divorced after seven years of marriage. Eventually, Françoise met Jonas Salk, a polio vaccine pioneer, and their mutual love of architecture led to their spending lots of time together and falling in love. One day, Jonas asked Françoise to marry him, but she declined, stating that she was not looking for someone to marry. But Jonas knew that they loved each other, so asked her to write down all the reasons why she would not marry him. After discussing her list, Jonas convinced Françoise that their marriage could work, so the pair were married in Paris in 1970.

During their marriage, the couple spent six months of every year apart, as Françoise travelled to paint across the world, and designed costumes, stage sets, and masks for productions at the Guggenheim in New York City. But their marriage was happy and lasted until Jonas' death. Since then, Françoise worked as the director of the *Virginia Woolf Quarterly* journal from 1973 and was on the board of the Department of Fine Arts at the University of Southern California, where she taught summer courses. In 1990, Françoise was made a member of the Légion d'Honneur in France and was promoted to an officer of the order in 2009. But with age, Françoise began to lose her sight, then suffered with heart and lung ailments which led to her death at the age of 101.

Françoise was a woman who knew her worth, and was not modest, accurately describing herself as "astonishingly good". Because of this, she bought back some of her art at auctions. Françoise claimed to not paint for the public, but herself, and even preferred it when people do not like her art, as it meant she was able to keep it. She was a woman who lived for her passion and continued to paint until her death, always preferring to be defined as an artist rather than "Picasso's lover" or "a friend of Matisse". As well as being an incredible artist, Françoise had an incredibly strong will and always chose not to dwell in the past, but to move forward and focus on her art.

Truus and Freddie Oversteegen (1923 – 2018 CE)

The Nazi-Killing Sisters

Inspired by their mother, Truus and Freddie knew that if they saw an injustice, it was up to them to do something about it. Because of their youthful and innocent appearances, Truus and Freddie were sought out by the Resistance to help them fight the Nazis and Dutch collaborators after the Nazi occupation of the Netherlands. This was an incredible risk, as if they were found out, they could have been executed. But despite their brave actions, neither sister received any recognition for their service to their country until recently.

Truus and Freddie grew up in Haarlem, in the Netherlands, on a barge, and before the outbreak of the Second World War, the family took in Lithuanian refugees. However, after their parents divorced, Truus and Freddie moved to a small apartment, living in poverty with their single, working-class mother. As children, their mother taught the girls about her communist ideals, which she demonstrated when the Second World War broke out.

In their small apartment, Truus and Freddie had to share a room to make room for the Jewish people, dissidents and homosexual people who had fled Germany and were sheltered by the small family. But in 1940, this became more dangerous after the German occupation of the Netherlands. Immediately, the family burned their radical literature which could criminalise them. At this time, Truus and Freddie were taught by their mother to always fight injustice.

With this in mind, Truus and Freddie helped their mother to distribute anti-Nazi newspapers and pamphlets. The sisters worked together, with one of them pasting an illegal poster on a wall over Nazi propaganda, while the other served as a lookout. Soon, a commander with the Haarlem Resistance Group noticed the two girls spreading their pamphlets before cycling away from the scene as fast as possible, and paid a visit to the house. He asked if he could recruit the two teenagers, just 16 and 14 at the time, to work with the Resistance. He believed that their youth and gender would be valuable in fighting the Nazis as they were less likely to be suspected. With their mother's blessing, the girls joined the Resistance.

Soon, the girls learned to sabotage bridges and railway lines, then they were taught to shoot Nazis. To make themselves appear less suspicious, they made themselves look more feminine with make-up, and Freddie braided her hair so she looked younger and more innocent. It was Freddie, the younger of the two sisters, who made the first kill. She was assigned to kill a Dutch woman who planned on handing over a list of Jewish people to the Germans. After approaching the woman in a park, and asking her name to confirm her identity, Freddie shot the collaborator.

After this, the sisters' most common method of attack was a drive-by, in which Truus would cycle a bike, while Freddie sat on the back and shot the target. One of the sisters' earliest missions was arson, as they burned down a Nazi warehouse and flirted with the guards to distract them.

At least once, Freddie seduced an SS officer in a tavern, seductively suggesting that they go for a stroll in the woods. Once she had brought him to the secluded woods, another Resistance officer shot him. In addition to seduction, Freddie was particularly good at following a target and keeping a lookout, as she never drew attention to herself. This enabled her to follow a target to their home and shoot them, or ambush them on bikes before shooting them.

Although the sisters killed many people during the war, Freddie expressed that each time she did so, she would have the urge to run to the victim as he fell, as she was disgusted by killing a human being. But they lived in a time when there was an incentive to kill.

One example of this was when Truus saw a Dutch SS soldier grab a baby and smash its head against the wall in front of the baby's father and sister. After the soldier had murdered the baby, Truus shot him right then and there, despite not being on a Resistance mission.

However, although attacking collaborators and soldiers was seen as a "necessary evil" by the sisters, they did face instances when they had to refuse a mission. Once, the Resistance asked them to take the children of a senior Nazi hostage, as they were to be exchanged for captured members of the Dutch Resistance. However, it was ordered that the children of the Nazi should be killed if negotiations failed, so Freddie and Truus refused, saying that Resistance fighters do not murder children.

In fact, Truus and Freddie considered rescuing children as the most important part of their job. They aided Jewish children by smuggling them out of the country and helping them to escape concentration camps. Truus and Freddie also helped the Resistance by working in the emergency hospital and guiding Jewish people to safe houses.

In 1943, Truus and Freddie were joined by a young woman called Hannie Schaft. She was a former university student, studying human-rights law, who had to drop out of university because she refused to sign a pledge of loyalty to Germany. Soon, the three girls became close friends, and went on assassination missions as a trio, luring, ambushing, and killing Nazis and collaborators. They knew that if they got caught, the consequence would be execution. This became a reality in 1945, when Hannie was arrested for working with the Resistance, and killed by the Nazis just three weeks before the war ended in Europe. Allegedly, during her execution, Hannie was initially just wounded by the executioner, so before he took the final fatal shot, Hannie's last words were "I'm a better shot."

After the war, Freddie served as a board member on the National Hannie Schaft Foundation, which was established by Truus. Both sisters married, Freddie to Jan Dekker, with whom she had three children, and Truus to Piet Menger, a fellow Resistance fighter, with whom she had four children, with the oldest named after Hannie Schaft. To cope with the events of the war, Truus spent much of her life speaking at universities and secondary schools about war, anti-Semitism, tolerance, and indifference. She also expressed her experiences of the war in a book, *Not Then, Not Now, Not Ever,* published in 1982. As well as expressing her grief through writing and speaking, Truus started sculpting after the war. Freddie on the other hand remained quieter about her experience in the Resistance, feeling haunted by those she killed. Both sisters suffered from insomnia after the war, and terrifying nightmares which caused them to scream and fight in their sleep, but neither regretted killing Nazis after witnessing the atrocities they committed. Both Truus and Freddie died at the age of 92, still haunted by their pasts.

After the war, neither sister was recognised for their role in the Resistance, instead, they were brushed aside as communists. However, in 2014, they both were elated to receive national recognition for their service to their country by being awarded the Mobilisatie-Oorlogskruis. Although both were teenagers at the time, Truus and Freddie were willing to risk their lives to fight the injustice that they witnessed after their home had been occupied, demonstrating their incredible courage and sense of justice.

Reference List

Pharaoh Hatshepsut
(1507 – 1458 BCE)

History.com Editors. "Hatshepsut." *HISTORY,* A&E Television Networks, 16 Dec. 2009, https://www.history.com/topics/ancient-history/hatshepsut

Tyldesley, Joyce. "Hatshepsut and Tuthmosis: a royal feud?" *History,* BBC, 17 Feb. 2011,

https://www.bbc.co.uk/history/ancient/egyptians/hatshepsut_01.shtml

Wilson, Elizabeth B. "The Queen Who Would Be King." *History,* Smithsonian Magazine, Sept. 2006, <https://www.smithsonianmag.com/history/the-queen-who-would-be-king-130328511/>

Sappho
(630 – 570 BCE)

Johnson, Marguerite. "Guide to the classics: Sappho, a poet in fragments." *The Conversation,* 12 Feb. 2018, https://theconversation.com/guide-to-the-classics-sappho-a-poet-in-fragments-90823

Mendelsohn, Daniel. "Girl, Interrupted: Who was Sappho?" *A Critic At Large,* The New Yorker, 16 Mar. 2015,

https://www.newyorker.com/magazine/2015/03/16/girl-interrupted

Poetry Foundation Editors. "Sappho." *Poetry Foundation,* n.d.,

https://www.poetryfoundation.org/poets/sappho

Empress Lü Zhi
(241 – 180 BCE)

Jacks, Lauralee. "Empress Lu Zhi of Han – China's first reigning Empress." *History of Royal Women,* 30 Sept. 2017, https://www.historyofroyalwomen.com/the-royal-women/empress-lu-zhi-han-chinas-first-reigning-empress/

Koon, Wee Kek. "Why one of China's first empresses was an able rule, despite psychopathic tendencies." *Opinion Reflections,* Post Magazine, 31 May 2018, https://www.scmp.com/magazines/post-magazine/short-reads/article/2148446/why-one-chinas-first-empresses-was-able-ruler

The Chairman's Bao Editors. "Chinese Emperors and Empresses: Lü Zhi of Han, China's First Empress." *The Chairman's Bao,* n.d., https://www.thechairmansbao.com/chinese-emperors-empresses-lu-zhi-han-chinas-first-empress/

Qian, Zhang. "Queen Lu was ruthless and cruel." *Shine,* 12 Sept. 2017, https://www.shine.cn/feature/art-culture/1709113495/

Trưng Trắc and Trưng Nhị
(12 – 43 CE)

Encyclopaedia Britannica Editors. "Trung Sisters: Vietnamese rebel leaders." *Encyclopaedia Britannica,* 1 Mar. 2016, https://www.britannica.com/topic/Trung-Sisters

Georgievska, Marija. "The Trung sisters: The national heroines of Vietnam, who successfully repelled a Chinese invasion for three years." *The Vintage News,* 20 Dec. 2016, https://www.thevintagenews.com/2016/12/20/the-trung-sisters-the-national-heroines-of-vietnam-who-successfully-repelled-a-chinese-invasion-for-three-years/?chrome=1

History 101 Editors. "Trung Sisters: The incredible story of Vietnam's rebel leaders." *History 101,* n.d., https://www.history101.com/trung-sisters-vietnamese-rebel-leaders/

Rajapaksha, Piumi. "Hai Bà Trưng: The Story of Vietnam's Elephant-Riding Warrior Princesses." *Culture Trip,* 16 Feb. 2018, https://theculturetrip.com/asia/vietnam/articles/hai-ba-trung-the-story-of-vietnams-elephant-riding-warrior-princesses/

Reese, M. R. "Hell Hath No Fury Like the Freedom Fighting Trung Sisters." *Ancient Origins,* 15 Apr. 2022, https://www.ancient-origins.net/history-famous-people/trung-sisters-002199

Empress Jingū
(169 – 269 CE)

Encyclopaedia Britannica Editors. "Jingū." *Encyclopaedia Britannica,* 11 Mar. 2019, https://www.britannica.com/topic/Jingu

Encyclopedia.com Editors. "Jingū (C. 201 – 269)." *Encyclopedia.com,* 25 Aug. 2022, https://www.encyclopedia.com/women/encyclopedias-almanacs-transcripts-and-maps/jingu-c-201-269

St Agnes of Rome
(291 – 304 CE)

Catholic Online Editors. "St. Agnes." *Catholic Online,* n.d., https://www.catholic.org/saints/saint.php?saint_id=106

Encyclopaedia Britannica Editors. "St. Agnes." *Encyclopaedia Britannica,* 25 Jul. 2021, https://www.britannica.com/biography/Saint-Agnes

Encyclopedia.com Editors. "Diocletian, Persecution Of." *Encyclopedia.com,* 25 Aug. 2022, https://www.encyclopedia.com/religion/encyclopedias-almanacs-transcripts-and-maps/diocletian-persecution

Hypatia of Alexandria
(370 – 415 CE)

Deakin, Michael. "Hypatia." *Encyclopaedia Britannica,* 25 Feb. 2022, https://www.britannica.com/biography/Hypatia

Mark, Joshua J. "Hypatia of Alexandria." *World History Encyclopedia,* 2 Sept. 2009, https://www.worldhistory.org/Hypatia_of_Alexandria/
O'Connor, J. J. and Robertson, E. F. "Hypatia of Alexandria." *Mac Tutor,* Apr. 1999, https://mathshistory.st-andrews.ac.uk/Biographies/Hypatia/
Zielinski, Sarah. "Hypatia, Ancient Alexandria's Great Female Scholar." *History,* Smithsonian Magazine, 14 Mar. 2010,
https://www.smithsonianmag.com/history/hypatia-ancient-alexandrias-great-female-scholar-10942888/

Liu Chuyu
(446 – 465 CE)

Wikipedia Editors, "Liu Chuyu." *Wikipedia,* 5 Mar. 2022, https://en.wikipedia.org/wiki/Liu_Chuyu
Wikipedia Editors, "Liu Song dynasty." *Wikipedia,* 11 Jun. 2022, https://en.wikipedia.org/wiki/Liu_Song_dynasty#Reign_of_Emperor_Xiaowu_and_Qianfei
WikiVisually Editors. "Liu Chuyu." *WikiVisually,* n.d., https://wikivisually.com/wiki/Liu_Chuyu

Queen Seondeok of Silla
(606 – 647 CE)

Cartwright, Mark. "Queen Seondeok." *World History Encyclopedia,* 14 Oct. 2016, https://www.worldhistory.org/Queen_Seondeok/
New World Encyclopedia Editors. "Queen Seondeok of Silla." *New World Encyclopedia,* n.d.,
https://www.newworldencyclopedia.org/entry/Queen_Seondeok_of_Silla
Rocket, Andrew. "Queen Seondeok of Silla." *Traditionaleastasia,* Badass Female Rulers, n.d.,
http://projects.leadr.msu.edu/traditionaleastasia/exhibits/show/badass-female-rulers/queen-seondeok-of-silla

Szczepanski, Kallie. "Who Was Queen Seondeok of the Silla Kingdom?" *ThoughtCo.,* 22 Oct. 2019, https://www.thoughtco.com/queen-seondeok-of-koreas-silla-kingdom-195722

Empress Wu Zetian
(624 – 705 CE)

Chao-Fong, Léonie. "10 Facts About Wu Zetian: The Only Empress of China." *HistoryHit,* 22 Jan. 2020, https://www.historyhit.com/facts-about-wu-zetian-the-only-empress-of-china/

Dash, Mike. "The Demonization of Empress Wu." *History,* Smithsonian, 10 Aug. 2012, https://www.smithsonianmag.com/history/the-demonization-of-empress-wu-20743091/

Factinate Editors. "Ruthless Facts About Wu Zetian, The Only Empress of China." *Factinate,* n.d., https://www.factinate.com/people/42-ruthless-facts-wu-zetian-empress-china/

Mark, Emily. "Wu Zetian." *World History Encyclopedia,* 17 Mar. 2016, https://www.worldhistory.org/Wu_Zetian/

Pope Joan
(818 – 857 CE)

ABC News Editors. "Looking for Pope Joan." *ABC News,* 19 Aug. 2015, https://abcnews.go.com/Primetime/pope-joan/story?id=1453197

Andrews, Evan. "Who was Pope Joan?" *History,* 10 Jun. 2015, https://www.history.com/news/who-was-pope-joan

Encyclopaedia Britannica Editors. "Pope Joan." *Encyclopaedia Britannica,* 11 Sept. 2020, https://www.britannica.com/topic/Pope-Joan

Mingren, Wu. "Pope Joan: The Female Pope Whose Gender was Revealed When She Gave Birth in a Procession." *Ancient Origins,* 22 Oct. 2020, https://www.ancient-origins.net/history-famous-people/female-pope-joan-020365

Murasaki Shikibu
(978 – 1014 CE)

Encyclopaedia Britannica Editors. "Murasaki Shikibu." *100 Women,* Encyclopaedia Britannica, n.d.,
https://www.britannica.com/explore/100women/profiles/murasaki-shikibu
Encyclopaedia Britannica Editors. "Murasaki Shikibu." *Encyclopaedia Britannica,* 1 May 2019,
https://www.britannica.com/biography/Shikibu-Murasaki
McMillan, Eric. "Murasaki Shikibu." *The Greatest Literature of All Time,* Editor Eric, n.d., http://www.editoreric.com/greatlit/authors/Murasaki.html
New World Encyclopedia. "Murasaki Shikibu." *New World Encyclopedia,* n.d.,
https://www.newworldencyclopedia.org/entry/Murasaki_Shikibu
Reese, Lyn. "Murasaki Shikibu." *Women in World History Curriculum,* n.d.,
http://www.womeninworldhistory.com/heroine9.html

Empress Matilda
(1102 – 1167 CE)

Castor, Helen. "Empress Matilda, daughter of Henry I: a queen in a king's world." *History Extra,* 10 Sept. 2020,
https://www.historyextra.com/period/medieval/matilda-daughter-of-henry-i-a-queen-in-a-kings-world/
Encyclopaedia Britannica Editors. "Matilda." *Encyclopaedia Britannica,* 6 Sept. 2022, https://www.britannica.com/biography/Matilda-daughter-of-Henry-I
English Monarchs Editors. "Maud, Daughter of King Henry I." *English Monarchs,* n.d., https://www.englishmonarchs.co.uk/normans_21.html
Ford, David Nash. "Empress Matilda (1101 – 1169)." *Royal Berkshire History,* David Nash Ford Publishing, n.d.,
http://www.berkshirehistory.com/bios/matilda.html
Johnson, Ben. "Empress Maud." *Historic UK,* n.d.,
https://www.historicuk.com/HistoryUK/HistoryofEngland/Empress-Maud/
Lewis, Jone Johnson. "Biography of Empress Matilda, Contender for the English Throne." *ThoughtCo.,* 4 Jun. 2019,

https://www.thoughtco.com/empress-matilda-biography-3528825

Spartacus Educational Editors. "Queen Matilda." *Spartacus Educational,* n.d., https://spartacuseducational.com/MEDmatilda.htm

Hōjō Masako
(1156 – 1225 CE)

Encyclopaedia Britannica Editors. "Hōjō Masako." *Encyclopedia Britannica,* 12 Aug. 2022, https://www.britannica.com/biography/Hojo-Masako

Japanese Wiki. "Hojo Masako." *Japanese Wiki,* n.d., https://www.japanese-wiki-corpus.org/person/Masako%20HOJO.html

Johnson, Linda L. "Hojo Masado (1157 – 1225)." *Encyclopedia.com,* n.d., https://www.encyclopedia.com/women/encyclopedias-almanacs-transcripts-and-maps/hojo-masako-1157-1225

New World Encyclopedia Editors. "Hojo Masako." *New World Encyclopedia,* n.d., https://www.newworldencyclopedia.org/entry/Hojo_Masako

Rejected Princesses Editors. "Masako Hojo." *Rejected Princesses,* n.d., https://www.rejectedprincesses.com/princesses/masako-hojo

Queen Tamar the Great
(1166 – 1213 CE)

Alexander and Roberts Editors. "Tamar the Great: Georgia's Queen of Kings." *Alexander and Roberts,* 7 Feb. 2018, https://www.alexanderroberts.com/blogs/blog/july-2018/tamar-the-great-georgias-queen-of-kings.aspx

Badass Ladies of History Editors. "Tamar the Great." *Badass Ladies of History,* n.d., https://badassladiesofhistory.wordpress.com/1000-ce-modern-day/leaders-politicians/tamar-of-georgia/

Chumburidze, Davit. "Queen Tamar The Great: 1184 – 1213." *History of Georgia,* 30 Jan. 2010, https://sites.google.com/site/historyofgeorgia/home/queentamarthegreat1184-1213

Dzagnidze, Baia. "A Brief History of Georgia's Only Female King." *Culture Trip,* 6 April 2021, https://theculturetrip.com/europe/georgia/articles/a-brief-history-of-georgias-only-female-king/

Georgian Journal Editors. "15 things to know about Tamar the Great – First female monarch of Georgia." *Discover Georgia,* Georgian Journal, 12 Jan. 2018, https://georgianjournal.ge/discover-georgia/34095-15-things-to-know-about-tamar-the-great-first-female-monarch-of-georgia.html

Goodyear, Michael. "Queen Tamar." *World History Encyclopedia,* 20 Jan. 2020, https://www.worldhistory.org/Queen_Tamar/

Mingren, Wu. "Queen Tamar: The Confident Female Ruler of the Georgian Golden Age." *Ancient Origins,* 3 May 2016, https://www.ancient-origins.net/history-famous-people/queen-tamar-confident-female-ruler-georgian-golden-age-005815

Queen Isabella
(1295 – 1358 CE)

Cavendish, Richard. "Edward II marries Isabella of France." *History Today,* 1 Jan. 2008, https://www.historytoday.com/archive/edward-ii-marries-isabella-france

Encyclopaedia Britannica Editors. "Isabella of France." *Encyclopaedia Britannica,* 19 Aug. 2022, https://www.britannica.com/biography/Isabella-of-France

English Monarchs Editors. "Isabella of France." *English Monarchs,* n.d., https://www.englishmonarchs.co.uk/plantagenet_27.html

History Extra Editors. "Isabella of France: the rebel queen." *History Extra,* 30 Jan. 2019, https://www.historyextra.com/period/medieval/isabella-france-rebel-queen-invasion-england-deposition-husband-edward-ii/

Jansen, Douglas C. "Isabella Of France (1296-1358)." *Encyclopedia.com,* n.d., https://www.encyclopedia.com/women/encyclopedias-almanacs-transcripts-and-maps/isabella-france-1296-1358

Miller, Mark. "The Wild Life of English Queen Isabella, She-Wolf of France aka the Rebel Queen Who Killed the King of England." *Ancient Origins,* 30 Dec. 2018, https://www.ancient-origins.net/history-important-events/isabella-france-0011247

Christine de Pizan
(1364 – 1430 CE)

Adams, Tracy. "Christine de Pizan." *French Studies,* Oxford Academic, 1 Jun. 2017, https://academic.oup.com/fs/article/71/3/388/3859856

Biography.com Editors. "Christine de Pisan Biography." *Biography.com,* A&E Television Networks, 10 Jul. 2020, https://www.biography.com/writer/christine-de-pisan

Brooklyn Museum Editors. "Christine de Pisan." *Brooklyn Museum,* n.d., https://www.brooklynmuseum.org/eascfa/dinner_party/place_settings/christine_de_pisan

Encyclopaedia Britannica Editors. "Christine de Pisan." *Encyclopaedia Britannica,* 18 Jul. 2022, https://www.britannica.com/biography/Christine-de-Pisan

King's College Editors. "Christine de Pizan." *Women's History,* King's College History Department, n.d., https://departments.kings.edu/womens_history/chrisdp.html

Mark, Joshua J. "Christine de Pizan." *World History Encyclopedia,* 26 Mar. 2019, https://www.worldhistory.org/Christine_de_Pizan/

Agnes Waterhouse
(1503 – 1566 CE)

Engole Editors. "Agnes Waterhouse, Witch." *Engole,* n.d., https://engole.info/agnes-waterhouse-witch/

Essex Voices Past Editors. "The Witches of Elizabethan Essex." *Essex Voices Past,* 1 Feb. 2014, http://www.essexvoicespast.com/tag/agnes-waterhouse/

Gorilla Cool Editors. "Agnes Waterhouse – The First "Witch" Executed In England." *Gorilla Cool,* n.d., https://gorillacool.com/agnes-waterhouse-witch/

Klimczak, Natalia. "Agnes Waterhouse: The First Woman Executed for Witchcraft in England." *Ancient Origins,* 21 Apr. 2016, https://www.ancient-origins.net/history-famous-people/agnes-waterhouse-first-woman-executed-witchcraft-england-005747

Luttmer, Frank. "The Examination and Confession of Certain Witches at Chelmsford in the County of Essex, before the Queen Majesty's Judges, the 26th day of July Anno 1566." *History Hanover,* 1566, https://history.hanover.edu/courses/excerpts/260chelm.html

Gráinne O'Malley
(1530 – 1603 CE)

Gillan, Joanna. "Grace O'Malley, The 16th Century Pirate Queen of Ireland." *Ancient Origins,* 3 Dec. 2019, https://www.ancient-origins.net/history-famous-people/grace-o-malley-16th-century-pirate-queen-ireland-001773

Mayo Ireland Editors. "Grace O'Malley the Pirate Queen, History in Co. Mayo." *Mayo Ireland,* n.d., https://www.mayo-ireland.ie/en/about-mayo/history/grace-omalley-the-pirate-queen.html

Murray, Theresa D. "Gráinne Mhaol, pirate queen of Connacht: behind the legend." *Early Modern History (1500 – 1700),* History Ireland, Mar./Apr. 2005, https://www.historyireland.com/grainne-mhaol-pirate-queen-of-connacht-behind-the-legend/

RMG Editors. "Grace O'Malley: The Pirate Queen of Ireland." *RMG,* n.d., https://www.rmg.co.uk/stories/topics/grace-o-malley-irish-female-pirate

Trowbridge, Benjamin. "Meeting Grace O'Malley, Ireland's pirate queen." *The National Archives,* 16 Jun. 2016, https://blog.nationalarchives.gov.uk/meeting-grace-omalley-irelands-pirate-queen/

Lady Katherine Grey
(1540 – 1568 CE)

De Lisle, Leanda. "Lady Katherine Grey." *Tudor Times,* 8 Jul. 2015, https://tudortimes.co.uk/people/lady-katherine-grey

English Monarchs Editors. "Lady Catherine Grey." *English Monarchs,* n.d., https://www.englishmonarchs.co.uk/tudor_24.html

Foster, Ann. "Lady Katherine Grey: The Epic Love Story Of A Forgotten Tudor Heiress." *Ann Foster,* n.d., https://annfosterwriter.com/2020/08/21/lady-katherine-grey/

Hales, Sally. "Tudor of the Month: Katherine Grey." *Britain Magazine,* n.d., https://www.britain-magazine.com/carousel/tudor-of-the-month-katherine-grey/

UK Mythology Editors. "Lady Catherine Grey, Almost a Queen." *UK Mythology,* n.d., https://ukmythology.wordpress.com/lady-katherine-grey-almost-a-queen/

Countess Elizabeth Báthory
(1560 – 1614 CE)

Cavendish, Richard. "Death of Countess Elizabeth Bathory." *History Today,* 8 Aug. 2014, https://www.historytoday.com/archive/months-past/death-countess-elizabeth-bathory

Chao-Fong, Léonie. "The Blood Countess: 10 Facts About Elizabeth Báthory." *History Hit,* 30 Sept. 2021, https://www.historyhit.com/the-blood-countess-facts-about-elizabeth-bathory/

History.com Editors. "Hungarian countesses' torturous escapades are exposed." *HISTORY,* A&E Television Networks, 20 Dec. 2019, https://www.history.com/this-day-in-history/bathorys-torturous-escapades-are-exposed

Kettler, Sara. "Elizabeth Bathory Biography." *Biography,* A&E Television Networks, 21 May 2020, https://www.biography.com/crime-figure/elizabeth-bathory

Pallardy, Richard. "Elizabeth Báthory." *Encyclopaedia Britannica,* 17 Aug. 2022, https://www.britannica.com/biography/Elizabeth-Bathory

Rejected Princesses Editors. "Elisabeth Bathory." *Rejected Princesses,* n.d., https://www.rejectedprincesses.com/princesses/elisabeth-bathory

Mary Frith
(1584 – 1659 CE)

Bibby, Miriam. "Moll Frith." *Historic UK,* n.d., https://www.historic-uk.com/HistoryUK/HistoryofEngland/Moll-Frith/

East End Women's Museum Editors. "Mary Frith, Or Moll Cutpurse, The Roaring Girl." *East End Women's Museum,* 20 Nov. 2016, https://eastendwomensmuseum.org/blog/mary-frith

Fearn, Esther. "Moll Cutpurse." *Britannica,* 22 Jul. 2022,
https://www.britannica.com/biography/Moll-Cutpurse

Historic Royal Palaces Editors. "Dangerous Women: The Cross-Dressing Cavalier Mary Frith." *Historic Royal Palaces,* 28 Feb. 2020,
https://blog.hrp.org.uk/curators/dangerous-women-the-cross-dressing-cavalier-mary-frith/

Van Huygen, Meg. "Mary Frith, 17th-Century London's Smoking, Thieving, Foul-Mouthed Roaring Girl." *Mental Floss,* 31 Oct. 2018,
https://www.mentalfloss.com/article/561584/retrobituaries-mary-frith-17th-century-londons-roaring-girl

Artemisia Gentileschi
(1593 – 1653 CE)

Barrington, Breeze. "The trials and triumphs of Artemisia Gentileschi." *Apollo Magazine,* 25 Apr. 2020,
https://www.apollo-magazine.com/artemisia-gentileschi-london/

Encyclopaedia Britannica Editors. "Artemisia Gentileschi." *Encyclopaedia Britannica,* 4 Jul.2022,
https://www.britannica.com/biography/Artemisia-Gentileschi

Jones, Jonathon. "More savage than Caravaggio: the woman who took revenge in oil." *The Guardian,* 5 Oct. 2016,
https://www.theguardian.com/artanddesign/2016/oct/05/artemisia-gentileshi-painter-beyond-caravaggio

The National Gallery Editors. "Artemisia." *The National Gallery,* 3 Oct. 2020,
https://www.nationalgallery.org.uk/exhibitions/past/artemisia

The National Gallery Editors. "Artemisia Gentileschi." *The National Gallery,* n.d., https://www.nationalgallery.org.uk/artists/artemisia-gentileschi

Queen Anne
(1665 – 1714 CE)

BBC Editors. "Anne (1665 – 1714)" *History,* BBC, n.d., https://www.bbc.co.uk/history/historic_figures/anne.shtml

Encyclopaedia Britannica Editors. "Anne." *Encyclopaedia Britannica,* 28 Jul. 2022, https://www.britannica.com/biography/Anne-queen-of-Great-Britain-and-Ireland

Johnson, Ben. "Queen Anne." *Historic UK,* n.d., https://www.historic-uk.com/HistoryUK/HistoryofBritain/Queen-Anne/

Kensington Palace Editors. "Queen Anne." *Kensington Palace,* n.d., https://www.hrp.org.uk/kensington-palace/history-and-stories/queen-anne/

Miller, Julie. *"The Favourite:* The Real-Life Power Struggle Between Queen Anne and Sarah Churchill." *Vanity Fair,* 25 Nov. 2018, https://www.vanityfair.com/hollywood/2018/11/the-favourite-movie-true-story-queen-anne

Royal UK Editors. "Anne (r. 1702 – 1714)" *Royal UK,* n.d., https://www.royal.uk/queen-anne

Nanny of the Maroons
(1686 – 1755 CE)

Bernard, Ian. "Queen Nanny of the Maroons (? – 1733)" *Black Past,* 1 Mar. 2011, https://www.blackpast.org/global-african-history/queen-nanny-maroons-1733/

Caribbean Elections Editors. "Nanny of the Maroons." *Caribbean Elections,* n.d., http://caribbeanelections.com/knowledge/biography/bios/nanny.asp

Jamaica Information Service Editors. "Nanny of the Maroons." *Jamaica Information Service,* n.d., https://jis.gov.jm/information/heroes/nanny-of-the-maroons/

Larasi, Maral. "The true story of Queen Nanny, rebel leader and Jamaican National Hero." *Visible Women,* Stylist, 2019, https://www.stylist.co.uk/visible-women/queen-nanny-of-the-maroons-jamaica-national-hero/235042

Morgan, Alex. "Queen Nanny of the Maroons." *Beyond the Single Story,* 14 Nov. 2018, https://beyondthesinglestory.wordpress.com/2018/11/14/queen-nanny-of-the-maroons/

Slavery and Remembrance Editors. "Nanny." *Slavery and Remembrance,* n.d., http://slaveryandremembrance.org/people/person/?id=PP023

Understanding Slavery Initiative Editors. "Nanny and the Maroons." *Understanding Slavery Initiative,* n.d., http://archive.understandingslavery.com/index.php-option=com_content&view=article&id=379&Itemid=245.html

Empress Elizaveta Petrovna
(1709 – 1762 CE)

Encyclopaedia Britannica Editors. "Elizabeth." *Encyclopaedia Britannica,* 1 Jan. 2022, https://www.britannica.com/biography/Elizabeth-empress-of-Russia

Encyclopedia.com Editors. "Elizabeth Petrovna (1709 – 1762)." *Women in World History: A Biographical Encyclopedia,* Encyclopedia.com, 25 Aug. 2022, https://www.encyclopedia.com/women/encyclopedias-almanacs-transcripts-and-maps/elizabeth-petrovna-1709 – 1762

Factinate Editors. "Decadent Facts About Empress Elizabeth of Russia, The Last Romanov." *Factinate,* n.d., https://www.factinate.com/people/empress-elizabeth/

Prodan, Olga. "Prominent Russians: Elizaveta Petrovna Romanova." *Russiapedia,* n.d., https://russiapedia.rt.com/prominent-russians/the-romanov-dynasty/elizaveta-petrovna/

Elizabeth Sugrue
(1740 – 1807 CE)

Farrell, Brendan. "Roscommon's Lady Betty-thief, murderer, and executioner." *Irish Central,* 17 Oct. 2020, https://www.irishcentral.com/roots/history/lady-betty-thief-murderer-executioner

Hume, Robert. "How Ireland's only female executioner got the job." *Irish Examiner,* 18 Apr. 2019, https://www.irishexaminer.com/lifestyle/arid-30918685.html

Sybil Ludington
(1761 – 1839 CE)

A Mighty Girl Editors. "Sybil Ludington: The 16-Year-Old Revolutionary Hero Who Rode Twice As Far As Paul Revere." *A Mighty Girl,* 4 Apr. 2022, https://www.amightygirl.com/blog?p=24115

American Battlefield Trust Editors. "Sybil Ludington." *American Battlefield Trust,* n.d., https://www.battlefields.org/learn/biographies/sybil-ludington

DeBenedette, Valerie. "Sybil Ludington: The 16-Year-Old Revolutionary Who Outrode Paul Revere." *Mental Floss,* 18 Apr. 2020, https://www.mentalfloss.com/article/78686/16-year-old-revolutionary-who-outrode-paul-revere

Encyclopaedia Britannica Editors. "Sybil Ludington." *Encyclopaedia Britannica,* 30 May 2022, https://www.britannica.com/biography/Sybil-Ludington

Encyclopedia.com Editors. "Ludington, Sybil (1761 – 1839)." *Women in World History: A Biographical Encyclopedia,* Encyclopedia.com, 25 Aug. 2022, https://www.encyclopedia.com/women/encyclopedias-almanacs-transcripts-and-maps/ludington-sybil-1761-1839

Kelly, Kate. "Sybil Ludington, 16, Helped Patriots in Revolutionary War." *America Comes Alive,* n.d., https://americacomesalive.com/sybil-ludington-16-helped-patriots-in-revolutionary-war/

Revolutionary War Editors. "Sybil Ludington." *Revolutionary War,* 4 Mar. 2020, https://www.revolutionary-war.net/sybil-ludington/

Wang Zhenyi
(1768 – 1797 CE)

Mehta, Devang. "The prolific life of Wang Zhenyi, autodidact, astronomer, and poet." *Massive Science,* 3 Nov. 2017, https://massivesci.com/articles/wang-zhenyi-poetry-venus-math/

Shah, Tia. "Trailblazers-The Age of Girls: Wang Zhenyi." *Girl Museum,* 24 May 2018, https://www.girlmuseum.org/trailblazers-age-of-girls-wang-zhenyi/

Ching Shih
(1775 – 1844 CE)

Arun, Vishnu. "Ching Shih; A Prostitute Who Became History's Deadliest Pirate." *History of Yesterday,* 22 Sept. 2020, https://medium.com/history-of-yesterday/ching-shih-a-prostitute-who-became-historys-deadliest-pirate-f596f7fcff23

Banerji, Urvija. "The Chinese Female Pirate Who Commanded 80,000 Outlaws." *Atlas Obscura,* 6 Apr. 2016, https://www.atlasobscura.com/articles/ching-shih-chinese-female-pirate

Factinate Editors. "Ruthless Facts About Ching Shih, China's Cunning Pirate Queen." *Factinate,* n.d., https://www.factinate.com/people/facts-ching-shih/

Reese, M.R. "Ching Shih-From Prostitute to Infamous Female Pirate." *Ancient Origins,* 12 Nov. 2020, https://www.ancient-origins.net/history-famous-people/ching-shih-prostitute-pirate-lord-002582

Rejected Princesses Editors. "Ching Shih." *Rejected Princesses,* n.d., https://www.rejectedprincesses.com/princesses/ching-shih

The Ministry of History Editors. "Ching Shih-From Poverty To Pirate." *The Ministry of History,* 9 Jul. 2020, https://www.theministryofhistory.co.uk/historical-biographies/ching-shih

Mary Baker
(1792 – 1864 CE)

Chadwick, Cassie. "Princess Caraboo." *Time,* n.d., http://content.time.com/time/specials/packages/article/0,28804,1900621_1900618_1900853,00.html

Evans, Zteve T. "The Curious Case of Princess Caraboo." *Folklore Thursday,* 21 Mar. 2019, https://folklorethursday.com/fakelore/the-curious-case-of-princess-caraboo/

Pekker, Michael. "Princess Caraboo from the Island of Javasu." *Jane Austen,* 26 Jul. 2020, https://janeausten.co.uk/blogs/authors-artists-vagrants/princess-caraboo-from-the-island-of-javasu

The History Press Editors. "The mysterious Princess Caraboo." *The History Press,* n.d., https://www.thehistorypress.co.uk/articles/the-mysterious-princess-caraboo/

Policarpa Salavarrieta
(1795-1817 CE)

Encyclopaedia Britannica Editors. "Viceroyalty of New Granada." *Encyclopaedia Britannica,* 11 Aug. 2018, https://www.britannica.com/place/Viceroyalty-of-New-Granada

Encyclopedia.com Editors. "Salavarrieta, Pola (1795 – 1817)." *Women in World History: A Biographical Encyclopedia,* Encyclopedia.com, 25 Aug. 2022, https://www.encyclopedia.com/women/encyclopedias-almanacs-transcripts-and-maps/salavarrieta-pola-1795 – 1817

Gomez, Guisell. "Policarpa Salavarrieta: The Colombian Heroine You Should Know About." *Be Latina,* 16 Jan. 2020, https://belatina.com/la-pola-colombian-revolutionary/

Google Arts and Culture Editors. "Policarpa Salavarrieta." *Google Arts and Culture,* n.d., https://artsandculture.google.com/entity/policarpa-salavarrieta/m0267388?hl=en

Mohney, Pete. "Policarpa Salavarrieta." *Find a Grave,* n.d., https://www.findagrave.com/memorial/4615/policarpa-salavarrieta

Sojourner Truth
(1797 – 1883 CE)

African American Odyssey Editors. "Sojourner Truth." *African American Odyssey,* n.d.,
https://www.loc.gov/exhibits/odyssey/educate/truth.html
Biography.com Editors. "Sojourner Truth Biography." *Biography.com,* A&E Television Networks, 2 Apr. 2014,
https://www.biography.com/activist/sojourner-truth
Encyclopaedia Britannica Editors. "Sojourner Truth." *Encyclopaedia Britannica,* 22 Nov. 2021,
https://www.britannica.com/biography/Sojourner-Truth
History.com Editors. "Sojourner Truth." *History.com,* 29 Oct. 2009,
https://www.history.com/topics/black-history/sojourner-truth
Michals, Debra. "Sojourner Truth." *National Women's History Museum,* n.d.,
https://www.womenshistory.org/education-resources/biographies/sojourner-truth

Mary Anning
(1799 – 1847 CE)

Bol, David. "New marine species named after Lyme Regis fossil hunter Mary Anning." *Bridport News,* 21 Feb. 2015,
https://www.bridportnews.co.uk/news/11809382.new-marine-species-named-after-lyme-regis-fossil-hunter-mary-anning/
Eylott, Marie-Claire. "Mary Anning: the unsung hero of fossil discovery." *Natural History Museum,* n.d.,
https://www.nhm.ac.uk/discover/mary-anning-unsung-hero.html
Lyme Regis Museum Editors. "Mary Anning." *Lyme Regis Museum,* n.d.,
https://www.lymeregismuseum.co.uk/collection/mary-anning/
Rafferty, John P. "Mary Anning." *Encyclopaedia Britannica,* 17 May 2022,
https://www.britannica.com/biography/Mary-Anning
Tappenden, Roz. "Ammonite: Who was the real Mary Anning?" *BBC News,* 17 Oct. 2020, https://www.bbc.co.uk/news/uk-england-dorset-54510746
Torrens, Hugh. "Mary Anning (1799 – 1847)." *UCMP Berkeley,* n.d.,
https://ucmp.berkeley.edu/history/anning.html

Pine Leaf
(1806 – 1854 CE)

Montana Women's History Editors. "Nineteenth-Century Indigenous Women Warriors." *Women's History Matters,* Montana Women's History, 6 Feb. 2014, https://montanawomenshistory.org/nineteenth-century-indigenous-women-warriors/

Radeska, Tijana. "Pine Leafe was a Woman Chief and warrior of the Crow people." *The Vintage News,* 20 Sept. 2016, https://www.thevintagenews.com/2016/09/20/pine-leaf-was-a-woman-chief-and-warrior-of-the-crow-people-2/?chrome=1

Ria Brodell Editors. "Biawacheeitche." *Butch Heroes,* Ria Brodell, n.d., https://www.riabrodell.com/biawacheeitche-or-woman-chief-aka-barcheeampe-or-pine-leaf

White Wolf Pack Editors. "Pine Leaf: A Two Spirit Woman War Chief of the Crow people You should know." *White Wolf Pack,* n.d., http://www.whitewolfpack.com/2016/09/pine-leaf-two-spirit-woman-war-chief-of.html

Frances Dickens
(1810 – 1848 CE)

Simpkin, John. "Fanny Dickens." *Spartacus Educational,* Sept. 1997, https://spartacus-educational.com/PRdickensFY.htm

Wikipedia Editors. "Fanny Dickens." *Wikipedia,* n.d., https://en.wikipedia.org/wiki/Fanny_Dickens

Rani Lakshmi Bai
(1828 – 1858 CE)

Bevan, Richard. "Lakshmi Bai and the Indian Rebellion of 1857." *Sky History,* n.d., https://www.history.co.uk/article/lakshmi-bai-and-the-indian-rebellion-of-1857

Encyclopaedia Britannica Editors. "Lakshmi Bai." *Encyclopaedia Britannica,* 12 Aug. 2022, https://www.britannica.com/biography/Lakshmi-Bai

History Extra Editors. "Rani Lakshmibai of Jhansi: the heroic queen dubbed India's 'Joan of Arc'." *History Extra,* 19 Feb. 2020, https://www.historyextra.com/period/victorian/manikarnika-who-was-rani-lakshmibai-how-did-she-die-hero-queen-jhansi-lakshmi-bai-east-india-company-bollywood/

McNamara, Robert. "A Timeline of India in the 1800s." *Thought Co.,* 30 Jun. 2018, https://www.thoughtco.com/timeline-of-india-in-the-1800s-1774016#:~:text=1700s%3A%20Britain%20Established%20Dominance&text=The%20British%20interests%20in%20India,even%20instituting%20a%20court%20system.

The New York Times Editors. "Overlooked No More: Rhani of Jhansi, India's Warrior Queen Who Fought the British." *The New York Times,* n.d., https://www.nytimes.com/2019/08/14/obituaries/laxmibai-rani-of-jhansi-overlooked.html

Toler, Pamela D. "Who is Manikarnika? The real story of the legendary Hindu Queen Lakshmi Bai." *History Net,* 9 May 2006, https://www.historynet.com/who-is-marnikarnika-legendary-hindu-queen-lakshmi-bai/?f

Your Dictionary Editors. "Lakshmi Bai." *Your Dictionary,* n.d., https://biography.yourdictionary.com/lakshmi-bai

Josephine Butler
(1828 – 1906 CE)

BBC Editors. "Josephine Butler (1828 – 1906)." *History,* BBC, n.d., https://www.bbc.co.uk/history/historic_figures/butler_josephine.shtml

English Heritage Editors. "Butler, Josephine (1828 – 1906)." *English Heritage,* n.d., https://www.english-heritage.org.uk/visit/blue-plaques/butler-josephine-butler/

Simkin, John. "Josephine Butler." *Spartacus Educational,* n.d., https://spartacus-educational.com/Wbutler.htm

University of Liverpool Library Editors. "Special Collections & Archives: Josephine Butler Collection." *University Library,* University of Liverpool, n.d., https://libguides.liverpool.ac.uk/library/sca/josephinebutler

Isabella Bird
(1831 – 1904 CE)

Activity Village Editors. "Isabella Bird." *Activity Village,* n.d., https://www.activityvillage.co.uk/isabella-bird

Lienhard, John H. "Isabella Bird." *Engines of Our Ingenuity,* n.d., https://uh.edu/engines/epi2074.htm

Scottish Places Editors. "Isabella Lucy Bird." *Scottish Places,* n.d., https://www.scottish-places.info/people/famousfirst3355.html

Simkin, John. "Isabella Bird." *Spartacus Education,* Sept. 1997, https://spartacus-educational.com/WWbirdbishop.htm

Woolf, Jo. "Isabella Bird-free spirit and fearless explorer." *Royal Scottish Geographical Society,* 24 Jun. 2015, https://rsgsexplorers.com/2015/06/24/isabella-bird-free-spirit-and-fearless-explorer/

Your Dictionary Editors. "Isabella Bird." *Your Dictionary,* n.d., https://biography.yourdictionary.com/isabella-bird

Dr Mary Edwards Walker
(1832 – 1919 CE)

Alexander, Kerri Lee. "Mary Edwards Walker." *National Women's History Museum,* Women's History, n.d., https://www.womenshistory.org/education-resources/biographies/mary-edwards-walker

Bishop, Jennifer D. and Pass, Alexandra R. "Mary Edwards Walker: Trailblazing feminist, surgeon, and war veteran." *American College of Surgeons,* n.d., https://www.facs.org/media/hixghdi4/06_walker.pdf

Encyclopaedia Britannica Editors. "Mary Edwards Walker." *Encyclopaedia Britannica,* 17 Feb. 2022, https://www.britannica.com/biography/Mary-Edwards-Walker

Ferry, Georgina. "Mary Edwards Walker: military surgeon who wore the trousers." *The Lancet,* 25 Jan. 2020, https://www.thelancet.com/journals/lancet/article/PIIS0140-6736(20)30102-1/fulltext

Lange, Katie. "Meet Dr. Mary Walker: The only female Medal of Honor recipient." *U.S. Army,* 7 Mar. 2017, https://www.army.mil/article/183800/meet_dr_mary_walker_the_only_female_medal_of_honor_recipient

Military.com Editors. "Medal of Honor Spotlight: Dr. Mary Edwards Walker." *Military.com,* n.d., https://www.military.com/history/dr-mary-edwards-walker.html

National Park Service Editors. "Dr. Mary Edwards Walker." *National Park Service,* n.d., https://www.nps.gov/people/mary-walker.htm

Yaa Asantewaa
(1840 – 1921 CE)

Anoba, Ibrahim. "African Heroes of freedom: Queen Mother Yaa Asantewaa of Ejisu." *Libertarianism,* 31 Jul. 2019, https://www.libertarianism.org/columns/african-heroes-freedom-queen-mother-yaa-asantewaa-ejisu

West, Racquel. "Yaa Asantewaa (Mid-1800s – 1921)." *Black Past,* 8 Feb. 2019, https://www.blackpast.org/global-african-history/yaa-asantewaa-mid-1800s-1921/

Edmonia Lewis
(1844 – 1907 CE)

Encyclopaedia Britannica Editors. "Edmonia Lewis." *Encyclopaedia Britannica,* 13 Sept. 2021,
https://www.britannica.com/biography/Edmonia-Lewis

George, Alice. "Sculptor Edmonia Lewis Shattered Gender and Race Expectations in 19th-Century America." *Smithsonian Magazine,* 22 Aug. 2019,
https://www.smithsonianmag.com/smithsonian-institution/sculptor-edmonia-lewis-shattered-gender-race-expectations-19th-century-america-180972934/

Hammersmith and Fulham Editors. "Black history month: Edmonia Lewis-a remarkable Hammersmith sculptor." *Hammersmith and Fulham,* 28 Sept. 2020,
https://www.lbhf.gov.uk/articles/news/2020/09/black-history-month-edmonia-lewis-remarkable-hammersmith-sculptor

Powers, Hermenia. "Who was Edmonia 'Wildfire' Lewis?" *Artuk,* 28 Oct. 2020,
https://artuk.org/discover/stories/who-was-edmonia-wildfire-lewis

Smithsonian American Art Museum Editors. "Edmonia Lewis." *Smithsonian American Art Museum,* n.d., https://americanart.si.edu/artist/edmonia-lewis-2914

The Art Story Editors. "Edmonia Lewis." *The Art Story,* n.d.,
https://www.theartstory.org/artist/lewis-edmonia/

Emily Hobhouse
(1860 – 1926 CE)

AngloBoerWar.com Editors. "Emily Hobhouse." *AngloBoerWar.com,* n.d.,
https://www.angloboerwar.com/other-information/16-other-information/1847-emily-hobhouse

British Empire Editors. "Emily Hobhouse." *British Empire,* n.d.,
https://www.britishempire.me.uk/emily-hobhouse.html

Encyclopaedia Britannica Editors. "Emily Hobhouse." *Encyclopaedia Britannica,* 4 Jun. 2022,
https://www.britannica.com/biography/Emily-Hobhouse

Goskar, Tehmina. "Emily Hobhouse Campaign." *The Hypatia Trust,* n.d.,
https://hypatia-trust.org.uk/emily-hobhouse-campaign

Men Who Said No Editors. "Emily Hobhouse." *Conscientious Objectors 1915 – 1919,* The Men Who Said No, n.d., https://menwhosaidno.org/context/women/hobhouse_e.html

New World Encyclopedia Editors. "Emily Hobhouse." *New World Encyclopedia,* n.d., https://www.newworldencyclopedia.org/entry/Emily_Hobhouse

Simkin, John. "Emily Hobhouse." *Spartacus Educational,* Sept. 1997, https://spartacus-educational.com/Whobhouse.htm

South African History Online Editors. "Emily Hobhouse." *South African History Online,* 17 Feb. 2011, https://www.sahistory.org.za/people/emily-hobhouse

Sultan, Mena. "Emily Hobhouse and the Boer war." *The Guardian,* 3 Jun. 2019, https://www.theguardian.com/gnmeducationcentre/from-the-archive-blog/2019/jun/03/emily-hobhouse-and-the-boer-war

Nellie Bly
(1864 – 1922 CE)

Biography.com Editors. "Nellie Bly Biography." *Biography.com,* A&E Television Networks, 19 Apr. 2021, https://www.biography.com/activist/nellie-bly

Encyclopaedia Britannica Editors. "Nellie Bly." *Encyclopaedia Britannica,* 1 May 2022, https://www.britannica.com/biography/Nellie-Bly

History Extra Editors. "Around the world in 72 days: how journalist Nellie Bly became the real Phileas Fogg." *History Extra,* n.d., https://www.historyextra.com/period/victorian/who-was-nellie-bly-race-around-world-80-days-real-phileas-fogg-jules-verne/

Irish Central Editors. "The Irish American journalist who faked her way into an insane asylum." *Irish Central.* 25 Jan. 2021, https://www.irishcentral.com/roots/history/nellie-bly-biography

Maranzani, Barbara. "Inside Nellie Bly's 10 Days in a Madhouse." *Biography,* 12 Nov. 2020, https://www.biography.com/news/inside-nelly-bly-10-days-madhouse

Winchester, Beth. "What Nellie Bly Exposed at Blackwell's Asylum, and Why It's Still Important." *Medium,* 26 Apr. 2016, https://medium.com/legendary-women/what-nellie-bly-exposed-at-blackwells-asylum-and-why-it-s-still-important-4591203b9dc7

Edith Cavell
(1865 – 1915 CE)

Cavell Nurses' Trust Editors. "Who was Edith Cavell?" *Cavell Nurses Trust,* n.d., https://www.cavellnursestrust.org/what-we-do/who-was-edith-cavell/

Edith Cavell Editors. "Edith Cavell 1865 – 1915." *Edith Cavell,* n.d., https://edithcavell.org.uk/

Encyclopaedia Britannica Editors. "Edith Cavell." *Encyclopaedia Britannica,* 30 Nov. 2021, https://www.britannica.com/biography/Edith-Cavell

History.com Editors. "British nurse Edith Cavell executed." *History,* A&E Television Networks, 28 Oct. 2009, https://www.history.com/this-day-in-history/british-nurse-edith-cavell-executed

Hore, Peter. "10 things you didn't know about Edith Cavell, nurses & Mary Lindell." *The History Press,* n.d., https://www.thehistorypress.co.uk/articles/10-things-you-didn-t-know-about-edith-cavell-nurses-mary-lindell/

IWM Editors. "Who Was Edith Cavell?" *IWM,* n.d., https://www.iwm.org.uk/history/who-was-edith-cavell

Edith Wilson
(1872 – 1961 CE)

Anthony, Carl. "Edith Wilson: The First Lady Who Became an Acting President Without Being Elected." *Biography,* 10 Mar. 2016, https://www.biography.com/news/edith-wilson-first-president-biography-facts

Caroli, Betty Boyd. "Edith Wilson." *Encyclopaedia Britannica,* 24 Dec. 2021, https://www.britannica.com/biography/Edith-Wilson

First Ladies Editors. "First Lady Biography: Edith Wilson." *First Ladies Editors,* n.d., http://www.firstladies.org/biographies/firstladies.aspx?biography=29

History Editors. "Edith Wilson, America's First (Acting) Female President." *History,* n.d., https://www.history.co.uk/articles/edith-wilson-america-s-first-acting-female-president

PBS Editors. "Edith Bolling Galt Wilson." *American Experience,* PBS, n.d., https://www.pbs.org/wgbh/americanexperience/features/wilson-edith-wilson/
White House Editors. "Edith Bolling Galt Wilson." *White House,* n.d., https://www.whitehouse.gov/about-the-white-house/first-families/edith-bolling-galt-wilson/

Constance Kopp
(1878 – 1931 CE)

Book Browse Editors. "Girl Waits with Gun by Amy Stewart." *Book Browse,* May 2016, https://www.bookbrowse.com/mag/btb/index.cfm/book_number/3280/girl-waits-with-gun
Library of Congress Editors. "Constance Kopp: Topics in Chronicling America." *Library of Congress,* n.d., https://guides.loc.gov/chronicling-america-constance-kopp
Rose, Shari. "How Constance Kopp Became First Female Sheriff's Deputy." *Blurred By Lines,* 14 Mar. 2021, https://blurredbylines.com/articles/constance-kopp-sisters-sheriff-heath-deputy/
Stewart, Amy. "The Real People Behind the Cast of Characters." *Amy Stewart,* n.d., https://www.amystewart.com/characters/

Raden Adjeng Kartini
(1879 – 1904 CE)

Biography.com Editors. "Raden Adjeng Kartini Biography." *Biography.com,* A&E Television Networks, 21 Apr. 2020, https://www.biography.com/activist/raden-adjeng-kartini
Dalton, Bill. "R. A. Kartini: Indonesia's First Woman's Emancipationist." *Bali Advertiser,* 2012, https://www.baliadvertiser.biz/kartini/
Encyclopaedia Britannica Editors. "Raden Adjeng Kartini." *Encyclopaedia Britannica,* 17 Apr. 2022, https://www.britannica.com/biography/Raden-Adjeng-Kartini

Encyclopedia.com Editors. "Kartini, Raden Ajeng." *Encyclopedia of World Biography,* Encyclopaedia.com, 26 Aug. 2022, https://www.encyclopedia.com/history/encyclopedias-almanacs-transcripts-and-maps/kartini-raden-ajeng

Lawrence, Annee. "R. A. Kartini and the 'Clover Leaf'." *Dangerous Women Project,* 27 Sept. 2016, https://dangerouswomenproject.org/2016/09/27/raden-adjeng-kartini/

Huda Sha'arawi
(1879 – 1947 CE)

Encyclopedia.com Editors. "Shaarawi, Huda." *Encyclopedia of World Biography,* Encyclopedia.com, 25 Aug. 2022, https://www.encyclopedia.com/history/encyclopedias-almanacs-transcripts-and-maps/shaarawi-huda

Engel, Keri. "Huda Shaarawi, Egyptian feminist & activist." *Amazing Women in History,* n.d., https://amazingwomeninhistory.com/huda-shaarawi-egyptian-feminist/

Hosken, Fran P. "Egyptian woman make progress despite pull for tradition." *The Christian Science Monitor,* 22 Jan. 1981, https://www.csmonitor.com/1981/0122/012212.html

Jaffer, Jennifer. "Huda Sharawi." *Encyclopaedia Britannica,* 19 Jun. 2022, https://www.britannica.com/biography/Huda-Sharawi

Rachidi, Soukaina. "Huda Sharawi: A Remarkable Egyptian Feminist Pioneer." *Inside Arabia,* 6 Jul. 2019, https://insidearabia.com/huda-sharawi-a-remarkable-egyptian-feminist-pioneer/

Weebly Editors. "Huda Shaarawi: "A Taste for Spectacular Gestures"." *Weebly,* n.d., https://shaarawi.weebly.com/

Anna Pavlova
(1881 – 1931 CE)

Biography.com Editors. "Anna Pavlova Biography." *Biography.com,* A&E Television Networks, 26 Mar. 2021, https://www.biography.com/performer/anna-pavlova

Royal Opera House Editors. "Anna Pavlova." *Royal Opera House,* n.d., http://www.roh.org.uk/people/anna-pavlova

Shelokhonov, Steve. "Anna Pavlova Biography." *IMDb,* n.d., https://www.imdb.com/name/nm0667816/bio?ref_=nm_ov_bio_sm

The Marius Petipa Society Editors. "Anna Pavlova." *The Marius Petipa Society,* n.d., https://petipasociety.com/anna-pavlova/

Victoria and Albert Museum Editors. "Anna Pavlova." *Victoria and Albert Museum,* n.d., http://www.vam.ac.uk/content/articles/a/anna-pavlova/

Walker, Kathrine Sorley. "Anna Pavlova." *Encyclopaedia Britannica,* 8 Feb. 2022, https://www.britannica.com/biography/Anna-Pavlova

Princess Alice of Battenberg
(1885 – 1969 CE)

Cope, Rebecca. "The extraordinary life of the Duke of Edinburgh's mother Princess Alice of Battenberg." *Tatler,* 15 Nov. 2019, https://www.tatler.com/article/who-was-princess-alice-of-battenberg-prince-philip-duke-of-edinburgh-mother

Foussianes, Chloe. "How Princess Alice of Battenberg, Prince Philip's Mother, Became the Royal Family's Black Sheep." *Town and Country Magazine,* 18 Nov. 2019, https://www.townandcountrymag.com/society/tradition/a29310694/who-is-princess-alice-prince-philip-mother-the-crown-facts/

Mackelden, Amy. "The Incredible True Story of Prince Philip's Mother, Princess Alice of Battenberg." *Harper's Bazaar,* 17 Nov. 2019, https://www.harpersbazaar.com/celebrity/latest/a29796667/who-is-prince-philip-mother-alice-battenberg/

Owoseje, Toyin. "What you need to know about Princess Alice of Battenberg, Prince Philip's tragic, heroic mother." *CNN,* 19 Nov. 2019, https://edition.cnn.com/2019/11/18/entertainment/prince-philips-mother-princess-alice-interesting-facts-intl-scli/index.html

Paunescu, Delia. "*The Crown:* Princess Alice of Battenberg's Life Was More Dramatic Than the Show Depicts." *Elle,* 9 Apr. 2021, https://www.elle.com/culture/movies-tv/a29849010/princess-alice-battenberg-the-crown-real-life/

Rodríguez, Patricia. "Princess Alice of Battenberg: the incredible true story of Prince Philip's mother." *El País,* 14 Apr. 2021, https://english.elpais.com/usa/2021-04-14/princess-alice-of-battenberg-the-incredible-true-story-of-prince-philips-mother.html

Vickers, Hugo. "Reunited with the mother who called him 'Bubbikins': Born in Windsor Castle, died in Buckingham Palace-and in between, an astonishing life as a nun battling Nazis. Now Hugo Vickers reveals her story, as told to him by her son Prince Philip." *The Daily Mail,* 16 Apr. 2021, https://www.dailymail.co.uk/news/article-9480353/Reunited-mother-called-Prince-Philip-Bubbikins-HUGO-VICKERS-reveals-story.html

Milunka Savić
(1888 – 1973 CE)

Bills, John William. "Milunka Savić: The Tragic Story of the Most Decorated Woman in Warfare." *The Culture Trip,* 27 Jul. 2018, https://theculturetrip.com/europe/serbia/articles/milunka-savic-the-tragic-story-of-serbias-gun-slinging-female-soldier/

Borenovic, Ina. "Milunka Savic: A great heroin of the Great War." *001 Info,* n.d., https://www.011info.com/en/belgraders/milunka-savic-a-great-heroin-of-the-great-war

Đorđević, Nikola. "History's most decorated female soldier: A Serb who defied the rules to fight in World War I." *Emerging Europe,* 26 Sept. 2020, https://emerging-europe.com/after-hours/historys-most-decorated-female-soldier-a-serb-who-defied-the-rules-to-fight-in-world-war-i/

In Your Pocket Editors. "Serbia's Real Life Mulan: The Story of Milunka Savić." *In Your Pocket,* n.d., https://www.inyourpocket.com/belgrade/serbias-real-life-mulan-the-story-of-milunka-savic_75533f

Serbia.com Editors. "Milunka Savić, the most awarded female combatant in the history of warfare." *Serbia.com,* n.d., http://www.serbia.com/about-serbia/serbia-history/world-war-one/milunka-savic/

Bessie Coleman
(1892 – 1926 CE)

Alexander, Kerri Lee. "Bessie Coleman." *National Women's History Museum,* Women's History, 2018,
https://www.womenshistory.org/education-resources/biographies/bessie-coleman

American Experience Editors. "Bessie Coleman." *American Experience,* n.d.,
https://www.pbs.org/wgbh/americanexperience/features/flygirls-bessie-coleman/

Encyclopaedia Britannica Editors. "Bessie Coleman." *Encyclopaedia Britannica,* 26 Apr.2022,
https://www.britannica.com/biography/Bessie-Coleman

Lauria-Blum, Julia. "Bessie Coleman." *Cradle of Aviation Museum,* 7 Jun. 2019,
https://www.cradleofaviation.org/history/history/women-in-aviation/bessie-coleman.html

Slotnik, Daniel. "Overlooked No More: Bessie Coleman, Pioneering African-American Aviatrix." *New York Times,* 12 Nov. 2019,
https://www.nytimes.com/2019/12/11/obituaries/bessie-coleman-overlooked.html

Dorothy Lawrence
(1896 – 1964 CE)

Karlins, Amber. "Dorothy Lawrence-War Correspondent." *The Heroine Collective,* 2 Oct. 2018,
http://www.theheroinecollective.com/dorothy-lawrence/

Pollard, Justin and Pollard, Stephanie. "Dorothy Lawrence." *History Today,* 10 Oct. 2017,
https://www.historytoday.com/archive/months-past/dorothy-lawrence

Weebly.com Editors. "Dorothy Lawrence-The Only English Woman Soldier." *Women in WW1,* Weebly.com, n.d.,
https://womeninthegreatwar.weebly.com/dorothy-lawrence.html

Wiltshire At War Editors. "'Sapper' Dorothy Lawrence: A forgotten Wiltshire Heroine." *Wiltshire At War,* n.d., http://www.wiltshireatwar.org.uk/story/sapper-dorothy-lawrence-a-forgotten-wiltshire-heroine/

Aloha Wanderwell
(1906 – 1996 CE)

Aloha Wanderwell Editors. "Aloha Wanderwell." *Aloha Wanderwell,* n.d., https://www.alohawanderwell.com/

Aloha Wanderwell Editors. "Aloha Wanderwell Biography." *Aloha Wanderwell,* n.d., https://www.alohawanderwell.com/biography/

DePrest, Jessica. "Aloha Wanderwell Baker." *Women Film Pioneers Project,* 2018, https://wfpp.columbia.edu/pioneer/aloha-wanderwell-baker/

Peters, Ed. "Around the world in a Model T: the adventures of Aloha Wanderwell, the first woman to circumnavigate the globe in a car." *History,* Post Magazine, 1 Mar. 2020, https://www.scmp.com/magazines/post-magazine/long-reads/article/3052601/around-world-model-t-adventures-aloha-wanderwell

Irena Sendler
(1910 – 2008 CE)

Dzięciołowska, Karolina. "Irena Sendler's Biography." *About the Righteous,* Museum of the History of Polish Jews, May 2018, https://sprawiedliwi.org.pl/en/o-sprawiedliwych/irena-sendlerowa/biografia-ireny-sendlerowej

Irena Sendler Editors. "Facts about Irena." *Life in a Jar: The Irena Sendler Project,* Irena Sendler, n.d., https://irenasendler.org/facts-about-irena/

Jewish Virtual Library Editors. "Irena Sendler." *Jewish Virtual Library,* n.d., https://www.jewishvirtuallibrary.org/irena-sendler

Mayer, Jack. "Irena Sendler and the Girls from Kansas." *National Endowment for the Humanities,* Summer 2020, https://www.neh.gov/article/irena-sendler-and-girls-kansas

POLIN Museum of the History of Polish Jews Editors. "Irena Sendler." *POLIN Museum of the History of Polish Jews,* Google Arts & Culture, n.d., https://artsandculture.google.com/story/zgWx_XNxPh8dLQ?hl=en

Yad Vashem, The World Holocaust Remembrance Center Editors. "Irena Sendler." *Women of Valor,* Yad Vashem, The World Holocaust Remembrance Centre, n.d.,
https://www.yadvashem.org/yv/en/exhibitions/righteous-women/sendler.asp

Noor Inayat Khan
(1914 – 1944 CE)

Alberge, Dalya. "Noor Inayat Khan: how British spy's love for blue betrayed her." *The Guardian,* 18 Jun. 2020,
https://www.theguardian.com/world/2020/jun/18/executed
Basu, Shrabani. "Noor Inayat Khan." *Second World War Experience Centre,* n.d., https://war-experience.org/lives/noor-inayat-khan-soe/
BBC Editors. "Noor Inayat Khan (1914 – 1944)." *History,* BBC, n.d.,
https://www.bbc.co.uk/history/historic_figures/inayat_khan_noor.shtml
Cope, Rebecca. "The remarkable story of the Muslim Princess who spied for the British during World War II." *Tatler,* 30 Oct. 2020,
https://www.tatler.com/article/noor-inayat-khan-muslim-spy-princess-a-call-to-spy
Dearnley, Elizabeth. "Musician, author, princess, spy: Noor Inayat Khan." *University of London,* n.d.,
https://www.london.ac.uk/news-and-opinion/leading-women/musician-author-princess-spy-noor-inayat-khan
Perrin, Nigel. "Noor Inayat Khan." *SOE Agent Profiles,* Nigel Perrin, n.d.,
https://nigelperrin.com/soe-noor-inayat-khan.htm
Siddiqui, Usaid. "Noor Inayat Khan: The forgotten Muslim princess who fought Nazis." *Aljazeera,* 28 Oct. 2020,
https://www.aljazeera.com/features/2020/10/28/noor-inayat-khan

Hedy Lamarr
(1914 – 2000 CE)

Biography.com Editors. "Hedy Lamarr Biography." *Biography.com,* A&E Television Networks, 19 Apr. 2021,

https://www.biography.com/actor/hedy-lamarr

Cheslak, Colleen. "Hedy Lamarr." *National Women's History Museum,* Women's History, 2018,

https://www.womenshistory.org/education-resources/biographies/hedy-lamarr

Encyclopaedia Britannica Editors. "Hedy Lamarr." *Encyclopaedia Britannica,* 15 Jan. 2022, https://www.britannica.com/biography/Hedy-Lamarr

Field, Shivaune. "Hedy Lamarr: The Incredible Mind Behind Secure WiFi, GPS And Bluetooth." *Forbeswomen,* Forbes, 28 Feb. 2018,

https://www.forbes.com/sites/shivaunefield/2018/02/28/hedy-lamarr-the-incredible-mind-behind-secure-wi-fi-gps-bluetooth/?sh=3f6c20bd41b7

George, Alice. "Thank This World War II-Era Film Star for Your Wi-Fi." *Ingenious Women,* Smithsonian Magazine, 4 Apr. 2019,

https://www.smithsonianmag.com/smithsonian-institution/thank-world-war-ii-era-film-star-your-wi-fi-180971584/

Hedy Lamarr Editors. "Hedy Lamarr Biography." *The Official Website of Hedy Lamarr,* n.d., https://hedylamarr.com/about/biography/

Édith Piaf
(1915 – 1963 CE)

Biography.com Editors. "Édith Piaf Biography." *Biography.com,* A&E Television Networks, 1 Nov. 2021,

https://www.biography.com/musician/edith-piaf

Encyclopaedia Britannica Editors. "Edith Piaf." *Encyclopaedia Britannica,* 15 Dec. 2021, https://www.britannica.com/biography/Edith-Piaf

Fancourt, Daisy. "Edith Piaf." *Music and the Holocaust,* n.d.,

https://holocaustmusic.ort.org/resistance-and-exile/french-resistance/edith-piaf/

IMDb Editors. "Édith Piaf Biography." *IMDb,* n.d.,

https://www.imdb.com/name/nm0681191/bio

Little Sparrow Editors. "Edith Piaf." *Little Sparrow,* n.d., http://www.little-sparrow.co.uk/marriage.html

Andrée Borrel
(1919 - 1944 CE)

Conscript Heroes Editors. "Andrée Borrel (1919-1944)." *Conscript Heroes,* n.d., http://www.conscript-heroes.com/Art02-Andree-Borrel-960.html

Encyclopedia.com Editors. "Borrel, Andrée (1919-1944)." *Dictionary of Women Worldwide: 25,000 Women Through the Ages,* Encyclopedia.com, 25 Aug. 2022, https://www.encyclopedia.com/women/dictionaries-thesauruses-pictures-and-press-releases/borrel-andree-1919-1944

McCue, Paul. "Lieutenant Andrée Raymonde Borrel." *Paul McCue Books,* 2014, https://www.paulmccuebooks.com/lt-andr-e-borrel

Military History Editors. "Andrée Borrel." *Military History,* n.d., https://military-history.fandom.com/wiki/Andr%C3%A9e_Borrel

Military Spouse Editors. "3 Unsung World War II Female Spies Who Helped Make D-Day a Victory." *News,* Military Spouse, n.d., https://www.militaryspouse.com/news/3-unsung-world-war-2-female-spies-who-helped-make-d-day-a-victory/

Spartacus Educational Editors. "Andrée Borrel." *Spartacus Educational,* n.d., https://spartacus-educational.com/SOEborrel.htm

Warnes, Kathy. "SOE Agent Andree Borrel Lived Several Lifetimes in Her 24 Years." *Windows to World History,* Weebly, n.d., https://windowstoworldhistory.weebly.com/soe-agent-andree-borrel-lived-several-lifetimes-in-her-24-years.html

Françoise Gilot
(1921–2023 CE)

Brockes, Emma. "'It was not a sentimental love': Françoise Gilot on her years with Picasso." The Guardian, 10 Jun. 2016, https://www.theguardian.com/artanddesign/2016/jun/10/francoise-gilot-artist-love-picasso

Darwent, Charles. "Françoise Gilot obituary" The Guardian, 7 Jun. 2023, https://www.theguardian.com/artanddesign/2023/jun/07/francoise-gilot-obituary

Goodman, Wendy. "Life With Françoise Gilot. The 98-year-old artist still paints every day in her Upper West Side apartment." Curbed, 9 Oct.2020, https://www.curbed.com/2020/10/inside-artist-franoise-gilots-apartment-and-art-studio.html

Kazanjian, Dodie. "Life After Picasso: Françoise Gilot." Vogue, 27 Apr. 2012, https://www.vogue.com/article/life-after-picasso-franoise-gilot

Truus and Freddie Oversteegen
(1923 – 2018 CE)

Little, Betty. "This Teenager Killed Nazis With Her Sister During WWII." *History.com,* 19 Sept. 2018, https://www.history.com/news/dutch-resistance-teenager-killed-nazis-freddie-oversteegen

O'Leary, Naomi. "'Her war never stopped': the Dutch teenager who resisted the Nazis." *The Observer,* The Guardian, 23 Sept. 2018, https://www.theguardian.com/world/2018/sep/23/freddie-oversteegen-dutch-teenager-who-resisted-nazis

O'Leary, Sarah. "The 14-year-old assassin who lured Nazis and traitors to their deaths." *Dutch Review,* 4 Nov. 2020, https://dutchreview.com/culture/history/dutch-history-freddie-oversteegen/

Poldermans, Sophie. "As Teenagers, These Sisters Resisted the Nazis. Here's What They Taught Me About Doing the Right Thing." *Time,* 30 Aug. 2019, https://time.com/5661142/dutch-resistance-friendship/

Printed in the USA
CPSIA information can be obtained
at www.ICGtesting.com
LVHW020814051023
760085LV00055B/1139